The Cosmopolitan Potential of Exclusive Associations

The Cosmopolitan Potential of Exclusive Associations

Criteria for Assessing the Advancement of Cosmopolitan Norms

Bettina R. Scholz

LEXINGTON BOOKS
Lanham • Boulder • New York • London

Published by Lexington Books
An imprint of The Rowman & Littlefield Publishing Group, Inc.
4501 Forbes Boulevard, Suite 200, Lanham, Maryland 20706
www.rowman.com

Unit A, Whitacre Mews, 26-34 Stannary Street, London SE11 4AB

British Library Cataloguing in Publication Information Available

Library of Congress Cataloging-in-Publication Data

Scholz, Bettina, 1971-
The cosmopolitan potential of exclusive associations : criteria for assessing the advancement of cosmopolitan norms / Bettina R. Scholz.
pages cm
Includes bibliographical references and index.
ISBN 978-0-7391-8997-9 (cloth : alk. paper) -- ISBN 978-0-7391-8998-6 (electronic) 1. Cosmopolitanism. 2. Non-governmental organizations--Influence. 3. Communities. 4. Globalization. 5. Civil society. I. Title.
JZ1308.S355 2015
369--dc23

2015021771

♾️™ The paper used in this publication meets the minimum requirements of American National Standard for Information Sciences Permanence of Paper for Printed Library Materials, ANSI/NISO Z39.48-1992.

Printed in the United States of America

Dedicated to my parents

Contents

Acknowledgments

I would like to acknowledge support from Harvard University, where this book originated as my dissertation in the Government Department, and Stonehill College. Both institutions provided grants to support my research and writing. Among the individuals who assisted me in this project, I would like first and foremost to acknowledge Nancy Rosenblum. She provided valuable encouragement for me to connect my interests in political theory and transnational associations. I would also like to thank Dennis Thompson whose suggestion that I consider sports organizations led me to focus on the Olympics. Michael Sandel also provided critical feedback, challenging me to think beyond the limits of existing liberal theories. Comments from participants at Harvard's Political Theory Workshop and many different conference discussants helped me to sharpen my arguments. My writing group colleagues at Stonehill provided incentives to find time to write amid my teaching responsibilities. Students in my "Citizens of the World" class challenged me to clarify my theoretical explanations of cosmopolitan theory. I also benefited from the thoughtful insights of Jospeh Kochanek during the final states of this project as well as from the assistance of Justin Race and his team at Lexington Press.

My deepest gratitude goes to family and friends for their love and encouragement, which appropriately came from all corners of the world. In particular, thank you to Frances Acosta, Paula Cosko, and Annie Chu. A special thank you goes to Antonia Scholz, who provided a place to stay during years of conference presentations, and to Max Scholz, who commiserated over writer's bloc. My parents, Rachel and Joachim Scholz, were an endless source of encouragement. They understood that sometimes the most helpful thing is providing the quiet to work. Last but certainly not least, I would like to thank Kirk Buckman, whose support made completing this project possible (through snow storms and emergency repairs).

Introduction

Médecins Sans Frontières (MSF), or Doctors Without Borders, provides emergency medical care across the globe without necessarily establishing a transnational community with those it aids. The International Olympic Committee (IOC) brings the world together around global games in which national teams compete against each other. Dissident members of the Anglican Communion have united globally around an interpretation of the Bible that excludes non-celibate gay men from ordained ministry and prohibits same-sex marriages. These three well-established and influential transnational voluntary associations span national borders and sponsor activities that involve outreach to individuals in communities other than their own. How should a cosmopolitan evaluate the effects of these associations? Saying they are influential does not answer the normative question of whether their influence is positive. Yet, this is the question one might want to answer when determining where to donate money or whether to join an association.

Since many individuals belong to associations, questions about which ones we ought to support are not merely abstract or theoretical puzzles. Among my students, for example, those who give a year of service after graduation often ask themselves normative questions. Should they serve at home or abroad? (A different question than could they serve abroad. Are there programs abroad? Is there funding available?) Which organization or association should they join? Even people not pondering what to do after graduation often belong to associations with transnational reach, whether they are sports clubs, professional associations, religious groups, or advocacy organizations, to name a few examples. Anyone who is a member of a transnational association ought to be interested in evaluating the effects of membership in the association and considering what obligations emerge as a result of participating in it. Asking normative questions that challenge us to evaluate the effects of associations requires choosing a standard to determine what constitutes a positive effect.

In order to answer the kinds of questions posed in the previous two paragraphs there are a variety of theoretical approaches from which to choose. One that stands out as particularly relevant is constructivism. A constructivist international relations approach in the vein of scholars like Margaret E. Keck and Kathryn Sikkink or Richard Price seeks to explain moral change on the international level by studying shifts in norms (standards of acceptable behavior), identities, or ideas that come about through repeated patterns of interaction among state and non-state actors.[1] This scholarship points to the reality that understanding international relations requires recognizing that states' interests are shaped not only by security concerns but also by norms and ideas. Governments can be pressured to change their actions if they come under international scrutiny for engaging in behavior that does not comply with international standards of human rights. Many states have even signed an international convention to ban landmines, weapons that could be used to help secure a state, because of international pressure to ban these indiscriminate weapons. Not only does the constructivist focus on norms and ideas seem to suit the project I am investigating well, but it is also the case that constructivists are more likely than scholars from other branches of international relations (particularly realists but also liberal institutionalists) to study the influence of non-state actors such as multinational corporations, media organizations, crime organizations, or advocacy networks. Although not always the case, a constructivist approach that studies norms can include the many different actors who have international influence on such standards. This can be very helpful when trying to uncover the impact of non-governmental associations.

Yet, as important as this constructivist scholarship is to understanding non-state actors' effects on the international level, it does not tell us whether the norm change is a change we should view positively or negatively. For example, if it were to become commonly accepted as legitimate to enslave certain people, one could study how that norm came to be accepted without necessarily concluding that one ought to support it. Even as he defends the importance of constructivist scholarship, Price acknowledges that constructivist "literature for the most part has not offered its own explicit normative or prescriptive defenses of particular changes as good."[2] What initially seemed a promising theoretical avenue has its limits.

There is another possible theoretical framework for evaluating the actions of associations, namely theories of global civil society (or transnational civil society). Here the focus is more directly on non-state actors and how they shape interests as well as public opinion. In some cases, normative positions are even more explicit if the *civil* in civil society entails an evaluative statement as it does for theorists like John Keane.[3] Associations that are part of civil society could be understood to include only those that behave in a civil, non-violent fashion or, in more limited cases, only those that cultivate democracy. While civil society theories have a direct focus on associations and may, in some cases, address more normative questions, there are significant limitations here as well. The concept of civil society was developed in a domestic context. Certain basic assumptions, such as the presence of a state to mediate between different interests in society and to enforce civil behavior, are missing on the global level. Constructivist approaches to associations begin from international theories but do not always explicitly develop a normative theory. Global civil society theories may more explicitly develop normative theories but do so using a concept developed for the domestic context.

If these two approaches are limited, where should one turn to find a strong normative basis for evaluating the effects of MSF, the IOC, or the Anglican Communion? I propose turning to cosmopolitanism. This term is used widely in a variety of fields including sociology, philosophy, anthropology, and literature as well as politics (not to mention its use in common parlance to refer to a drink and a magazine). The normative cosmopolitan theories, particularly moral cosmopolitan political theories, that I will draw from focus on the obligations we all have as fellow humans to ensure justice irrespective of state boundaries. The origins of cosmopolitanism can be traced back to ancient Greece where the idea of being a cosmopolitan challenged the traditional concepts of political loyalty. Rather than defining your identity and your responsibilities in terms of being a citizen of a particular city, such as Athens or Sparta, a person should imagine him or herself to be a citizen of the cosmos, the world. The idea of cosmopolitanism surfaces again and again in different time periods. Cicero's Rome and Kant's Enlightenment Europe are two prominent historical examples.[4] The obligations and meanings of this term can be quite complex as theorists disagree over exactly what obligations a citizen of the world should have and even whether or not being a citizen of the world implies global political, legal, or economic institutions. In some cases the moral or normative question is not the primary focus at all. Constructivist approaches to international relations that employ the term cosmopolitanism are often interested in whether projects based on cosmopolitan moral ideas are "easier to implement as policy than projects based on more parochial ideals."[5] Although such a question may have normative elements in that moral projects are being investigated, the focused is on what policies are easier to implement not the question of which policies we should want to implement. After all, it might be that we have to work hard to implement the right moral project against difficult odds rather than simply settle for what is easier or efficient.

The theories of cosmopolitanism I address are largely normative theories that engage in outlining moral obligations and prescriptions. At the core of the cosmopolitan ideal, as I will be employing it, is an understanding that humans are moral equals and as such are members of a transnational community of fellow humans who share a universal morality. From this basic assumption theorists derive different implications for the kinds of equal treatment that are required of morally equal individuals particularly when interacting with those who are not citizens of their country. A very weak cosmopolitanism may argue that I should not kill or harm foreigners simply because they are not citizens of my country—an idea no longer particularly controversial. Even a critic of most cosmopolitan theories, such as David Miller, argues that, with very few exceptions, contemporary theorists are weak cosmopolitans in the sense that they assume humans worthy of some concern simply because they are human.[6] What makes those who embrace the label of cosmopolitan different from Miller's weak cosmopolitans are the more robust requirements that result from a belief in moral equality—usually some form of moral obligation to equal treatment or consideration. The individual not the state or other group is the primary unit of concern. Thomas Pogge's definition of cosmopolitanism is based on three similarities cosmopolitans share, despite other differences.

> First, *individualism*: the ultimate units of concern are human beings, or persons—rather than, say, family lines, tribes, ethnic, cultural or religious communities, nations, or states. . . . Second, *universality*: the status of ultimate unit of concern attaches to every living human being equally. . . . Third, *generality*: this special status has global force. Persons are ultimate units of concern for everyone.[7]

Stronger forms of cosmopolitanism may expand the requirement that one not physically harm strangers to include more indirect actions that affect others.[8] Perhaps, I ought to change my consumption patterns if they contribute to environmental degradation that impacts the people in Bangladesh or the ozone layer over Australia. Stronger forms might also include duties to aid fellow humans who are facing conditions, such as starvation, that no human should have to endure. In addition to duties of not harming and/or aiding there may be duties to construct more transnational communities either through travel and cultural exchanges or global governance institutions that would ensure fair and democratic decision-making on the transnational level.[9] Cosmopolitanism has normative theory at its core. Unlike constructivist theories, it can serve as a source for standards to evaluate associations. Unlike global civil society, it is rooted in a global not domestic philosophical tradition.

However, even with cosmopolitan theory there are limitations. Although cosmopolitan theory has the potential to establish standards for associations, comprehensive cosmopolitan theories that defend the core principles of cosmopolitanism rarely talk about associations. How might cosmopolitan theory evaluate the three associations mentioned at the beginning: MSF, the IOC, and the Anglican Communion? If cosmopolitan ideals, broadly understood, envision a world in which communities are increasingly transnational and where the equal moral worth of all humans is respected, then certainly some aspects of the three associations fit cosmopolitan ideals. At the same time, the three associations have non-cosmopolitan components that should not be overlooked: reinforcement of an image of expatriate elite saviors rescuing victims in the developing world, cultivation of nationalist sentiments, and discrimination against gay and lesbian individuals. Given the complexity of these associations it is not immediately clear how one would assess whether they are advancing cosmopolitanism. The main goal of this book is to connect scholarship on the impact of associations with cosmopolitan theory's normative framework to establish criteria nuanced enough for evaluating whether the effects of associations advance cosmopolitan ideals. The real challenge will be to evaluate the impact of associations that are not straightforwardly cosmopolitan, such as the three just described.

Rather than establishing a comprehensive theory of cosmopolitanism, which would develop and defend fundamental principles, I instead begin from the assumption that a more cosmopolitan world is desirable. Drawing on existing cosmopolitan moral theories, I ask: How ought one assess whether norms, dispositions, or identities compatible with cosmopolitanism are being generated and maintained? This is a critical question because one cannot assume that cosmopolitanism will inevitably arise from the working of some invisible order. If cosmopolitanism is not inevitable then it behooves cosmopolitans to consider what actions are advancing not only increased global interactions but also respect for moral equality and which are not. Criteria for evaluating the effects of associations can help cosmopolitans respond to the challenge that their theories are too abstract to be useful in understanding the world. Cosmopolitan moral theory is often critiqued for its abstract idealistic nature. All theory is abstract to some extent, because it generalizes, but not all moral theories are as abstract as cosmopolitanism. Its ideal world does not look much like the one that exists today.[10] Yet, many normative theories describe ideals that do not match the actual behavior of actors in the world. Democratic theories, such as deliberative democracy, for example, paint pictures of ideal democratic behavior that actual democracies fail to fully realize. Nevertheless, there are democratic governments. Cosmopolitanism is much less institutionalized in the world. There are no corresponding political institutions. Although there is a United Nations, there is no world government in which all humans are represented equally or any actual global citizenship. Few individuals identify themselves first as humans as opposed to Americans, or Canadians, or even Bostonians. It is true that economic decisions in one part of the world affect people across the globe; however, the effects are not on equal terms. There are also few avenues for demanding rectification. Progress has been made toward ever-greater recognition of the importance of human rights or human dignity, but whether rights are protected still depends a great deal on the state in which an individual lives. Even constructivist scholars, who argue that moral progress on the international level is possible, seek to distinguish their projects from cosmopolitanism's utopianism[11] or its idealism.[12]

As a partial response to such critiques, I establish a middle-level theory of cosmopolitanism that bridges the gap between more abstract ideals of contemporary moral cosmopolitan political philosophy and studies in global civil society or constructivist international relations on norm changes.[13] Global civil society as a theoretical framework may be problematic, as previously mentioned, but research on associations contributes to our understanding of the plurality and diversity of non-state actors. As already mentioned, constructivists increasingly acknowledge that their projects do not explicitly explore normative assumption;[14] however, the strength of this scholarship does not lie in developing a full-fledged normative theory. Constructivists can contribute an understanding of the actions of associations. According to John Gerard Ruggie, its inductive approach means that constructivism's concepts are "intended to tap into and help interpret the meaning and significance that actors ascribe to the collective situation in which they find themselves."[15] Attention to particular situations is unlikely to emerge from "universalizing theory-sketch or from purely nominal definitions."[16] Or in the words of Price, constructivism's attention to context requires humility because providing ethical guidelines in one type of situation may come at the expense of new moral dilemmas.[17] The situated, context-specific, thick description and explanation of constructivist scholarship on transnational norm changes can help inform cosmopolitanism's normative ideals. A middle-level theory combines abstract foundational principles and empirical research on the impact of associations. This can contribute to international relations research, since as

> long as international relations remains a practical discourse, one ultimately (though often implicitly) concerned with the question of 'how we should act,' . . . closer attention to the variety of ethical underpinnings in the field can strengthen our understanding of what we do and, channeled properly, can motivate research progress as it enhances our ability, individually or collectively, to speak to the most pressing issue of political action in contemporary world politics.[18] $

Cosmopolitan theory is better able to understand actors in our imperfectly cosmopolitan world and potentially locate allies among transnational non-governmental associations that seek to transform the world.

Since addressing the impact of transnational voluntary associations is critical to my project it is important to be clear on what I mean by that term. Just as the term cosmopolitanism is used in a variety of ways, associations on the international level are classified and categorized in many different ways. Let me briefly indicate what I mean by transnational voluntary associations before turning to how these associations might be understood within cosmopolitan theory. The complex relationship between cosmopolitanism and associations will be discussed in much greater detail in subsequent chapters as I construct my middle-level theory. However, some preliminary remarks can be helpful. Using the term *association* allows me to encompass different ways individuals associate beyond states. Some common categories include social movements, advocacy networks, non-governmental organizations (which themselves often encompass different regional, national, or local branches), religious groups, professional organizations, multinational corporations, and even criminal organizations. Adopting a broad term like associations means addressing types of organizations that are often distinguished.

However, I do not mean to imply that there are no relevant distinctions. One distinction to which I generally adhere is the separation of for-profit and not-for-profit organizations. I do not address transnational business. Yet, even this seemingly easy demarcation ignores the complexity of organizations such as the Olympics, which raises questions about the ability to draw a strict line between for-profit and not-for-profit when understanding effects of associations.[19] There are also often important differences drawn between violent and non-violent groups. My focus will be on associations that do not employ violence or actively seek to violate human rights. Yet, here too there are complexities as some associations that do not intend to may nevertheless give rise to situations in which rights are violated. This will be discussed in the case of the Olympics and the Anglican Communion's crisis over homosexuality. Categories of not-for-profit and non-violent groups encompass other common distinctions between epistemic communities based in professional scientific communities and, for example, social movements that connect associations and individuals around an interest in a social change cause.[20] The term non-governmental organization (NGO) itself, although seemingly broad, can invoke the narrower definition the United Nations (UN) employs. The UN includes in its definition of an NGO a concern for the general global interest rather than that of a particular community or group.[21] I wish to develop criteria for cases of associations that do not necessarily fit this requirement. My use of the term non-governmental association means a non-state actor rather than the UN's more narrowly defined understanding of the term. What scholarship on all of these ways of associating shows is that non-state associations have important effects on shaping international norms or dispositions. I do not focus primarily on drawing distinctions between types of associations because my goal is to develop criteria that can address the effects of a variety of associations with transnational membership. It is precisely associations not obviously in line with cosmopolitan ideals that can serve as a test for whether a broad range of associations have cosmopolitan effects.

So far, I have sought to explain what I mean by association. What about the voluntary element of transnational voluntary associations? This stems from a tradition within domestic civil society theories that focuses on non-state actors, which individuals freely join in order to pursue common interests. Although an emphasis on the voluntary nature of associations may be historically rooted in a Western philosophical tradition of association in political community, specifically the Greek polis,[22] later historical periods emphasize the voluntary aspect of an association as a way to distinguish certain forms of organization from the state. Contemporary scholarship on free associations in a democratic context often draws on Alexis de Tocqueville's *Democracy in America*, particularly passages where he argues, "an association consists simply in the public assent which a number of individuals give to certain doctrines and in the engagement which they contract to promote in a certain manner the spread of those doctrines."[23] Or where he writes that the "right of freedom of association therefore appears to me almost as inalienable in its nature as the right of personal liberty."[24] In this context, associations are distinct from but critical to a democratic state because they protect individual liberty and at the same time connect individuals to each other, ensuring that they do not become entirely self-interested. However, scholars such as Cheryl B. Welch caution that invoking Tocqueville can "become a shorthand substitute for the claim that associations have positive moral and social consequences for democratic politics," rather than really representing his actual arguments.[25] I hope to avoid the assumption that voluntary associations are necessarily beneficial to cosmopolitanism. When using the term *voluntary*, I mean it primarily in a descriptive sense that individuals are not forced to join the association and can leave if they choose (without as many costs to exit as there are to denouncing citizenship in one country and gaining it in another, for example). I will develop my use of the term *transnational voluntary association* in greater depth in chapter 1. For the moment, I wish to make clear that the term *transnational voluntary association* denotes a broad category of nonstate actors that individuals freely form or join and can freely exit.

The relevance of individual liberty draws the connection with associations back to cosmopolitanism. Insofar as cosmopolitanism's focus on the individual is expressed in terms of individual liberties, cosmopolitanism often falls in the category of a liberal philosophical theory. Liberal philosophy prizes individual liberty and usually protects it by establishing a private sphere in which a broad array of practices can be tolerated. Although not all cosmopolitan theorists I will draw on embrace all of liberal philosophy, what they share is some recognition of the importance of individual liberty, even if it is for different reasons or with different implications. Moreover, they all argue that liberty is relevant beyond state boundaries. I will talk in terms of basic liberties as essential human rights, of which freedom of association is one.[26] The "right to freedom of peaceful assembly and association" is a basic human right enshrined in international documents such as the Universal Declaration of Human Rights.[27] Membership in associations may not pose any problem to cosmopolitan theory's focus on the individual if membership is based on individual choice. Given that individual liberty can usually encompass freedom of association, it seems as though cosmopolitanism can tolerate associations. The debates over partial allegiances that usually arise have to do with political association—the state. Debates rage over the dangers or benefits of patriotism.[28] Contemporary cosmopolitans that conceive of associations in broader terms than the state argue more generally that membership in associations is "characteristic of a meaningful and re-warding life."[29] Most cosmopolitans today (and certainly the ones I dis-cuss in chapter 2) do not want to be seen as imposing principles that do not respect diversity and difference—or at least they want to establish a form of cosmopolitanism in which universal principles can be applied in different and unique ways.

Some cosmopolitan theorists go farther to actually embrace partial ties in their theories, referring to ideas of rooted cosmopolitanism, patriotic cosmopolitanism, vernacular cosmopolitanism, and so on. David Hol-linger calls these the "new cosmopolitans" in order to distinguish them from previous versions that prioritized universalism at the expense of partiality.[30] In the new cosmopolitanism a tension between universalism and partiality lies at the very center of the theory. Yet, the diversity of transnational voluntary associations is much less likely to be the focus of cosmopolitan philosophers. Lacking the power and privileges of mem-bership in a state, membership in freely chosen non-state associations is not seen as potentially threatening or beneficial. In cases where it is ad-dressed, it is often in terms of an instrumental role to realize cosmopoli-tan political projects (such as when NGOs play governance roles working in conjunction with the UN to craft and implement policy[31]). Cosmopoli-tan David Held lists "the development of transnational, grass-roots movements with clear regional or global objectives, such as the protec-tion of natural resources and the environment, and the alleviation of disease and ill-health" as a critical element in "the establishment of a cosmopolitan model of democracy."[32] Democratic theorist Jürgen Haber-mas also maintains that non-state actors are critical to creating the condi-tions for transnational democracies. For the European Union to succeed, he argues, there needs to be a pan-European civil society of non-state actors to create the conditions for democratic government.[33] These views focus on how associations assist in realizing cosmopolitan political insti-tutions, not primarily on the effects of membership in associations that extend beyond global governance. Moreover focusing on the purpose of the association, as Held does, tends to address only certain kinds of asso-ciations.

Exclusive transnational associations without a cosmopolitan purpose should be tolerated under freedom of association, but they also make particularly interesting test cases for the viability of cosmopolitan ideals in an incompletely cosmopolitan world. Such associations often draw members from more than one country, thus connecting individuals across borders at the same time they remain only partial associations. They do not encompass all humans and do not necessarily embody or advance universal principles. Furthermore, one cannot argue that their partiality is merely due to practical limitations. Some transnational asso-

ciations aim to define membership in non-universalist terms (professionals, athletes, *etc.*). To put it more starkly, their membership criteria exclude. Not all transnational associations necessarily advance cosmopolitanism simply by virtue of membership crossing state borders. How
ought a cosmopolitan evaluate these partial, exclusive associations? I
argue that one needs to determine what constitutes core cosmopolitan
values and how associations realize them.

In achieving this goal, the variety within moral cosmopolitan theory
actually helps in evaluating the potential of associations, but only if one
shifts away from defending particular comprehensive theories of cosmopolitanism. Instead I categorize theories in terms of the different elements
or expressions of cosmopolitanism they emphasize, whether it be establishing just institutional relations, expanding imaginations to recognize a
common humanity, creating transnational shared identities, or participating in global public deliberations. This raises certain tensions because the
theories may well take what seem like either/or positions. (Either your
obligations originate from institutional relations or they originate simply
from human fellowship.) However, I am not addressing cosmopolitanism from the perspective of an individual moral agent who might be
asking the question—what moral obligations do I have? Instead, I am
interested in understanding how associations can contribute to advancing cosmopolitanism. An association has no moral obligation to advance
cosmopolitanism (despite not being justified in violating core principles
such as human rights, either). Even advancing only some elements of
cosmopolitanism may nevertheless be worth noting.

Drawing on different theories of cosmopolitanism in evaluating associations does ensure that tensions remain. Yet, comprehensive cosmopolitan theories themselves, as I will argue in chapter 2, are not without their
tensions. Partiality and universality will require negotiation, given that
freedom of association means allowing individuals to choose to join non-
cosmopolitan associations that do not include all humans and do not aim
to advance cosmopolitan principles. To require that that all associations
aim at advancing cosmopolitan ideals of individual liberty or human
rights would undermine free choice unnecessarily since many forms of
exclusion do not necessarily threaten human rights. One does not have a
human right to join a specific religious organization or to be married in a
particularly religious tradition. The result of a liberty to associate is a
tension between universal principles such as freedom of association,
which apply to all individuals equally, and partial associations that do
not treat all individuals equally. Moreover this tension will not disappear
so long as one assumes that free people will not all make the same decisions on which associations to form or join. The liberal bias in my understanding of cosmopolitanism remains but by focusing on exclusive cases
rather than human rights associations I hope to develop criteria that allow for the cosmopolitan contribution of a wide range of associations.

Emphasizing toleration and diversity is a critical contribution contemporary theorists have made to our understanding of the moral obligations of cosmopolitanism. (It helps theorists to escape the "huge shadow of . . . the cosmopolitanism associated with the Enlightenment."[34]) However, when it comes to associations, simply establishing a threshold of toleration misses the potential for them to actually generate or advance cosmopolitan norms. In addition, the goal should not be to determine whether the association is successful in achieving its purpose but also whether it has cosmopolitan effects. This opens up the possibility for incredible complexity. At the same time it opens up the possibility that exclusion need not mean there are no cosmopolitan effects in some elements of the association. Associations are actually good places to explore partial forms of cosmopolitanism because the weightier implications of citizenship rights are not at issue. Therefore, rather than reiterating the debates between cosmopolitans defending universalism and communitarians defending the moral value of national communities, I begin from cosmopolitanism and adapt it to create a middle-level theory of cosmopolitan criteria based on the different expressions of cosmopolitanism one could expect of associations. Mark E. Warren's middle-level theory of democracy and association on the domestic level is the inspiration for my work. Warren asks: What effects can democratic theorists expect from associations?[35] My version of this question is: What kinds of effects should cosmopolitans expect from associations? This in turn raises the question: What kinds of effects do associations have and can one generalize about their effects? In his analysis Warren focused on whether or not associations help to support democratic norms by providing spaces to practice democratic skills or learn how to deliberate or craft democratic institutions. My goal will be to draw from existing theories of cosmopolitanism to locate what cosmopolitan norms or standards associations might advance.

If a framework of cosmopolitan criteria for associations represents various expressions of cosmopolitanism, then scholarship on actual examples of associations helps to illustrate what satisfying cosmopolitan criteria might look like. What, for example, would it mean for associations to advance cosmopolitanism through institutional effects, or by creating public spheres or shared identities? Assuming a basic threshold of toleration that associations must pass, namely that violating human rights is unacceptable, still leaves forms of exclusion that do not violate human rights. Cosmopolitan criteria that respect associational pluralism need to be broad enough to recognize and assess the potential of a range of associations while not being so broad as to lose their critical moral force. After drawing out core values or expressions of cosmopolitanism in chapter 2 and assessing the lessons from studying theories of associations in chapter 3, chapter 4 develops the criteria by connecting four types of cosmopolitan theory with four types of associational effects.

These criteria can assess the different ways associations might foster a greater sense of moral equality and more transnational communities among fellow humans. In order to understand what the cosmopolitan effects look like in associations, I illustrate the criteria using a series of actual associations. I begin with the easier case of the anti-slave trade movement in Britain, whose mission fits cosmopolitan ideals of moral equality more clearly. The cases discussed in part II (MSF, the Olympics, and the Anglican Communion) involve greater complexity and are not as straightforwardly cosmopolitan. They exhibit tensions between cosmopolitan and non-cosmopolitan elements of the association helping to explore what partial or indirect expressions of cosmopolitanism might entail.

By focusing on effects rather than the self-conscious mission of the association, a few critical conclusions will emerge. Even those associations whose goals are more compatible with cosmopolitanism's respect for moral equality (such as ending the slave trade) raise the possibility that associations with a cosmopolitan purpose may not advance all elements of cosmopolitanism. Cosmopolitans can also consider the possibility that associations generate cosmopolitan norms and dispositions without avowing explicit cosmopolitan purposes or exhibiting all expressions of cosmopolitan effects. Developing a sense of partial cosmopolitanism should not be viewed as weakening cosmopolitanism to the point that any group could be considered cosmopolitan in some way. Partial expressions of cosmopolitanism still need to retain some meaningful moral and therefore normative component drawn from theories of cosmopolitanism. Instead of focusing on developing an ideal type of the perfect cosmopolitan association, which would miss certain sources of cosmopolitanism, perhaps even painting a misleading picture of how cosmopolitanism comes about in the world, my goal is to develop criteria that can be applied to transnational voluntary associations that do not have an explicit purpose of advancing cosmopolitan norms. Focusing on associations with tensions forges a middle ground not only between normative and empirical scholarship but also between associations that advocate for cosmopolitanism and those that directly threaten it.

Even though my main argument is for reorienting how cosmopolitan theory applies to associations, it does not mean that there are no implications for individuals. Individuals interested in advancing cosmopolitanism should begin to think not only of how to build a common human community or about what cosmopolitan obligations they have but also about the effects membership may have on them and how they might reform their associations in more cosmopolitan directions. I will argue that cosmopolitan ideals need not only be expressed through membership in advocacy organizations. There might even be reasons to encourage actions like hosting the Olympics or like transforming medical research practices. One could consider how to bring associations in line with cosmopolitan norms without necessarily altering their purpose.

Before I embark on the project of establishing criteria for assessing the effects of a broad array of associations, it is important to note some limitations to my approach. Focusing on established associations, such as the cases in part II, ensures there is substantial research on the effects of the association. However, all three cases of transnational associations originated in the northern hemisphere and, in fact, all three started in Western Europe. These associations do play an important role at the global level and their effects should not simply be seen as positive or quickly condemned based on their origin. However, more work is also needed to address newer associations as well as ones that originate in other parts of the world. Considering whether individuals are able to access liberties such as freedoms of association may also reveal that membership in associations is tied to socioeconomic status, like on the domestic level.[36] From some perspectives this could give rise to additional cosmopolitan obligations of justice in order to help individuals realize freedom of association. Another limitation arises from the fact that cosmopolitanism is not itself without controversy. I will continue to flesh out this concept in chapters 1 and 2, but the theories I draw on are from Western philosophical traditions. As cosmopolitanism is redefined and altered to incorporate greater diversity, the criteria may need to shift. Because my methodology connects normative and empirical research I could also imagine some adaptations to the criteria occurring as a result of new information about associations.

One example of the complexity of studying associations outside of the United States and Western Europe is that associations may be more intertwined with state power (not only in receiving funding but also in being partially state sponsored) or intertwined with market powers. Such challenges emerge in scholarship studying how associations in China are joining international networks and forging transnational linkages.[37] While there has been a significant increase in associations in China they are "best understood as a mix of state-sponsored social control and spontaneous grassroots activity."[38] Further research into the flexibility of my criteria could explore the extent to which they would have to be altered to include associations more intertwined with state power. Nothing in the criteria, as they exist now, requires that the association be completely separate from the state, although ensuring the underlying goal of individual liberty could be threatened by too much government oversight or control.

Even if future shifts and amendments to the criteria become necessary, the critical point for now is to begin the process of developing criteria for evaluating associations in a way that respects diversity. Cosmopolitan theories need to be broken down into different expressions of core ideals. This has significant implications for those seeking to reform associations in which they are members as well as for scholars studying associations or cosmopolitanism. If partial and indirect expressions of cosmopolitanism could be established then cosmopolitanism could be spread piecemeal through a plurality of associations that advance cosmopolitanism in different ways. For those skeptical of cosmopolitan theory, particularly those worried about the homogenizing threat of liberal cosmopolitan universalism, I aim to demonstrate one way in which cosmopolitan theory could be more open to diversity and partiality. Approaching tensions inherent in cosmopolitanism from the perspective of non-state actors is a way to consider how a diverse array of associations could help spread cosmopolitan norms and dispositions. A concept of indirect cosmopolitanism understood in the context of free and voluntary transnational associations can actually broaden the possibility for cosmopolitanism to be spread without depending on the explicit belief in cosmopolitan principles.

NOTES

1. Margaret E. Keck and Kathryn Sikkink, *Activists Beyond Borders: Advocacy Networks in International Politics* (Ithaca, NY: Cornell University Press, 1998); Richard Price, ed., *Moral Limit and Possibility in World Politics* (New York: Cambridge University Press, 2008); Richard Price, "The Ethics of Constructivism," in *The Oxford Handbook of International Relations,* ed. Christian Reus-Smit and Duncan Snidal (New York: Oxford University Press, 2010), 1–52.

2. Price, "The Ethics of Constructivism," 318.

3. John Keane, *Global Civil Society?* (Cambridge: Cambridge University Press, 2003).

4. For a discussion of the historical use of cosmopolitanism, see Derek Heater, *World Citizenship and Government: Cosmopolitan Ideas in the History of Western Political Thought* (New York: St. Martin, 1996). For a specific focus on Kant, see Pauline Kleingeld, *Kant and Cosmopolitanism: The Philosophical Ideal of World Citizenship* (New York: Cambridge University Press, 2011).

5. Chaim D. Kaufmann and Robert A. Pape, "Explaining Costly International Moral Action: Britain's Sixty-Year Campaign against the Atlantic Slave Trade," *International Organization* 53, no. 4 (1999): 642.

6. David Miller, *National Responsibilities and Global Justice* (New York: Oxford University Press, 2007), 27.

7. Thomas W. Pogge, "Cosmopolitanism and Sovereignty," *Ethics* 103, no. 1 (1992): 48–49.

8. Thomas Pogge, *World Poverty and Human Rights: Cosmopolitan Responsibilities and Reforms* (Malden, MA: Polity, 2002).

9. Kwame Anthony Appiah, *Cosmopolitanism: Ethics in a World of Strangers* (Princeton, NJ: W.W. Norton & Company, 2006); Daniele Archibugi, "Cosmopolitan Democracy and Its Critics: A Review," *European Journal of International Relations* 10, no. 3 (2004); David Held, *Democracy and the Global Order: From the Modern State to Cosmopolitan Governance* (Stanford, CA: Stanford University Press, 1995).

10. Catherine Lu's work is an interesting exception to cosmopolitanism's tradition of idealism. She rejects the idea that cosmopolitanism needs to be idealistic. Instead it can be "realistic" in recognizing that there is a "common human condition marked by frailty and fallibility." She defends this realistic cosmopolitanism in "The One and Many Faces of Cosmopolitanism," *The Journal of Political Philosophy* 8, no. 2 (2000): 265.

11. Price, "The Ethics of Constructivism," 300.

12. John Gerard Ruggie, "What Makes the World Hang Together? Neo-Utilitarianism and the Social Constructivist Challenge," *International Organization* 52, no. 4 (1998): 858.

13. In using the term *middle-level theory* I am drawing on the term Mark E. Warren uses to describe his theory of associations and democracy. Mark E. Warren, *Democracy and Association* (Princeton, NJ: Princeton University Press, 2001). He is not alone in seeking to delineate a theoretical methodology between first-order principles and empirical studies. Amy Gutmann and Dennis Thompson refer to a "second-order" theory in *Why Deliberative Democracy?* (Princeton, NJ: Princeton University Press, 2004). Elizabeth Ellis discusses the importance of "provisional theory" in *Provisional Politics: Kantian Arguments in Policy Context* (New Haven, CT: Yale University Press, 2008).

14. Kathryn Sikkink makes this comment regarding her own work in "The Role of Consequences, Comparison, and Counterfactuals in Constructivist Ethical Thought," in Price, *Moral Limits*, 83. Richard Price also references the "normative bias" in much of transnational civil society scholarship in a review article entitled "Transnational Civil Society and Advocacy in World Politics," *World Politics* 55, no. 4 (2003): 601–2.

15. Ruggie, "What Makes the World Hang Together?" 880.

16. Ibid.

17. Price, "The Ethics of Constructivism," 324–25.

18. Christian Reus-Smit and Duncan Snidal, "Introduction: Between Utopia and Reality: The Practical Discourses of International Relations," in Reus-Smit and Snidal, *Oxford Handbook of International Relations*, 17.

19. Lester M. Salamon employs this distinction in "The Rise of the Nonprofit Sector," *Foreign Affairs* 73, no. 4 (1994), 109. Keane is an example of someone who rejects this distinction in *Global Civil Society?*

20. For theories of advocacy networks, see Keck and Sikkink, *Activists Beyond Borders*. For a discussion of social movements, see Jackie Smith, "Global Civil Society? Transnational Social Movement Organizations and Social Capital," *American Behavior Scientist* 42, no. 1 (1998). Peter Haas discusses epistemic communities in "Introduction: Epistemic Communities and International Policy Coordination" *International Organization* 46, no. 1 (1992).

21. Shamima Ahmed and David Potter discuss how NGOs are defined through UN documentation. They write that for the UN "any international organization which is not established by intergovernmental agreement shall be considered as an NGO," and that NGOs are expected to be not-for-profit, not to advocate for violence, not be schools, universities, or political parties, and "any concern with human rights must be general rather than restricted to a particular communal group, nationality, or country," *NGOS in International Politics* (Bloomfield, CT: Kumarian Press, 2006), 8.

22. John W. Chapman, "Voluntary Associations and the Political Theory of Pluralism," in *Voluntary Associations Nomos XI*, ed. J. Roland Pennock and John W. Chapman (New York: Atherton Press, 1969), 89.

23. Alexis de Tocqueville, *Democracy in America,* trans. and ed. Harvey C. Mansfield and Delba Winthrop (Chicago: University of Chicago Press, 2002), 181.

24. Ibid., 184.

25. Cheryl B. Welch, *De Tocqueville* (New York: Oxford University Press, 2001), 239.

26. The importance of freedom of association is not necessarily as central to forms of cosmopolitanism that do not have the protection of individual liberties as a central goal. For example, certain forms of utilitarian cosmopolitanism could argue that we should seek to maximize utility on the global level whether or not this involved respecting individual liberties.

27. *The Universal Declaration of Human Rights*, United Nations, accessed January 14, 2010, http://www.un.org/en/documents/udhr/index.shtml.

28. For an example of such a debate over cosmopolitanism and patriotism see Joshua Cohen, ed., *For Love of Country?* (Boston: Beacon Press, 2002).

29. Kok-Chor Tan, "The Demands of Justice and National Allegiances," in *The Political Philosophy of Cosmopolitanism,* ed. Gillian Brock and Harry Brighouse (New York: Cambridge University Press, 2005), 164.

30. David A. Hollinger, "Not Universalists, Not Pluralists: The New Cosmopolitans Find Their Own Way," *Constellations* 8, no. 2 (2001): 237.

31. Only one of many examples is the role environmental groups are playing in the implementation of international rules governing fisheries. This is explicitly indicated on the website for the Food and Agricultural Organization of the United Nations. Under its section on governance the role of NGOs is specifically highlighted as having increased dramatically starting in the 1980s but particularly in the 1990s. "The role of NGOs in the governance of fisheries," Food and Agricultural Organization of the United Nations, accessed April 25, 2014, http://www.fao.org/fishery/topic/13310/e.

32. Held, *Democracy and the Global Order,* 237.

33. Jürgen Habermas, *The Postnational Constellation: Political Essays,* trans. and ed. Max Pensky (Cambridge, MA: MIT Press, 2001), 103.

34. Hollinger, "Not Universalists, Not Pluralists," 237.

35. Warren, *Democracy and Association,* 13.

36. Ibid., 73. Warren cites as evidence for this Sidney Verba, Kay Lehman Schlozman, and Henry E. Brady, *Voice and Equality: Civic Voluntarism in American Politics* (Cambridge, MA: Harvard University Press, 1995), chapter 17, and Theda Skocpol, "Associations without Members," *American Prospect* 45 (1999): 66–73.

37. Katherine Morton, "The Emergence of NGOs in China and Their Transnational Linkages: Implications for Domestic Reform," *Australian Journal of International Affairs,* 59, no. 4 (2005): 522.

38. Ibid., 520.

Part I

Tensions between Cosmopolitan Universalism and Partial Associations

ONE

The Meaning of Cosmopolitanism and Its Relation to a Plurality of Associations

If a middle-level theory of cosmopolitan criteria for assessing the effects of associations is to draw from different theories of cosmopolitanism, one might ask: Which theories of cosmopolitanism are relevant to an analysis of transnational voluntary associations? Moreover, if the goal is not to determine an ideal type of cosmopolitan association but to establish criteria that apply to the broad range of associations individuals freely join, a second question also emerges: Can cosmopolitanism's universalism actually be balanced with valuing a plurality of associations that are not fully universal? My discussion of cosmopolitanism is focused on contemporary political theories of cosmopolitanism and even more specifically on those that address moral questions. These theories share a basic belief in the universal moral equality of all humans, a focus on individuals rather than states as the fundamental moral unit, and toleration of diversity. Differences arise because theorists do not all draw the same conclusions from these core beliefs. This brings me back to the importance of exploring which understandings of cosmopolitanism are relevant to evaluating associations, particularly a plurality of associations.

Political theorists often point to two broad understandings of cosmopolitanism. These are: (1) a view of cosmopolitanism as setting out the responsibilities and duties we have to others, and (2) an understanding of cosmopolitanism as an identity or way of life. This distinction follows Samuel Scheffler's argument that cosmopolitanism entails two main strands: "one strand presents it primarily as a doctrine about justice. The other presents it primarily as a doctrine about culture and the self."[1] Gillian Brock and Harry Brighouse create a similar categorization. In their introduction to *The Political Philosophy of Cosmopolitanism* they describe cosmopolitanism as a "thesis about identity" and a "thesis about responsibility."[2] Therefore, while the majority of cosmopolitan political theories have some underlying normative ideal—the ought—that motivates their demand that individuals recognize their international moral obligations, some also see cosmopolitanism as relevant to shaping identities. My project is not a contribution to the already lively debates over how global political structures could foster cosmopolitan identities or help fulfill cosmopolitan responsibilities. Instead my focus is on the effects of membership in associations.

Associations realize cosmopolitanism not merely through shifting norms toward acknowledging global moral responsibility or advocating for human rights but also through shaping members' dispositions to see themselves as global actors and their concerns as relevant to the broader human community. If cosmopolitan theory is to assess the effects of associations, then the two strands of cosmopolitan theory need to be combined. Cosmopolitanism as a way of life or identity addresses how associations could cultivate dispositions that are crucial to supporting cosmopolitan norms, which in turn could support universal moral principles. Explaining the importance of both approaches to cosmopolitanism foreshadows the analysis in chapter 2 where cosmopolitan theories of moral obligation as well as of identity and deliberation become sources for criteria to assess associations.

As I just did for the first question, let me now foreshadow how I will approach the second question from the beginning of this chapter. Can cosmopolitanism's universalism actually be balanced with valuing a plurality of associations that are not fully global? Since my goal is to consider what cosmopolitan theory implies for a range of associations—not only an ideal type—it is also important to ask how cosmopolitanism, with its universal moral principles, could relate to a plurality of associations. As a starting point, it is helpful to delineate different possible relations between universalism and partiality: prioritizing universalism, prioritizing pluralism, or combining universalism and plurality. Cosmopolitan theories are often categorized into the first approach, which privileges universal principles over particular identities or ties. However, simply assuming that contemporary cosmopolitan theory prioritizes universalism does not best describe what are actually complex theories that take into account diversity and partial relations. In fact, some theorists even defend cosmopolitan patriotism, a seemingly contradictory concept.

Cosmopolitan theories are often distinguished from an approach that prioritizes some form of pluralism because pluralism focuses less on individuals and more on groups. Pluralism has different meanings. In some definitions, pluralism rejects an understanding of social and political activity as aiming at "the realization of a single and manifestly supreme value, in light of which all other moral ambitions may be empirically and conclusively evaluated."[3] As a normative ideal pluralism refuses to prioritize one set of universal principles. Instead, it represents the benefits of cultural and social diversity. As an explanatory theory rather than a normative one, pluralism helps to understand how policy is developed through the actions of different actors.[4] For example, in American theories of democracy, pluralism explains how democracy functions through the interactions of different interest groups rather than primarily through the actions of the public as a whole or even through independent individual voters.[5] Global civil society theorists, who defend the value of a variety of transnational associations, represent a pluralism approach relevant to my topic. Some of these theorists specifically critique prioritizing universalism as hubristic and threatening to diversity. Like with the approach that prioritizes universalism, the pluralism approach goes too far in one direction. As I will show in chapter 3, it helps to illustrate the weaknesses of focusing too much on plurality. Transnational voluntary associations must be assessed for "cosmopolitanism cannot simply gape in admiration before the brave new world of international civil society."[6] Therefore, pluralism, as I will employ the term, is not meant to explain specific policy developments. I use the term to indicate that a diversity of non-state actors may contribute different elements of cosmopolitanism without necessarily prioritizing or establishing a hierarchy of those values of cosmopolitanism.

A third approach seeks to connect universalism and pluralism and is much better able to accommodate many of the contemporary cosmopolitan theories I employ. It argues that a plurality of associations can contribute to generating norms that establish cosmopolitan responsibilities and advance cosmopolitan universal moral principles. While existing contemporary theories can easily be classified into this middle ground approach the implications for transnational voluntary associations are not always fully explored.

The introduction outlined a self-consciously broad definition of associations as transnational (drawing membership from more than one state) and voluntary (usually meaning non-state associations that individuals are free to join and leave). Relying on a very general definition of transnational voluntary associations allows for considering a plurality of associations. This includes more formally organized advocacy associations such as Amnesty International, religious organizations, or professional groups, as well as more loosely or temporarily organized social movements and advocacy networks—all of which scholars have shown play an important role in impacting norms on the global level. As a result of this diversity, coming up with one definition for the term *association* is difficult. Even on the domestic level establishing one definition that encompasses all the different types of associations is like defining a "moving target."[7] Nevertheless, let me say a few more words about common ways of categorizing associations. They are, after all, central to my project.

Associations are sometimes categorized in terms of the means they employ. This is often done to distinguish associations from states or the market. Voluntary non-governmental organizations do not have a legitimate monopoly of violence, unlike states, and do not necessarily operate in terms of profit, unlike businesses. Instead they tend to employ persuasion and emphasize normative argument and justification.[8] The United Nations' definition of non-governmental organizations (NGO) embodies some of these points. To be considered a NGO an association needs to be not-for-profit and "principally independent from government."[9] It also needs to be "task-oriented and made up of people with a common interest" even limiting the common interest to "issues in support of the public good."[10] Despite this common definition, Nancy L. Rosenblum and Mark E. Warren caution that trying to distinguish associations from the state and market is too blunt an approach. Warren is right to point out that voluntary membership around a particular task does not mean that associations are without power.[11] Transnational associations often act in areas where those they aid have little say in the actions of the association. Rosenblum reminds us of the fact that associations may have other goals or purposes that are valuable to individuals besides advancing the public good. Although I will refer to transnational associations as voluntary and non-governmental, my goal in doing so is to focus on evaluating membership in associations that individuals are free to join and leave. The goal is not to classify associations based on their purposes but instead to focus on a plurality of associations with different purposes. Focusing on goals that support the public interest overlooks the possibility that membership in associations that do not seek to persuade people to work for the public good might nevertheless advance certain elements of cosmopolitanism.

Rather than addressing the means or purpose of an association, some theorists distinguish them in terms of types of membership. This may seem particularly helpful given my focus on the effects of membership. The associations I am interested in are often distinguished from first-order intimate relationships—or what Amy Gutmann refers to as "primary associations"—between family and friends.[12] However, Warren cautions against missing ties of intimacy within associations.[13] In addition to intimate relations, distinctions are made between "'secondary' associations . . . whose central functions entail bringing members together in local chapters for regular meetings" and "'tertiary' associations that are distant from their members in their daily operations."[14] The examples that Gutmann gives of tertiary associations include organizations like Amnesty International and Oxfam, where many members are not actively involved in running the organization but instead donate money or participate sporadically in group-sponsored activities. As the examples of tertiary associations show, choosing to focus on secondary at the expense of tertiary groups would eliminate many associations on the international level, which ought to be studied for their cosmopolitan potential. Instead my project is inspired by the work of Roseblum, who explores "the personal uses of pluralism,"[15] and of Warren, who explores the "rich tapestry"[16] of associations. Both theorists emphasize plurality rather than categories of membership. The difference in my approach is that I take the evaluation of associations to the transnational level.

Defining transnational associations is not easy, especially if one seeks a broad definition. Associations are organizations of individuals that "constantly confront us with their mixed nature and purposes."[17] Therefore, I employ a general definition of associations as non-state actors in which individuals organize for a variety of purposes (thereby excluding the transnational influence of powerful individual actors, for example). Put another way, the associations at the heart of this project represent "pluralistic forms of social organization."[18] Members must be consciously organized. Just because one could tally up a group of individuals in terms of class, race, ethnicity, or gender does not mean that they form an association, although sometimes these commonalities motivate people to organize. Common interests, such as opposing the use of landmines (a famous example of transnational coordination), can lead people to organize transnationally. Given all of the difficulties with how to classify associations, one might argue that differences among associations make it impossible to generalize about their effects. Warren worries about this as well but concludes that one can generalize about associations if one makes "the right kinds of distinctions—distinctions that capture the diversity of associational goods."[19] For my purposes, I will generalize about associational effects that advance cosmopolitanism.

In order to use universal ideals to account for a plurality of associations a broad definition of cosmopolitanism is needed or else the assessment of associations is too narrow and diversity is sacrificed. At this point connections between the answers to the two central questions of this chapter become even clearer. Cosmopolitanism understood as a theory of identity and responsibility can help to develop criteria that acknowledge the potential of a plurality of associations to advance ideals of moral equality and transnational community. Therefore, it is important to defend the claim that a cosmopolitanism of responsibility and identity can be combined and that cosmopolitanism ought to include both elements of universalism and pluralism. These two critical background claims will be explored in greater detail now.

DEFINING COSMOPOLITANISM

Understanding what type of cosmopolitanism ought to be used to evaluate associations is critical because it will determine which theories of cosmopolitanism ought to be explored in more detail to derive the cosmopolitan content for criteria to assess associations. Therefore, let me now address the two strands of cosmopolitanism I have mentioned.

Cosmopolitanism as Responsibility

The first way to categorize contemporary cosmopolitan theories is to note that many theorists see cosmopolitanism as first and foremost about theorizing moral responsibilities or obligations. What cosmopolitan duties do we have? The focus is specifically on the moral obligations individuals have to those beyond their state borders and to non-citizens within their local communities. Thomas Pogge's definition referenced in the introduction describes cosmopolitan individualism as challenging the common view that states are the primary morally relevant unit on the global level. Instead, the status of ultimate moral concern "attaches to every living human being equally," and "has global force."[20] Not only do humans have equal moral worth but this status also entails moral responsibilities that extend beyond state borders. Cosmopolitans differ on the specific obligations but most robust theories extend obligations to some form of equal treatment. The very basic cosmopolitan responsibility I assume will be respecting human rights. As Charles Beitz writes, "to whatever extent contemporary international political life can be said to have a 'sense of justice,' its language is the language of human rights" even if their application and enforcement is uneven and at times in effective.[21] Although many prominent cosmopolitans including Beitz and Pogge connect cosmopolitanism and human rights, my assumption of a responsibility to respect human rights is not necessarily an uncontroversial stance. In some cases theorists go farther to argue that we ought to help ensure individuals can fully access the capabilities that lead to flourishing human lives.[22] Even among those who develop theories of human rights, there are debates about which rights should be human rights. Some could argue, for example, that freedom of association should not be a human right. Debates over human rights have been and continue to be discussed in other contexts. Rather than entering into such debates, which would potentially side track me from the goal of considering whether cosmopolitan theories could be applied to associations, I simply begin from the assumption that freedom of association is a human right and that cosmopolitanism, at its minimum, consists of a responsibility to ensure that we do not violate the rights of others no matter how distant. The general thesis of responsibility to respect human rights to individual liberties embraces theoretical distinctions that cosmopolitans often debate—such as strong versus moderate views on the extent of our obligations to others.

An obligation to respect the human right to freedom of association is actually not usually discussed in terms of transnational voluntary associations. Cosmopolitans that address associations often focus on the nation or the state as the partial association most in need of theoretical analysis. An example of such an approach can be found in the following quote: "if the cosmopolitan idea of justice is to have any appeal for human beings, it must acknowledge the local attachments and commitments people have that are characteristic of most meaningful and rewarding human lives. Among the special ties and commitments that people share are those of nationality."[23] Nationality or attachments to a state are considered particularly significant because states remain powerfully influential actors in our world today. Moreover, states make claims of loyalty and duty on their citizens, a particularly strong example of which is military service. In the words of someone skeptical of cosmopolitanism: "one who knows no heroes in his own land will feel nothing but contempt for the naïveté of those who honor heroes elsewhere. Before a child can learn to value others he needs to learn to value."[24] The state's demand for loyalty leads some cosmopolitans to argue that patriotism is "morally dangerous"[25] because national identity and patriotic state allegiance obstruct our recognition of universal commonalities among fellow humans. There are contemporary cosmopolitans who do not accept this sharp distinction between cosmopolitanism and partiality, instead arguing that one can have obligations to partial associations and to fellow humans (a point I will discuss in the next section of this chapter).

It is the aim of this book to argue that cosmopolitanism understood as a theory of responsibility to respect and protect universal rights to individual liberty ought to explore how associations help advance cosmopolitanism. Associations can play an instrumental role in contributing to cosmopolitan goals of protecting human rights or reinforcing international norms of human rights by providing opportunities for individuals to fulfill obligations. One expatriate doctor from Médecins Sans Frontières (MSF) describes his gratitude for the opportunity MSF provided for him to work in Sudan. He writes that the experience, "allowed me to stay firm in the world, to make peace with things I may otherwise have tried to ignore."[26] Scholarship focusing on the goals of associations with the purpose of advancing human rights often asks questions like: What is a morally appropriate way to advocate for human rights? In David A. Bell and Jean-Marc Coicaud's edited volume *Ethics in Action: The Ethical Challenges of International Human Rights Nongovernmental Organizations*, essays address topics such as "Northern INGOs [International Non-governmental Organizations] and Southern Aid Recipients: The Challenge of Unequal Power," or "INGOs and Governments: The Challenges of Dealing with States that Restrict the Activities of INGOs."[27] As these titles indicate, the main focus is on how obligations are best fulfilled in challenging contexts. Associations certainly can be studied for their instrumental role in supporting international standards of human rights.[28] However, this focus does not see membership in associations as generating cosmopolitan norms and dispositions even if indirectly or unintentionally. As chapter 4 will flesh out in detail, associations can actually create cosmopolitan obligations by bringing people together in new ways such that duties arise as a result of membership in an association even without a goal of advocating for human rights. Highlighting the creative potential of associations sees them as more than assistants to governmental institutions or enforcers of existing international law. A thesis of responsibility certainly can involve exploring what cosmopolitan obligations associations help to fulfill but it should also consider how associations might give rise to and shape cosmopolitan obligations. Chapter 2 will consider more specifically what cosmopolitan obligations ought to entail and how associations might advance them.

Cosmopolitanism as Identity

Theories that focus on responsibility often aim to keep that view of cosmopolitanism distinct from a concept of identity. The liberal cosmopolitan Kok-Chor Tan defends such a separation arguing that cosmopolitanism as an identity is problematic "if the truly free individual on the cosmopolitan view is one who is culturally detached, and one who must be able to provide impersonal and general justifications for the social ties and commitments that she has."[29] Instead cosmopolitanism should be "understood primarily as a doctrine about justice" because then it is "agnostic about how individuals are to understand their own conceptions of the good and their special allegiances."[30] And Tan is not alone in this view. Beitz also argues that the benefit of moral cosmopolitanism is that it entails responsibilities without requiring specific claims about what constitutes a cosmopolitan identity.[31] Pogge's definition of the three central components of cosmopolitanism (individualism, universalism, generality) says nothing about a cosmopolitan identity or a global sense of belonging.[32] Imposing the rigorous demands of universal moral responsibilities on identity would require that individuals detach themselves from all special identifications and base their attachment on "only reason and the love of humanity."[33] In order to avoid this and protect diversity, the argument goes, one must reject the ideal of a universal cosmopolitan identity. Of course there are certain cosmopolitan theorists, such as Martha Nussbaum, who see cosmopolitan identity as requiring that individuals step back from partial ties. In that case, cosmopolitanism is a "lonely business."[34] Yet, those who worry that cosmopolitan identity requires impartial detachment are employing a limited understanding of what cosmopolitan identity can actually entail.

There are theorists who argue that cosmopolitanism need not require detachment from parochial attachments. There are some who rightly argue that "the current usage of cosmopolitanism as a moral perspective, in fact, requires some recourse to the original, non-pejorative idea of cosmopolitanism as a mode of life."[35] It is necessary to "resist the sharp distinction that is sometimes made between 'moral' and 'cultural' cosmopolitanism, where the former comprises those principles of moral universalism and impartialism, and the latter comprises the values of the world traveler."[36] The danger of this distinction is that it misses the necessary connection between our identities and living up to our responsibilities. After all, "if we care *about* others who are not part of our political order — others who may have commitments and beliefs that are unlike our own — we must have a way to talk *to* them."[37] When it comes to understanding how associations can contribute to cosmopolitan ideals, attempts to separate responsibility and identity are counterproductive. They overlook the full potential of associations.

In order to defend a combination of responsibility and identity it is necessary to be clearer about what cultural cosmopolitanism or cosmopolitan identity ought to entail. Not all definitions of cosmopolitan identity are compatible with moral principles. One incompatible view is the ideal of a world traveler as merely someone "who savors cultural diversity" for aesthetic purposes.[38] This image of cosmopolitanism as a lifestyle based on familiarity with "the manners, habits, languages and social customs of cities throughout the world" results in a cosmopolitan becoming nothing more than "a parasite, who depends upon the quotidian lives of others to create the various local flavours and identities in which he dabbles."[39] This view could be compatible with moral obligations if a conscious decision to enjoy diversity was adopted in order to better live up to cosmopolitan ideals of universalism, although this does not seem to fit the description of a dabbler in diversity. A purely aesthetic view does not require a strong connection to a sense of responsibility.[40] A slightly more normative understanding of detached cosmopolitan identity involves an intellectual elite exchanging ideas in a global republic of letters. There might be some sense of solidarity among fellow intellectual cosmopolitans, however narrowly defined, but obligations do not necessarily extend beyond that group.

A very different concept of cosmopolitan identity is directly linked to understanding moral or responsible ways of forming solidarities and respecting diversity. It need not require individuals give up partial attachments or realize a single set of intellectual virtues. Instead, recognizing the complexity of local, transnational, and global components of an individual's identity becomes vital to respecting individuals. Theorists have given this version of cosmopolitanism many qualifications in order to distinguish it from more universalist Enlightenment versions of cosmopolitanism and their problematic imperialistic tendencies. Some such

qualifications include rooted cosmopolitanism or vernacular cosmopolitanism and often link cosmopolitanism with national or cultural communities.[41] Kwame Anthony Appiah defends a rooted cosmopolitanism
where cosmopolitans can even be patriots. Homi Bhaba writes of vernacular cosmopolitanism in which individuals at the margins of society revise "the 'universal' or the general" through protesting imperialist projects or refusing to fit in with accepted standards of globalization and in
doing so transform "what is local and what is global."[42] A cosmopolitan
disposition can mean recognizing that one's cultural identity is shaped
over time through a process of interactions with others rather than seeing
one's culture as a pure and unchanging whole. Cosmopolitan identities
emerge through the melding of and reshaping of cultures resulting in
hybrid ways of life, which may be accessed through migration and travel
or through living in certain cosmopolitan local communities such as
world cities like New York, Paris, and Bombay.[43] Cosmopolitanism can
even be found in "the testing of boundaries and limits as part of a communal, collective process, so that choice is less an individualistic internal
desire, than it is a public demand and duty."[44] Clearly certain discussions
of cosmopolitanism and culture are infused with the language of obligation and duty.

Rather than joining in debates on the cosmopolitanism of cultural
communities, I draw from these arguments the idea that a cosmopolitan
identity is more complex than merely embracing the most universal of
identities—human—or reveling in diversity for aesthetic purposes.
Transnational not merely global identities should be considered relevant
for cosmopolitans. (Transnational, as I use it, indicates that associations
have cross-border membership but do not encompass all humans. It does
not imply a normative claim about the importance of national borders.)
Determining the scope of an identity as transnational or global is not
enough to make it cosmopolitan, as transnational terrorist groups clearly
demonstrate. Chapter 2 will explore in a bit more detail what makes
certain partial and hybrid identities cosmopolitan. Establishing how partial identities could nevertheless be compatible with cosmopolitanism is
one of the reasons criteria for associations are necessary. Acknowledging
the cosmopolitan potential of partial identities can allow for a more inclusive, less elitist understanding of who could develop a cosmopolitan
identity because it does not require radical detachment from all partial
ties.

In conclusion, the two understandings of cosmopolitanism—identity
and responsibility—can be distinguished; however, it is important to eschew strict demarcations between them when analyzing associations in
order to avoid a tendency toward elitism and an underappreciation of the
value of membership. Connecting the responsibility and identity strands
will aid in bridging the gap "between identity constructions and normative development processes that have tended to fall outside the lenses of

traditional moral theories."[45] How identity is constructed has significant moral implications. Yet, it need not follow that the identity formed should be purely universal. As the cases in part II help to illustrate, membership in associations can cultivate cosmopolitan dispositions by drawing out connections and commonalities that transcend state borders. This in turn could cultivate a sense of transnational responsibility to members of the association.

RELATIONSHIPS BETWEEN UNIVERSALISM AND PLURALISM OF ASSOCIATIONS

Connecting responsibility and identity strands of cosmopolitanism raises additional questions because combining them requires accepting significant tensions. Universalism and partial identities are not obviously mutually supportive, as earlier quotes from cosmopolitan theorists Tan and Beitz make clear.[46] If universal principles require respecting individuals' freedom of association then tensions likely emerge because not all freely formed associations are necessarily going to aim at fostering cosmopolitanism. It is necessary to address the second question this chapter began with: Can cosmopolitanism embrace universalism and a plurality of associations? Note that in asking this I side step the much debated question of whether it is desirable to form connections across borders. Rather than participating in the more common debate between cosmopolitans and statists or communitarians (those who reject the global scope of obligations and the value of transnational identity), my discussion begins by assuming that cosmopolitanism is acceptable and considers its implications for associations.

Within theories that value global connections there are still significant differences over the appropriate relationship between universal principles and membership in partial associations. These can be summarized in terms of three main approaches. Approach one and two are drawn from theories of cosmopolitanism and global civil society respectively. They require prioritizing an ideal—universalism or pluralism of associations. This prioritizing has weaknesses my middle ground approach of supplemented cosmopolitanism seeks to address. The middle ground approach does not aim to resolve the tension in favor of either universalism or partial associations but claims "cosmopolitanism should be supplemented not abandoned: we should honour our cosmopolitan duties to others *and* respect cultural diversity."[47] Or in the words of another representative of this view: "it would be wrong, however, to conflate cosmopolitanism and humanism . . . [because] cosmopolitanism is not just the feeling that everyone matters. The cosmopolitan also celebrates the fact that there are different local human ways of being."[48] In other words, respectfully engaging with diversity is crucial to a cosmopolitan life. Diversity and plurality are compatible with cosmopolitan conceptions of liberty. Tensions may remain but that does not mean cosmopolitan theory is untenable. Because the middle ground approach argues universalism and pluralism are compatible, it best allows for considering the potential of a variety of associations.

My goal in outlining the three approaches is to foreshadow the framework I will be using in the next three chapters. Chapter 2 analyzes cosmopolitan theories. Chapter 3 assesses global civil society theories. Chapter 4 develops my cosmopolitan criteria, which supplements existing cosmopolitan theories. Before explaining the middle ground approach in more detail, outlining the universalism and pluralism approaches is useful because they show the weaknesses of views that privilege one or the other. Lessons can be learned from exploring those views.

Universalism Approach

This approach argues that universalism should trump diversity. Cosmopolitan theories may seem obviously to fall into this approach. Universal principles are certainly a central part of cosmopolitanism understood as a thesis about responsibility. Critics of cosmopolitanism attack it for granting global force to what is really just a "reassertion of Greek or Enlightenment values, of (European) philosophical universalism"[49] in the tradition of imperialist projects that involve spreading culture and universal principles in the name of civilizing people. In such views, the diversity found in many parts of the world is considered backward and not worth saving. Cosmopolitanism's normative project fails to really embrace toleration. Instead it is merely "the universalization of a culturally particular conception of justice" that imposes "a framework of twentieth-century American liberalism" on the world.[50] The great liberal philosopher John Rawls famously opposed cosmopolitan justice because of the threat of cultural and political imperialism that he saw underlying an international application of his theory. Universalizing liberal values would result in a situation where "nonliberal societies are always properly subject to some form of sanctions," sanctions that denied their freedom.[51] A picture of universalism that imposes homogeneity on the world is easy to attack. Yet, contemporary cosmopolitans do not oppose diversity. Certainly forms of diversity (for example, those that violate rights) are unacceptable but not many other forms of diversity. Imperialist homogeneity would violate the very goals of respecting human dignity, human rights, or human flourishing. More complex views of cosmopolitanism are not as easily rejected outright. Nevertheless, there are still weaknesses one can find in approaches that claim to respect diversity but prioritize universalism.

Martha Nussbaum's cosmopolitanism acknowledges the importance of diversity but still aims to prioritize universalism. She argues that partial allegiances are acceptable if justified in impartial universal terms.[52] Tensions between universalism and partiality are therefore resolved. Associations whose exclusive membership could not be justified in universal terms (for example, racist justifications) would not be acceptable. One could justify membership in associations on impartial terms if one were to argue that, given the lack of global governmental institutions, human rights or environmental associations are the best avenues for individuals to fulfill their moral obligations to people in other parts of the world.

Collapsing the tensions between universalism and partiality results in a failure to recognize the potential of certain associations without cosmopolitan goals to advance cosmopolitanism. The universalism approach does not provide a path for people to come to act on cosmopolitan norms in any way other than through a self-conscious decision to do so. Yet, perhaps I join an association because I want to participate in its athletic games. Coming up with universal justifications may be possible but they would likely be far removed from the actual motivation of members. This leaves the association tolerable but not relevant to advancing cosmopolitanism. Incorporating non-cosmopolitan associations into a theory of cosmopolitanism would certainly bring tensions back into the theory.

Pluralism Approach

Another approach to the relation between cosmopolitanism and partial associations emphasizes pluralism, understood to mean valuing a plurality of diverse associations. Pluralism ought to be protected first and foremost—trumping cosmopolitan universalism. Used in this way pluralism represents not a descriptive view of what the world actually looks like but a normative claim about what the world ought to look like. One example of this can be found in certain global civil society theories. John Keane, for example, defends the essential role played by pluralism in global civil society.[53] He argues not simply that individuals should be free to join different associations, but that there ought to exist different kinds of associations. Heterogeneity in global civil society is necessary for protecting against dangerous forms of hubris that lead people to believe their views are the only truth and therefore ought to be imposed on the whole world. A plurality of associations can encourage people to question their own positions or at least recognize theirs is not the only view.[54] As a result, Keane's theory of global civil society does not aim to establish one specific global community but instead aims to provide the conditions necessary for creating a culture of self-awareness and hybridity. Cosmopolitanism, he maintains, is not compatible with pluralism precisely because of its universalism. His concept of global civil society "sticks a pin in the bottom of cosmopolitan universalism" and deflates cosmopolitanism's ideal of one common global community.[55]

However, Keane's position has its limitations, as will be discussed in greater detail in chapter 3. The pluralism Keane presents is missing a strong basis from which actually to defend pluralism, and despite recognizing some forms of pluralism as a threat, does not have a strong justification for drawing acceptable limits to this pluralism.[56] A position that prioritizes pluralism to too great an extent is left with only a vague sense of ethical behavior to govern global interactions. In Keane's case the global ethic is one that consists of respecting difference and practicing nonviolence. Keane assumes that pluralism will remove the dangers of hubris but he does not explain why or how diversity will result in respect for diversity and how individuals will come to espouse the ethics he proposes.

The right approach to cosmopolitanism could provide a much stronger basis for recognizing the possibilities and limits of a plurality of associations. Not all associations will necessarily have beneficial effects but cosmopolitanism can establish a framework for determining what forms of pluralism are beneficial for spreading its global ethic. A view that rejects cosmopolitanism as homogenizing underestimates the potential of cosmopolitanism to address a broad range of associations.

Middle Ground Approach to Cosmopolitanism

Cosmopolitanism can defend itself from global civil society theorists' critiques if it can accommodate pluralism rather than always privilege universalism. There are different ways of carving out a middle path between universalism and pluralism. An aesthetic view could argue that a plurality of associations ensures human flourishing by providing people opportunities to tap into ways of life as a kind of freedom of experimentation. A cosmopolitan world is not "a homogenized, bland, world of stultifying uniformity"[57] because otherwise, the cosmopolitan could not enjoy experiences necessary for living a full life. However, such a view remains unsatisfactory for reasons discussed earlier. It is incompatible with my definition of cosmopolitanism because it fails to involve a robust concept of responsibility. It also seems to imply a perfectionist view of the appropriate kind of cosmopolitan life—that of a world traveler. While that kind of life is described as free, it may not be accessible to all people and excludes certain choices of associational life. The middle route needed here is one that can embrace freedom of membership in associations beyond the cosmopolitan traveler who dabbles in diversity.

One such middle ground view could argue that cosmopolitanism can tolerate a range of associations with non-cosmopolitan purposes. Pluralism is relevant if one realizes that: "human rights [such as freedom of speech and association] do not simply not generate uniformity: they positively facilitate pluralism."[58] However, tensions between cosmopolitan universal principles of liberty and participation in partial associations seem likely to occur; "What is freedom if not the ability to do what others may think not worth doing?"[59] One way to resolve theoretical tensions is to establish a threshold of toleration. This is possible because cosmopolitan responsibilities represent only a bare minimum that allows for a plurality of additional allegiances. "Cosmopolitan distributive ideals are not destructive of diversity," cosmopolitan Simon Caney writes, "because they do not aim to set out a full and general ethics or political morality: they simply set out some minimum standard."[60]

If a plurality of associations is to be evaluated on cosmopolitan terms, a threshold of toleration can determine which effects threaten cosmopolitanism but not which effects advance cosmopolitanism. Associations with explicitly anti-cosmopolitan goals, such as transnational religious terrorist organizations, need not be tolerated. Despite their global scope they seek to dehumanize others and violate human rights. Those with clearly cosmopolitan goals could also be picked out using cosmopolitan theory. Associations like Amnesty International or Human Rights Watch consciously aim to advance human rights. This mission is congruent with cosmopolitan theory's principle of the moral equality of all humans. Between these two types of associations—cosmopolitan ones and anti-cosmopolitan ones—there are a vast number of associations that do not self-consciously aim at advancing cosmopolitan ideals and do not threaten its principles either. A set of criteria is needed for more nuanced assessment of the creative potential of such associations to advance cosmopolitanism. It is precisely the impact of associations without an explicitly cosmopolitan goal that is most likely to be overlooked by a focus on toleration. Furthermore, studying a broad range of associations benefits from a broadly defined understanding of cosmopolitanism that includes a concept of responsibility and identity. This can account for different possible contributions to cosmopolitanism from groups that do not fully embrace its principles. Not all associations need to become fully cosmopolitan to help cultivate greater respect for moral equality or transnational community. This raises the possibility that cosmopolitanism need not be advanced as a whole, an idea I will test with actual cases of associations in part II. In order to apply cosmopolitanism to associations, it is necessary to carve out a middle ground between universalism and pluralism with criteria drawn from cosmopolitan theory for evaluating common effects of associations.

Before moving forward to develop a middle-level theory of criteria, one should acknowledge that there certainly are arguments for keeping cosmopolitan theory abstract and ideal. If we return to the claim about the power of moral cosmopolitanism, it rests in its universalism not its partiality. Universal principles serve as critical standards to use in judging practices in our world. However, if one is interested in how cosmopolitanism could come about in the world in a way that respects the diversity resulting from individual liberty, it is also important to find ways of applying cosmopolitan theory in an incompletely cosmopolitan world. This is the goal of some theories of cosmopolitan identity. A middle-level theory of cosmopolitan criteria for associations can provide a way of considering how to evaluate the norm changes and identities developed through the actions of a plurality of associations. Cosmopolitan theory ought to include not only a claim about the *limits* of toleration but also a way of evaluating the cosmopolitan *potential* of associations that do not have a self-consciously cosmopolitan purpose.

Much greater specificity is needed before it is possible to delineate criteria for evaluating the effects of associations but what I have argued so far hints at some very general ways membership in associations can have cosmopolitan effects. Norm development is a way associations could spread cosmopolitanism. Associations could shape what norms are acceptable in transnational public deliberation through awareness-raising campaigns. They could help to institutionalize certain norms in international law. Or associations could establish standards that help advance moral equality through garnering greater respect for women, overcoming racial divides, or recognizing obligations to those negatively affected by the global market, to name a few examples. In addition to norm development, the potential cosmopolitanism of associations could also exhibit itself in terms of shaping dispositions. Associations mobilize different groups of people on the transnational level for reasons besides love of diversity or cosmopolitan principles. They invoke particular commonalities that can generate empathy across borders. Transnational associations provide opportunities for individuals to experience being global actors and, in some cases, re-frame local concerns in a global context. Although it may seem like developing norms and shaping dispositions can be broken up to map onto the strands of responsibility and identity cosmopolitanism, it becomes clear that even those two types of effects weave together obligations and dispositions. In order to abide by moral obligations certain dispositions may be required. Categorizing cosmopolitan theories in terms of theories of responsibility and identity is inadequate for understanding associations. It is important that both theories of responsibility and identity be addressed but in terms of categories that more directly relate to the goal of assessing associations.

Connecting the two understandings of cosmopolitanism—responsibility and identity—and embracing a plurality of associations does not mean developing a new comprehensive theory of cosmopolitanism that begins by defining and defending new foundational principles. My goal is not to establish theoretical justifications for freedom of association. Instead I begin from the premise that cosmopolitan theory respects individual liberty to form and join associations in order to understand the implications of such a theoretical position. Respecting individual liberty to form associations is not best supported by a theory that focuses on an ideal type of association. A plurality of transnational voluntary associations may be compatible with but also could be crucial to realizing cosmopolitanism in the world. If different associations exhibit different expressions of cosmopolitanism then it can arise piecemeal—a norm changed here, a disposition transformed there, and so on. If the focus remained on ideal associations the cosmopolitan potential of those without explicitly cosmopolitan goals would likely be overlooked. It is precisely these associations that hold the potential for spreading cosmopolitanism.

Membership in associations needs to be seen as relevant to realizing cosmopolitan obligations and forming cosmopolitan identities. Linking morality and identity can ensure that universal principles are not defined at the expense of pluralism or pluralism at the expense of moral standards. While not all theorists believe the thesis of responsibility and the thesis of identity should be combined, a middle-level theory consisting of criteria compatible with diverse ways of expressing cosmopolitanism is made possible by an understanding of cosmopolitanism that draws inspiration from both theses. The two strands or theses are still too general to lead easily to criteria. Therefore, I focus next on particular cosmopolitan theories of obligation and of ethical ways of living to draw out specific expressions of cosmopolitan duties and identities.

NOTES

1. Samuel Scheffler, "Conceptions of Cosmopolitanism," *Utilitas* 11, no. 3 (November 1999): 225.

2. Gillian Brock and Harry Brighouse, introduction to *The Political Philosophy of Cosmopolitanism,* ed. Gillian Brock and Harry Brighouse (New York: Cambridge University Press, 2005), 2.

3. John W. Chapman, "Voluntary Associations and the Political Theory of Pluralism," in *Voluntary Associations Nomos XI,* ed. J. Roland Pennock and John W. Chapman (New York: Atherton Press, 1969), 92.

4. For this distinction see John Dryzek and Patrick Dunleavy, *Theories of the Democratic State* (New York: Palgrave Macmillan, 2009), 2. Also see chapter 2, "Pluralism," for a discussion of theories of pluralism in relation to democracy.

5. Nancy L. Rosenblum describes pluralism as commonly understood to entail multiple centers of power. She then goes on to argue that the centers of power need not be found only in political forms of power. Nancy L. Rosenblum, *Membership and Morals: The Personal Uses of Pluralism in America* (Princeton, NJ: Princeton University Press, 1998), 4.

6. Bruce Robbins, "Actually Existing Cosmopolitanism," in *Cosmopolitics: Thinking and Feeling Beyond the Nation,* ed. Pheng Cheah and Bruce Robbins (Minneapolis: University of Minnesota Press, 1998), 9.

7. Rosenblum, *Membership and Morals,* 5.

8. Mark E. Warren, *Democracy and Association* (Princeton, NJ: Princeton University Press, 2001), 39.

9. "Non-Governmental Organizations," United Nations Rule of Law Website, accessed April 22, 2014, http://www.unrol.org/article.aspx?article_id=23. This is a website maintained by the Rule of Law Unit in the Executive Office of the Secretary General of the UN. It serves as a repository for UN law materials and information.

10. Ibid.

11. Warren, *Democracy and Association,* 52. Rosenblum makes a similar point, *Membership and Morals,* 6.

12. Amy Gutmann categorizes associations in "Freedom of Associations: An Introductory Essay," in *Freedom of Association,* ed. Amy Gutmann (Princeton, NJ: Princeton University Press, 1998), 10.

13. Warren discusses the different categorizations of associations, including Amy Gutmann's, and their drawbacks. *Democracy and Association,* 39.

14. Gutmann, "Freedom of Association," 10. Gutmann is discussing associations in the context of a liberal democracy, the United States. However, the associations she references, such as Amnesty International, clearly have a scope beyond the United States.

15. Rosenblum, *Membership and Morals,* 22.

16. Warren, *Democracy and Association,* 16.

17. Rosenblum, *Membership and Morals,* 7.

18. Warren, *Democracy and Association,* 40.

19. Ibid., 11.

20. Thomas Pogge, "Cosmopolitanism and Sovereignty," *Ethics* 103, no. 1 (1992): 48.

21. Charles Beitz, "Human Rights as a Common Concern," *The American Political Science Review* 95, no. 2 (2001): 269.

22. Martha Nussbaum discusses the importance of ensuring all humans have the capabilities necessary to lead a flourishing life in *Frontiers of Justice: Disability, Nationality, Species Membership* (Cambridge, MA: Belknap Press of Harvard University Press, 2006). Beitz also argues that we have a human right to democracy in his article "Human Rights as a Common Concern." Whatever the particular argument defended, cosmopolitans often develop theories with more extensive moral obligations than simply the command "do no harm."

23. Kok-Chor Tan, "The Demands of Justice and National Allegiances," in Brock and Brighouse, *The Political Philosophy of Cosmopolitanism,* 164.

24. Michael W. McConnell, "Don't Neglect the Little Platoons," in *For Love of Country,* ed. Joshua Cohen (Boston: Beacon Press, 2002), 80.

25. Martha Nussbaum, "Patriotism and Cosmopolitanism," in Cohen, *For Love of Country,* 4.

26. James Maskalyk, *Six Months in Sudan: A Young Doctor in a War-torn Village* (New York: Speigel & Grau, 2009), xii.

27. From the table of contents of David A. Bell and Jean-Marc Coicaud, ed., *Ethics in Action: The Ethical Challenges of International Human Rights Nongovernmental Organizations* (New York: Cambridge University Press and United Nations University, 2007), vii–viii.

28. One example of this is David Held's argument in *Democracy and the Global Order: From the Modern State to Cosmopolitan Governance* (Stanford, CA: Stanford University Press, 1995), 237, 277–278.

29. Tan, "Demands of Justice," 177.

30. Ibid.

31. Charles Beitz, *Political Theory and International Relations* (Princeton, NJ: Princeton University Press, 1979), 181.

32. Pogge, "Cosmopolitanism and Sovereignty," 48.

33. Nussbaum, "Patriotism and Cosmopolitanism," 15.

34. Ibid.

35. Christine Sypnowich acknowledges that this will require some push and pull as the two, moral universalism and worldly aestheticism, do not necessarily go together. After all, a world of diversity can also be a world with great inequality. Christine Sypnowich, "Cosmopolitans, Cosmopolitanism, and Human Flourishing," in Brock and Brighouse, *The Political Philosophy of Cosmopolitanism,* 56, 58.

36. Kwame Anthony Appiah, *The Ethics of Identity* (Princeton NJ: Princeton University Press, 2005), 222.

37. Ibid. (Italics in original.)

38. Sypnowich, "Cosmopolitans," 56-57.

39. Roger Scruton, "Cosmopolitanism," *The Palgrave Macmillan Dictionary of Political Thought*, 3rd ed. (New York: Palgrave Macmillan, 2007), 146.

40. Steven Vertovec and Robin Cohen, "Introduction: Conceiving Cosmopolitanism," in *Conceiving Cosmopolitanism: Theory, Context, and Practice*, ed. Steven Vertovec and Robin Cohen (New York: Oxford University Press, 2002), 6–7.

41. Appiah, *Ethics of Identity*, chapter 6; Homi K. Bhaba, "Unsatisfied: Notes on Vernacular Cosmopolitanism," in *Text and Nation: Cross-Disciplinary Essays on Cultural and National Identities*, ed. Laura García-Moreno and Peter C. Pfeiffer (Columbia, SC: Camden House, 1996), 196; Pnina Werbner, "Vernacular Cosmopolitanism," *Theory Culture and Society* 23 (May 2006).

42. Bhabha, "Unsatisfied," 202.

43. Jeremy Waldron, "What is Cosmopolitan?" *The Journal of Political Philosophy* 8, no. 2 (2000); 232.

44. Bhabha, "Unsatisfied," 205.

45. Richard M. Price, "Moral Limit and Possibility in World Politics," in *Moral Limit and Possibility in World Politics*, ed. Richard M. Price (New York: Cambridge University Press, 2008), 32.

46. See endnotes 29, 30, and 31.

47. Simon Caney, "Cosmopolitan Justice and Cultural Diversity," *Global Society* 14, no. 4 (2000): 541. Caney is a cosmopolitan theorist who mounts a defense of cosmopolitanism against the criticism that "cosmopolitan distributive schemes are objectionable because they constitute a form of ideological hegemony," 534. His work provides a good representation of how cosmopolitan theorists seek to reconcile cosmopolitanism and diversity. See also Simon Caney, *Justice Beyond Borders: A Global Political Theory* (New York: Oxford University Press, 2005), 76.

48. In the same passage Appiah defines humanism as "consistent with the desire for global homogeneity. Humanism can be compatible with cosmopolitan sentiments, but it can also live with a deadening urge to uniformity." Appiah, "Cosmopolitan Patriots," in Cohen, *For Love of Country*, 25.

49. Robbins, " Actually Existing," 9.

50. Richard Shapcott, "Anti-cosmopolitanism, Pluralism and the Cosmopolitan Harm Principle," *Review of International Studies* 34 (2008): 190.

51. John Rawls, *The Law of Peoples with "The Idea of Public Reason Revisited"* (Cambridge, MA: Harvard University Press, 1999), 82. In fact, he continues in this same section, "on this account, the foreign policy of a liberal people—which is our concern to elaborate—will be to act gradually to shape all not yet liberal societies in a liberal direction, until eventually (in the ideal case) all societies are liberal. But this foreign policy simply assumes that only a liberal democratic society can be accepted," 82.

52. Nussbaum, "Patriotism and Cosmopolitanism," 9, 13.

53. John Keane, *Global Civil Society?* (Cambridge: Cambridge University Press, 2003), 66, 196–197. By global civil society Keane means a normative ideal of extra-governmental organizations behaving in a non-violent manner respectful of plurality. Also see pages 8–17 for more detail.

54. Ibid., 15.

55. Ibid., 125.

56. Keane's discussion includes not only different kinds of associations but also different moralities. He describes global civil society as marked by moral ambivalence, *Global Civil Society?* 15.

57. Caney, *Justice Beyond Borders*, 91.

58. Ibid.

59. George Kateb, "The Value of Association," in *Freedom of Association*, ed. Amy Gutmann (Princeton, NJ: Princeton University Press, 1998), 40.

60. Caney, "Cosmopolitan Justice and Cultural Diversity," 543. For a similar sentiment see also Nussbaum, *Frontiers of Justice*, 310.

TWO

From Comprehensive to Partial Cosmopolitanism

A view that associations are incompatible if not dangerous to cosmopolitan universalism because of their partiality—partial in the sense of not encompassing all humans and in the sense of oriented toward the interests of certain people—is misleading. As I argued in the previous chapter, increasingly cosmopolitans are defending a universalism in which a diversity of affiliations can be tolerated. This is an important improvement over imperialistic, homogenizing concepts of universalism. However, this improved cosmopolitan theory stops after establishing a threshold of toleration. It does not provide a way of assessing the contribution of transnational voluntary associations to the advancement of cosmopolitan norms, especially if the association does not have a cosmopolitan purpose. A more complex and nuanced picture of what cosmopolitanism requires of associations is needed. In order to develop such a theory this chapter addresses the question: What are the implications existing cosmopolitan theories have for studying the effects of associations?

Answering this question could take quite a while if every cosmopolitan theory (even if only every contemporary moral cosmopolitan theory) were explored, so narrowing down the task is critical. The broad definition of cosmopolitanism I outlined in chapter 1 directs one toward theories of global responsibilities as well as culture and identity. It helps to establish a relevant starting point even as it calls for greater theoretical explication before cosmopolitanism can serve as a source of criteria for applying to associations. This chapter will explore specific theories that fall into the categories of cosmopolitanism understood as about responsibility and about identity. The theories are comprehensive normative political theories because even though I am not addressing political institutions, my focus is studying organizations of individuals—transnational non-state associations—rather than individual morality or aesthetic views of cosmopolitanism. The political theories are comprehensive theories that defend first principles of cosmopolitanism and the implications for individual morality and/or social justice. Since none of the theories claim to provide criteria for evaluating associations, my goal is not to argue for one comprehensive theory over another but rather to consider how elements of these comprehensive theories could contribute to developing types of partial expressions of cosmopolitanism.

Ensuring that I include theories of responsibility as well as identity, I outline four main categories of cosmopolitan theory: institutional, natural duties, cultural, and deliberative democratic cosmopolitanism. The first two deal primarily with the source of obligations. The last two emphasize the ethical implications of membership in cultural or democratic communities. The theorists represented in each category may actually develop arguments that overlap the categories. However, the goal is to draw out aspects of cosmopolitanism that partial associations might realize rather than analyze theories as a whole. Even though the theory itself may not address transnational voluntary associations, I have chosen theories from which implications for partial associations can be drawn. What types of behavior, responsibilities, or identities might different theories emphasize that could be applied to associations? In exploring the implications of these theories for associations I make reference to possible effects associations might have. These references will be quite abstract at this point, as the theories under discussion do not depend upon empirical examples. It is also important to ask: How do cosmopolitan theories handle tensions between universalism and partiality? Drawing from different cosmopolitan theories means that tensions are certain to remain. In fact, the tensions may not only arise from cosmopolitanism's universalism and the partiality of associations but now also from combining different comprehensive theories of cosmopolitanism. Rather than choose between types of cosmopolitan theory to pick the best one for evaluating associations, each category represents particular expressions of cosmopolitanism an association could realize.

CATEGORIES OF COMPREHENSIVE COSMOPOLITANISM

Institutional Cosmopolitanism

This category presents cosmopolitan moral obligations as arising through relations within coercive global institutions. Charles Beitz, A. J. Julius, Darrel Moellendorf, and Thomas Pogge argue that international institutional rules and standards ought to be structured so that individuals operating within and individuals affected by such institutions could consent to them. There are certainly differences among these theorists' arguments, but they all help illustrate an approach to moral cosmopolitanism that defines our responsibility in terms of realizing fair and just global institutions.

In this view, cosmopolitanism entails obligations that emerge not "simply by virtue of the nature of [an individual's] personhood. On the contrary, duties of justice arise between persons when activities such as politics or commerce bring persons into association."[1] Beitz argues that institutions of the global economy require justification because they "have such deep and pervasive effects on the welfare of people to whom they apply regardless of consent."[2] Pogge considers us all to be "participants in a single, global institutional scheme—involving such institutions as the territorial state and a system of international law and diplomacy as well as a world market" and as a result "human rights have come to be, at least, potentially, everyone's concern."[3] One need not go so far as to conclude a single global institutional scheme exists in order to argue cosmopolitan obligations can arise from institutional ties. Julius does not believe that our interdependency has progressed to a stage where one can talk of establishing a single fair global system of institutional structures.[4] Nevertheless, he too argues moral obligations arise from coercive institutional relations that exist on the transnational level. When individuals form institutions they do so in order to direct the action of others.[5] Those setting up institutions need to justify the terms of coercion to those they will direct, even if the institutional relations cross state boundaries.

The non-voluntary and coercive character of international economic institutions is a common example of particularly problematic institutional relations. From a moral point of view, global economic institutions connect individuals transnationally in often grossly unjust ways that fail to adequately account for the moral equality of individuals.[6] In other words, these institutions constitute an economic system that oppresses some for the benefits of others.[7] Many individuals are reduced to a dire poverty that deprives them of the basic goods necessary for freedom. Even national governments often remain powerless to protect their citizens from injustices, as withdrawing from the global economy is not necessarily a feasible option. Individuals can be affected even if their state is not an active or powerful member of global economic institutions. The normative solution is to create cosmopolitan institutional relations to which people could consent. Beitz argues for cosmopolitan liberalism, which "applies to the whole world the maxim that choices about what policies we should prefer, or what institutions we should establish, should be based on an impartial consideration of the claims of each person who would be affected."[8] Freely consenting impartial individuals would not consent to conditions of gross injustice or exploitation.

As part of this solution, tensions between universal principles and particular relations are resolved. As global economic and political institu-

tions become more liberal and cosmopolitan, those reformed global institutions cultivate liberal principles and convictions in individuals. If they
did not it would be difficult to ensure the survival of such institutions.[9]
Once a fair institutional scheme is established an individual should
"come to value the resulting order in its own right. . . . The commitment
to a mutually acceptable scheme would then further deepen as a consequence of the transition itself (through the experience of mutual trust and
cooperation), while the overlap of genuinely shared values expands."[10]
Certain basic institutional structures, it seems, can be depended upon to
shape shared values.[11] The goal is to reform institutions that are establishing unjust values in order to develop just relationships among individuals. The central place of John Rawls's theory in such an argument is
clear because Rawls argued: "if citizens of a well-ordered society are to
recognize one another as free and equal, basic institutions must educate
them to this conception of themselves, as well as publicly exhibit and
encourage this ideal of political justice."[12] It is important to ensure that
institutions are in place to cultivate a just society rather than an unjust
one. In order to show that this is not merely a utopian dream, Pogge
draws on Rawls's example of religious toleration emerging as a shared
moral value out of initially fragile bargains to end bloodshed in relations
among Christian faiths after the Protestant Reformation.[13] Cosmopolitan
theorists, like Pogge, extend these conclusions to international institutions in order to argue for a more just world.

What are the implications of institutional cosmopolitanism for transnational voluntary associations? Associations are voluntary, which may
seem to remove some of the concerns of coercion that apply to states or
international economic institutions. As a result of such a difference, associations need not be held to the exact same standards of justice. Instead a
range of different associations could be tolerated within a framework of
fair cosmopolitan institutions, as long as members are free to exit and the
actions of the association do not violate human rights (two ways in which
coercion is reduced). In fact, Pogge provides an example of how cosmopolitan institutions could create conditions in which partial ties cease to
threaten cosmopolitanism. Pogge imagines that loyalty to particular collectives could be diffused.[14] Individuals could feel attachments to a range
of collectivities (city, state, national, transnational, regional, global . . .).
As long as one is not considered more important than another, they do
not pose a threat. Extending this idea of diffusing loyalties to non-state
associations means that partial attachments need not pose a threat so
long as they do not become so dominant that an allegiance to them blinds
members to their cosmopolitan obligations. This approach does not recognize a necessary tension between the partial associations that arise
through individuals acting on their freedom of association and the cosmopolitan demands for establishing universal fair institutional relations.
The focus is only on toleration. Associations need not pose a threat if

loyalty to them is diffused. This does not recognize the potential of associations to generate cosmopolitan obligations or norms. Introducing the possibility of associations advancing cosmopolitanism does bring back in possible tensions because not all associations will advance cosmopolitanism.

Despite not addressing the potential of transnational voluntary associations, institutional cosmopolitanism does have implications for such groups. Transnational associations often have global institutions of their own. In certain cosmopolitan theories they even play a role in global governance.[15] This is certainly one way to make a connection between institutional cosmopolitanism and associations. Yet, what about institutions less focused on governance? It is necessary to adapt the institutional approach in order for it to apply more broadly. The adaptations stretch cosmopolitan institutionalism but aim to remain within the original intent—locating the institutional source of cosmopolitan obligations

Voluntary associations can play a role in institutionalizing global rules, standards, or codes of conduct that support cosmopolitan norms. Human rights advocacy associations or consumer rights groups, for example, can monitor the compliance of powerful actors such as governments, companies, and other non-governmental organizations (NGOs) to international law. Even if they are not affecting the "highest order moral interests" such rules and standards can take some steps toward advancing respect for moral equality.[16] In the case of the Olympics, which I discuss later, international codes of fair play can generate cosmopolitan norms. In this way associations could be assessed in terms of whether they help to develop as well as to enforce rules that make institutional relations more just.

In other cases transnational non-state associations may have their own institutional relations that could be evaluated in terms of the obligations they create or generate. Transnational obligations may arise through membership if joining an association requires agreeing to abide by codes of conduct or by certain norms embodied in the associations. Just because the obligations are voluntarily accepted does not mean the duty can be easily dismissed. Voluntarily accepted obligations may even have force that over time can expand beyond the original intent. Joshua Cohen and Charles Sabel argue that cosmopolitan obligations can be generated through customs or precedents organizations set.[17] This leads them to argue that the implications of consequential rule-making need to be broadened beyond the state. The specific example they discuss is the International Labor Organization, which has accepted the responsibility of working to develop fair labor standards. It ought not suddenly decide that it is not responsible for workers in the informal sector. Expectations have built around the organization's claims of responsibility to labor that can bind its actions even if the original set of expectations was optional.[18] This is one significant way that cosmopolitan norms can arise from voluntary associations. Individuals are not necessarily morally obligated to form transnational voluntary associations; however, Cohen and Sabel's argument could be used to argue that once they are formed, certain obligations toward individuals emerge. It seems also that institutional responsibilities may extend beyond members if others seek membership or the association interacts with non-members. In cases where groups establish relations with non-members the understanding of these associations as purely voluntary becomes complicated. Relief organizations, such as Médecins Sans Frontières (MSF), have struggled to deal with differences in institutional relationships between expatriate volunteers and local workers they hire.

An institutional approach can provide some guidance toward assessing associations once one moves beyond attempts to resolve the differences between states and voluntary associations. It tells us that transnational institutional relations can generate transnational obligations. Some of these obligations exist irrespective of the associations (due to participation in global economic or political institutions) but associations can help to fulfill or enforce those obligations. Some obligations only come to exist with the creation of the association. Assessing associations means taking both types of obligations into account. This means that the transnational ties associations create can be assessed in terms of whether they facilitate adherence to certain cosmopolitan justice obligations, such as to global poverty reduction, or whether they generate new cosmopolitan obligations due to transnational relations between members of the association. In the first case, a cosmopolitan theory of associations ought to consider whether an association helps to standardize rules or codes of conduct that foster cosmopolitan norms or perspectives. This entails evaluating the kinds of transnational rules being institutionalized through the association or that an association advocates for being institutionalized in more formal international law. In the second case, it is important to consider whether voluntary associations are more than instrumentally valuable to cosmopolitanism. Do they generate obligations of their own? Forging transnational ties could lead to transformations within an association's understanding of membership obligations. As discussed in chapter 7, recent changes in the Anglican Communion have challenged the prevailing practice of regional autonomy in favor of stressing responsibilities to the global Anglican Communion.

Adapting existing institutional theories in order to apply them to associations is important but to stop with questions of institutions would leave the potential of associations incomplete. There are associations that do not establish institutional standards and some that do not even have robust institutional structures. Institutional cosmopolitanism represents two possible ways of expressing cosmopolitanism rather than a full picture of what associational effects could be. Exploring other theories of cosmopolitanism is necessary. The next category I turn to defends cosmopolitan moral obligations to fellow humans irrespective of institutional ties.

Natural Duties Cosmopolitanism

In the natural duties approach to cosmopolitanism, moral obligations do not arise out of institutional relations, but rather the "very birth of a person into the human community" entitles him or her to considerations based on equal moral worth.[19] Martha Nussbaum and Catherine Lu have cosmopolitan theories that, while different in many ways, help to illustrate how cosmopolitan moral obligations can arise irrespective of institutional relations. Nussbaum writes that when it comes to our moral obligations, "the relevant entitlements are pre-political, not merely artifacts of laws and institutions."[20] Because the source of obligations in this category is characterized as pre-political, recognition of our responsibilities requires shaping dispositions to recognize commonalities and empower individuals to act on them. For Lu, who attempts to rescue cosmopolitanism from criticisms of utopianism, our "common or shared humanity entails common circumstances that make the idea of a *human* condition intelligible."[21] For both theorists the common condition of humanity is one of vulnerability; therefore, cosmopolitans should focus on how to prevent cruelty and suffering.[22] This is not achieved first and foremost through reforming institutions. Institutional relations are relevant but only in order to sustain the development of individuals not to generate the appropriate dispositions. Or as Nussbaum puts it "institutions do not come into being unless people want them, and they can cease to be if people stop wanting them."[23]

How does one cultivate a cosmopolitan disposition that can recognize and motivate individuals to act on global duties? Cosmopolitanism calls for the moral cultivation of individuals through broadening imaginations and training us to feel empathy. All this is possible because "compassion contains thought," and therefore, "it can be educated."[24] Nussbaum acknowledges that it is a challenge to live according to cosmopolitan morality. Reason may tell us all humans are moral equals but humanity is a vague concept compared to the more intimate ties we have to particular loved ones (parents, siblings, friends, spouses . . .). Even if we sought to interact more with those beyond our intimate circles, we do not usually interact with humanity but rather with particular individuals. Therefore, it is critical to cultivate empathy for those beyond our borders who seem different from us by focusing on commonalities that lie beneath the differences.

With cultivating moral dispositions as her goal, Nussbaum turns to education reform, particularly early childhood development, as the key place for advancing cosmopolitan norms. Students must "learn to recognize humanity wherever they encounter it, undeterred by traits that are strange to them, and be eager to understand humanity in all its strange guises."[25] Diversity and difference are part of this education but always with the goal that students "learn enough about the different to recognize common aims, aspirations, and values, and enough about these common ends to see how variously they are instantiated in the many cultures and their histories."[26] Only once we realize that humans share certain things in common can we imagine what it would be like to be in another person's shoes. For Nussbaum, recognizing shared commonalities despite differences is critical to motivating people to act on obligations toward others. In asking ourselves what is morally good we ought to ask ourselves whether an action is something I "can commend as such to all human beings."[27]

Although in many ways quite different from Nussbaum, in her own way Lu also draws on the idea that cosmopolitanism ought to be found in common humanity. She argues that individuals need to recognize common vulnerabilities among humans. If all individuals come to see "the significance of cruelty as a moral vice," they can come to see "humans as potential victims and sufferers," but also, "the unpleasant realty of humans as agents responsible for such vice and malice."[28] It is important that we cultivate "a moral allegiance, not to an abstract community of humankind, but to the humanity in all those with whom we can claim to be human, friend, stranger or foe."[29] With this last statement differences become apparent between Nussbaum's universal impartiality and Lu's cosmopolitanism of one and many faces.

What implications might a cosmopolitanism focused on common humanity or moral development have for associations that are partial rather than encompassing all humanity? As with the previous category, partial associations can be tolerated. Nussbaum's theory sees nothing wrong with special relations among individuals as long as one can see the commonalities behind them. Her approach is located closer to the universal end of a universalism/pluralism spectrum. In fact, one scholar argues that for Nussbaum, "universalism and cosmopolitanism are synonyms."[30] How does she reconcile universalism with partiality? For Nussbaum partial allegiances must be justified in terms of universal principles. It is fully acceptable to give our own children more love and attention, she argues. We must, however, justify this by arguing: "it is good for children, on the whole, that things work this way, and that is why our special care is good, rather than selfish."[31] Nussbaum's approach requires a direct form of cosmopolitanism based on committed belief in cosmopolitan principles. Associations could be tolerated if they provide an important universal good. If associations raise awareness of crimes against humanity and shared vulnerability to environmental dangers, such as global warming, they could be cultivating cosmopolitan compassion and helping fulfill obligations. They would aid directly in cosmopolitan training by teaching people to recognize common humanity. Even though she recognizes that associations can provide a more fleshed-out ethics beyond a minimum standard for human dignity,[32] this additional ethic still needs to fit the threshold of universal justification. The tension between universal moral principles and partial associations is resolvable—with priority given to universal principles. Tensions would not arise if members in associations have the proper motivation.

What about associations without a cosmopolitan mission or that do not justify themselves in terms of universal principles? Even here tensions could be resolved, Samuel Scheffler argues, so long as Nussbaum's requirements are relaxed a little to allow individuals to draw on common *experiences* rather than common *principles*. Particular attachments could be justified in terms of common experiences of special attachment. For example, individuals could come to a shared understanding that family relations are significant no matter a person's nationality or no matter the particular cultural understandings of family.[33] However, expecting individuals to justify membership in associations based on the recognition of common experiences still seems to require that members already have a cosmopolitan disposition. Although Scheffler's view gets closer to acknowledging the challenges of resolving tensions between universalism and partiality, there does not seem to be room for indirect cosmopolitanism spread among those not already committed to the goal of recognizing common humanity. What about cases where individuals do not actually embrace cosmopolitan principles and cases where experiences are less commonly shared than family? Indirect cosmopolitanism is necessary once one considers tensions that result from forms of membership that may not be as universalizable.

Lu's theory does not focus to as great an extent on demands for impartial universal justifications but instead stresses the importance of recognizing the inherent complexities of the human condition. Because of this she is more open to the tensions found in trying to lead a cosmopolitan life of "peaceful social *plurality*" in a non-cosmopolitan world.[34] If we did live in a cosmopolitan world then our particular obligations would not conflict with our cosmopolitan obligations because special allegiances would not be used to justify turning a blind eye to suffering.[35] Outside such conditions one cannot expect to fully reconcile tensions by justifying membership in universal terms. Instead, we need to live with a "permanent state of inner doubt and contestation" as we wrestle with our different allegiances and obligations.[36] The goal of cosmopolitanism should entail evaluating how we relate to different forms of partiality.

Although more open to navigating particularity, Lu's focus on individual moral responsibility also seems to require self-conscious cosmopolitanism. She argues that individuals ought to relate to their particular loyalties in a way that nourishes critical reflection on them.[37] Her cosmopolitanism constitutes "an ethical primer coat of sorts; it is not the be-all and end-all of moral life, but without it our most noble and well-meaning moral masterpieces will peel and crumble."[38] Can her insights on the primer coat version of cosmopolitanism say anything about associations and how membership in associations might contribute to fleshing out the masterpiece? In other words, if we were to evaluate not only the motivation of actors in associations but also the effects of associations could one gain insights from her arguments? The straightforward way might be to consider whether associations alleviate suffering but that may be too limited a view. It again focuses primarily on the instrumental role of associations. Could they contribute to cultivating cosmopolitan dispositions in other ways? How might associations help to cultivate the moral courage necessary to act like a cosmopolitan in a non-cosmopolitan world? Answering this question requires shifting the focus from individuals to associations while retaining the idea of individual moral development.

What lessons for associations can be learned from a natural duties approach to cosmopolitanism? Could associations play a role in cultivating the cosmopolitan disposition or ethical perspective defended by this approach? Transnational associations are not always all-inclusive and may not address all humanity; yet, one can assess whether associations cultivate a sense of commonality across borders in a way that helps generate a sense of empathy or basic equality across global cleavages or national boundaries (even if it does not extend to all humanity). Associations may be able to advance cosmopolitan dispositions in ways that recast or redefine our obligations. MSF's re-interpretation of the Hippocratic Oath, for example, re-conceives the role of doctors as obligated to help the vulnerable in emergencies anywhere in the world. We need criteria to understand what it would mean for membership in associations to cultivate cosmopolitan dispositions on a transnational (rather than only fully universal) scale.

Cosmopolitanism is not only about acknowledging commonalities with strangers or victims but also about acknowledging our responsibilities to stop suffering. It is difficult for individuals to see themselves as responsible global actors in the abstract. One possible implication of a role for associations is that participation in them could provide opportunities for people to act transnationally or see their local problems in global terms. Global political and economic institutions are closed or inaccessible to many individuals or groups. One could evaluate whether transnational associations link local projects to larger global endeavors not only by establishing institutions but also through shifting language in ways that stress common humanity. Part of individuals becoming efficacious actors, for Nussbaum, requires fostering capabilities. Could associations help individuals learn skills for participating in global arenas? Bishops from countries in Africa learned to navigate within the Anglican Communion in ways that lead to their empowerment outside local parishes. How they viewed their role in the Communion began to shift.

Without certain skills or a sense of empowerment access to institutions may be meaningless.

When conceived most broadly, this approach to cosmopolitanism could help in assessing whether associations have educative effects like expanding imaginations or whether associations provide opportunities for global action. Both of these would be ways to help train individuals to recognize moral obligations across borders as well as encourage and enable people to fulfill those obligations. None of these goals rest on a utopian picture of all people coming to love each other as one big family. Sometimes recognizing shared vulnerabilities, Lu argues, can connect certain individuals across vast differences. Associations may have a committed belief in basic cosmopolitan principles and as a result help to aid individuals in ending suffering or raise awareness of suffering so that others step in to stop it. Considering membership in associations also opens up all kinds of other reasons individuals may choose to work together. One can evaluate the effects of even these more partial points of commonality and transnational action. Addressing effects, especially indirect effects, does mean dropping the expectation that partial associations need to be justified in terms of cosmopolitan universal principles. Nevertheless, natural duties cosmopolitanism points to the need to consider whether associations contribute to developing more global moral perspectives. This is an important insight but like the institutional approach a natural duties approach lacks a broad enough view of the potential for associations to advance cosmopolitanism.

Cultural Cosmopolitanism

Cultural cosmopolitanism shifts the focus from impartial universal obligations of justice to transnationally engaged ways of life and complex, hybrid identities. Lumping cultural cosmopolitans together does gloss over a range of different answers to the question of what makes an identity cosmopolitan. The theories I address are those where moral considerations remain central. This means that ties to culture and identity are discussed in the context of what it means to lead a morally acceptable life not just a worldly or transnational one. This might sound quite similar to what natural duties cosmopolitans argue. The difference lies in the reason for connecting, which is not primarily to fulfill moral obligations but to have a sense of belonging, to be in solidarity with others. Amartya Sen sees evidence of a thin global identity forming through actions by the United Nations, but he also has hope for the "possibility of committed work, which has already begun, by citizen's organizations, many non-governmental institutions, and independent parts of the news media" to advance a sense of global identity.[39] Kwame Anthony Appiah argues that one can view art as well as other intellectual and cultural contributions as not only deriving from or belonging to a particular culture but as part of a world culture.[40] However, as I already discussed these are not purely aesthetic theories. In cultural cosmopolitanism identities are not only evaluated based on scope. Global identities could be cosmopolitan but are not necessarily so. There are moral implications of theories like Appiah's. Seeing art in terms of world culture means one ought not claim to possess a culture or seek to maintain cultural purity.

What is a cosmopolitan identity if global scope is not the only or primary defining feature? Cultural cosmopolitans contend that respecting the humanity of every individual requires recognizing individuals have local and trans-local identities simultaneously. What makes these identities cosmopolitan? For some theorists it means taking a particular attitude toward one's identity. Jeremy Waldron argues that a cosmopolitan identity need not be based on an all-encompassing global group or community. In fact, claiming such an identity is disrespectful to the individual liberty of those who choose other forms of identity. A cosmopolitan is someone who takes a particular attitude toward his or her partial identities or rather does not take the position of presenting "oneself and one's cultural preferences *non-negotiably* to others in the present circumstances of the world."[41] Cultures and identities are not authentic unchanging wholes but are constantly being shaped and changed through experiences with others. A cosmopolitan recognizes that "it is the rule, not the exception, that ideas and ways of doing things are propagated and transmitted, noticed and adapted."[42] This has moral implications because it means individuals need to treat their culture as consisting of "intelligent and intelligible structures of reasoning."[43] When we offer reasons and explanations for our way of doing things we are speaking the universal language of cosmopolitanism as opposed to simply presenting our ways of life as "brute aspects of one's identity, like one's sex or one's color."[44] A person's identity consists of a set of solutions to problems that he or she may share with others. This does not go so far as to demand Nussbaum's universal justification but it does require taking a somewhat more objective new of our partial identities.

Appiah considers cosmopolitan identity to be closely connected to particular communities but he goes a step further toward pluralism. He defends a rooted form of cosmopolitanism, in which partial identities play an even greater role in actually realizing cosmopolitanism than they do for Waldron. Appiah understands cosmopolitanism as connected to many different ways of living one's life.[45] It entails embracing differences not merely commonality because communicating and working with others means interacting with particular others. He rejects arguments like Nussbaum's that claim our particular relations need to be understood as accidental or coincidental ways of realizing universal moral principles and arguments like Scheffler's that people are bound to locate equal moral worth in an equal respect for common experiences.[46] Instead cosmopolitans must see that partiality itself can be valuable. A relation to someone is special precisely because she is my friend not because friendship is valuable: "the pronoun 'my' *is* magical."[47] Cosmopolitans need to see the world as social and individuals as constructing solidarity and building identities. His model of cosmopolitanism is a life spent learning to live with diverse ways of life. A cosmopolitan values his or her particular relations but also engages with others in "conversations across boundaries of identity."[48] This means not simply "literal talk but also . . . engagement with the experience and the idea of others."[49] Moreover, "conversation doesn't have to lead to consensus about anything, especially not values; its enough that it helps people get used to one another."[50]

Appiah is not alone in arguing that morality requires that cosmopolitanism embrace partiality more fully. Toni Erskine also defends an embedded cosmopolitanism, which is "radically situated in particularist associations" and which "eschew[s] impartiality in moral reasoning," while at the same time remaining "inclusive and self-critical enough to take seriously the equal moral standing of compatriots, comrades, foreigners, and foes alike."[51] Such arguments are not simply defenses of pluralism but rather attempts to locate a cosmopolitan path through the complex relationships between diversity and universality. Appiah stresses that cosmopolitanism does not establish a condition under which universal justifications must be prioritized over local concerns in *all* cases.

This approach differs from the previous types of cosmopolitanism because diversity ought not always be sacrificed to achieve respect for universally justifiable moral demands. Appiah asks: "What would the world look like if people always spent their money to alleviate diarrhea in the Third World and never on a ticket to the opera?"[52] He answers his own question, stating, "It would probably be a flat and dreary place." Yet none of this means moral equality ceases to exist. Appiah cautions us not to conclude that "the lives of the children you could have saved were just worth less than your evening at the ballet." Instead he poses a final question asking us to consider whether we really want to "live in a world in which the only thing anyone had ever cared about was saving lives." The conclusion he draws is that there should not be a single standard for ranking all values—including one that would necessarily privilege universal justifications. To establish such standards would close off possibilities for individuals freely choosing ways of life not congruent with cosmopolitanism.[53]

Diversity and culture are not valuable for their own sake but because we cannot adequately respect human dignity if we constantly seek what is common to all humans subsuming particular differences. Respecting diversity is required if freedom is to be respected. Appiah is explicit about his support for liberal ideals of individual liberty, stating, "the roots of cosmopolitanism I am defending are liberal" continuing that this means specifically "liberalism's insistence on human dignity."[54] In order to protect dignity and liberty it is important to recognize our own fallibility for it is disrespectful and wildly hubristic to expect that one has found the best way of living. Nevertheless, one need not accept all forms of diversity. Some forms of diversity threaten individual liberty with violence or oppression. Sen cautions that sharply bifurcated identities (us *vs.* them) "crowd out, often enough, any consideration of other, less confrontational features of the people on the opposite side of the breach, including, among other things, their shared membership in the human race."[55]

With its respect for diversity rooted in partial attachments, cultural cosmopolitanism seems clearly applicable to associations. Rich with local attachments, different cultures, and diverse ways of life, this approach seems like it should be easily extended from talk of culture to associations. Perhaps the solution to evaluating partial associations has been found in a particular type of cosmopolitanism after all. This view has the hope of "reconcil[ing] a kind of universalism with the legitimacy of a least some forms of partiality" because "a tenable cosmopolitanism, in the first instance, must take seriously the value of human life, and the value of particular human lives, the lives people have made for themselves within the communities that help lend significance to those lives."[56] Appiah even questions the tensions I describe as emerging due to exclusive membership. He says, "solidarity worries us" only "because we take its obverse face to be exclusion; but should we?"[57] Solidarities can exclude without being morally exclusive. States are bound by social justice to treat all fairly but as an individual I can "give you your due and still treat my friends better."[58]

My focus is on the effects of associations not cultural communities and/or individual moral development so I want to consider what can be learned from cultural cosmopolitanism for evaluating associations. It is not hard to imagine how associations, especially a plurality of them, play a role in individuals shaping hybrid and complex identities. How do we understand what kinds of associational diversity advance cosmopolitanism and which do not? If we are not going to lose the moral force of cosmopolitanism and simply accept all forms of diversity, then cosmopolitan criteria are necessary. Cultural cosmopolitanism emphasizes that there are different ways to evaluate the cosmopolitan nature of identities. Similar in some ways to the natural duties approach, one can focus on the global community of fellow humans. However, rather than addressing obligations, the focus is on membership and ways of building solidarity. Some transnational associations aim at building global communities. The case of the Olympics will highlight how shared rituals, practices, and symbols (the Olympic flag and anthem, for example) are designed to reinforce the idea of one common world community even as national teams compete. These symbols might even be considered part of a kind of world culture. Yet global identity is not the primary focus of cultural cosmopolitan theorists. They ask: What kind of partial identities are compatible with cosmopolitanism?

What matters for a cosmopolitan can be traced to how one relates to a given shared identity (even a partial one). An association that attempted to forbid members other identities would be a problem for individual liberty. Associations may showcase their particular group's culture or provide ways to preserve shared practices in ways that are more or less cosmopolitan. Engaging in a cosmopolitan way of life requires a degree of fallibility and open-mindedness. One has to be willing to admit to not possessing the whole truth on a matter. Learning about others through sharing differences is also critical. Demands of purity and authenticity are unacceptable because they can block learning from others, and they can also fail to recognize internal hybridity. How members relate to each other also matters. Focusing on solidarity and building community means considering whether associations encourage shared practices that unite individuals in respectful relations. Solidarity needs to be built on respect and a sense of reciprocity. Shifting away from a focus on commonalities to acknowledge differences more centrally allows for one also to consider different roles or valuable contributions individuals could make within a given association. Associations may bring different individuals together in ways that make the most of particular talents or experiences.

As in the previous two categories, one can summarize the cosmopolitan implications of cultural cosmopolitanism for associations. First of all, one can assess an association by asking if it forms a cosmopolitan identity by connecting individuals transnationally around shared practices that bridge diverse differences like race or religion or class. If exclusivity itself is not dangerous, one can, second of all, ask whether members relate to each other in ways that generate respectful reciprocity. Relations within an association based purely on charity, where some members are considered passive recipients, would not be based on reciprocity. Creative opportunities for members to make different kinds of contributions could better ensure solidarities are formed in a way that cultivates cosmopolitan interactions. It is also crucial that membership not generate a sense of hubris but rather acknowledge fallibilism, which could be evidenced by critical self-reflection on the association's identity and practices. Cosmopolitanism can evaluate not only the scope of institutional relations, as I mentioned earlier, or evaluate the breadth of moral imaginations but also whether a cosmopolitan identity and sense of solidarity emerges among individuals within an association.

Deliberative Democratic Cosmopolitanism

Deliberative democratic cosmopolitanism also addresses ethics and membership but specifically ethics of deliberation in the context of democratic political communities. Certain forms of public deliberation have the potential to generate cosmopolitan norms even among strangers. In defending a deliberative democratic cosmopolitanism theorists like Seyla

Benhabib and James Bohman extend democratic theories of deliberation to the cosmopolitan level. Jürgen Habermas's very influential deliberative democratic theory, particularly his views on the kind of communication that can take place among strangers, is the inspiration for many deliberative democratic cosmopolitans like Benhabib. Therefore, I will begin with a very brief explanation of some key terms from Habermas's theory. This will not do justice to the complex relationship his theory has to cosmopolitanism, which Anand Bertrand Commissiong describes as grounded in the "context of modern national democratic community."[59] Yet, some key terms from Habermas's theory of a particular kind of deliberation will help in understanding how cosmopolitan theorists adapt his view.

Habermas argues that in a democracy citizens working to find solutions to common problems need to justify their position on issues using language that respects fellow citizens. This means offering reasons fellow citizens could understand (even if they disagree with the reasons). The willingness for people to participate in common democratic projects depends on the "communicative power of the public of citizens," which in turn depends on a particular kind of deliberation.[60] This is not an empirical claim about how politics works but a normative claim about a particular kind of communication that is appropriate for public discussion.

Communication in a public language can take place among strangers in complex relationships precisely because it is not the language of intimate relations among those who know each other well.[61] A public language speaks to people not as mother, sister, friend, or neighbor but as fellow rational individual. Deliberation in public spaces where contributing members are respected as equals and where inclusion is based on who is affected by a problem or decision forms a public sphere. A public sphere is a "social phenomenon" that can "best be described as a network for communicating information and points of view . . . in such a way that they coalesce into bundles of topically specified *public* opinions."[62] It is in public spheres that public opinions are formed, which in turn play a role in shaping acceptable standards of behavior (norms) or even what counts as legitimate language for discussing an issue. For Habermas it is critical that these forms of communication be institutionalized in actual procedures.[63] Non-state associations play an important role in shaping public spheres because being on the periphery of power means that associations have "the advantage of greater sensitivity in detecting and identifying new problem situations."[64] Habermas is skeptical of the benefits of eliminating states if there is no common public culture to unite people in the kind of solidarity that would generate public deliberation.

Cosmopolitans take Habermas's ideas of deliberation among strangers global. They emphasize the cosmopolitan potential of discourse ethics. If one is really to respect others as potential rational co-deliberators one "cannot limit the scope of the *moral conversation* only to those who reside within nationally recognized boundaries"; instead, one "must view the moral conversation as potentially extending to all of *human-ity*."[65] In addition, James Bohman, a democratic cosmopolitan, argues that on the transnational level associations are critical to creating spaces for innovation. They help create a plurality of interlocking publics even though they alone remain unable to solve the problems of domination in our world.[66] Yet, even if one considers creative deliberation and "moral conversation as potentially extending to all of *humanity*,"[67] cosmopolitan theorists like Seyla Benhabib do not argue that deliberation ought to always or even primarily be among a universal community under one cosmopolitan democratic world government. Habermas and Bohman develop theories that are more dependent on particular institutional structures of democratic government or governance even though they come to different conclusions as to what the governance would look like. Benhabib explores implications of the universalist moral standpoint for deliberation in bounded political communities. Her focus on membership is particularly interesting for a discussion about the implications of membership in associations.

Cosmopolitanism, Benhabib argues, requires continual mediation between how we define our membership in a community and our moral obligations to non-members. Deliberation is critical to navigating the tension between universal principles and partial affiliations.[68] Addressing democratic political communities, she concludes that citizens are obligated to justify the terms of exclusive membership in states—namely, the terms of citizenship—because this form of membership dramatically affects the rights of individuals. Without the global enforcement of international law an individual without citizenship often has no protection for his or her human rights. In requiring the justification but not the elimination of exclusive membership, the goal of cosmopolitan theory ought not be to resolve the tension (or paradox, as she calls it) between moral universalism and exclusive associations but rather to determine how to navigate it in a just fashion. There are ethical forms for deliberating over membership criteria.

Despite her focus on the state and citizenship, her arguments about membership can be applied to voluntary associations. The mechanism to achieve mediation between moral obligations and membership—democratic iterations—is not limited to only legal or even political communities but can be tied to other forms of democratic deliberation. She writes: "Democratic iterations are linguistic, legal, cultural, and political repetitions-in-transformation, invocations that also are revocations. They not only change established understanding but also transform what passes as the valid or established view of an authoritative precedent."[69] This mediation will take the form of deliberation in public spaces about what constitutes membership (who qualifies and who does not but also which qualifications matter). Although such deliberation is more difficult to realize outside the state, for lack of institutionalized public spaces, it is certainly not impossible.

The arguments of theorists like Habermas, Bohman, and Benhabib provide further insight into how one might assess associations' effects. One can evaluate their effects in cultivating public spheres of deliberation. There is no single global public sphere for political action like there might be on the domestic level (a point to be discussed further in the next chapter). Bohman argues that if there is no single global public sphere then we might need to start thinking in terms of public spheres.[70] This requires establishing "public spheres around various institutions with the goal of making the forms of inquiry more transparent, accessible, and open to greater variety of actors and perspectives."[71] There is a role for non-governmental associations in crafting such public spheres.[72] There may not be one public opinion on the global level but groups craft public opinions around particular institutions or establish public spaces that are more inclusive and open to different voices. Parallel summits are a way to create spaces in which associations can gather to raise issues ignored in more formal international forums—an example of this is the World Social Forum. Associations may also share information in existing public debates that results in influencing public opinions on an issue.[73]

When discussing voluntary associations one needs a concept of deliberation broader than more formal, structured debates in political institutions. The actions of associations may indirectly generate public spheres if their actions or advocacy result in the formation of opposition or splinter groups raising their voices in disagreement. Later chapters will discuss examples of this in the cases of Olympic protest groups and Anglican gay and lesbian associations opposing Communion rulings against same-sex unions. What all this means is that associations can help establish new spaces for public deliberation. They may also advance public spheres in more cosmopolitan directions by introducing ideas into transnational public deliberation that are ignored in other forums. The example of MSF campaigns, to be discussed in chapter 5, will help to illustrate this point.

Benhabib's discussion of membership leads to another consideration in evaluating the effects on public spheres. One can extend the example of a political community engaging in deliberation on membership to consider how associations could deliberate on membership in a way that enables the group to reconstitute itself—even redefining itself in more inclusive, respectful terms. Rather than contributing to or transforming public spheres external to the association, deliberation on matters of membership could foster skills of deliberation within the association. The institutional organization of an association can serve as a place for deliberation. At first this may appear to create more of a private sphere than a public sphere since the deliberation may not extend beyond the association itself. However, the deliberation within associations can have broader implications beyond how membership in that particular association is understood. I will use the Olympics to show how excluded groups, such as women, have petitioned for more inclusive membership, even sometimes using the language of the association itself. This can have broader implications on public opinion about the place of women in sports.

In conclusion, deliberative democratic cosmopolitanism does have implications for non-state associations. First of all, one can ask whether associations contribute to global public spheres of deliberation by introducing discussion of ideas, themes, or language that challenge the narrow focus of national interest. MSF, for example, bears witness to ignored human rights violations through awareness-raising campaigns. Contributions to public spheres can be indirect if large associations become a focal point for debate, deliberation, or protests not initiated by the association. Second of all, associations may provide opportunities for individuals to deliberate transnationally through the association's own institutions. It may foster the practice of deliberative ethics—providing justification and reasons that could be understood by others in the conversation—or create forums that establish spaces for transnational deliberation. Even debating issues as seemingly exclusive as membership limitations can foster cosmopolitan attitudes if reasoned justification is required. A requirement for committed belief in cosmopolitanism may be more central to the first element of deliberation since the causes associations promote would be more or less cosmopolitan. However, indirect cosmopolitanism effects are possible if associations become the focal point of discussions that advance cosmopolitanism, even if the association itself did not initiate the discussion. The two possible expressions of cosmopolitanism do not need to go together. Raising awareness does not necessary speak to or require the association to be internally deliberative. The partial and on-going nature of deliberation in theories like Benhabib's makes an important contribution to carving out a middle ground between cosmopolitan universalism's ethical deliberation requirements and the needs of community to define membership in partial associations. Theorists like Benhabib recognize tensions will remain and need to be constantly navigated and renegotiated.

CONCLUSION: THE COSMOPOLITAN
CONTENT OF CRITERIA FOR ASSOCIATIONS

Two critical trends emerge from considering the implications these four types of cosmopolitanism have for associations. First, despite a trend to try and resolve or ignore tensions between cosmopolitan universalism and partial associations there are some exceptions. Resolving the tension may be possible if one merely expects associations not to thwart cosmopolitanism (for example, requiring they do not violate human rights or employ violence). Aiming to resolve the tension is not a fruitful goal if one wants to understand whether associations can advance cosmopolitan ideals. Certain theories like Benhabib's seek to carve out space for a continued mediation between the values of universalism and partial membership. My project aims to provide a way to understand and evaluate the effects of associations rife with such tensions.

The second trend that emerges is theorists expecting committed belief in cosmopolitan principles or cosmopolitan dispositions. Individuals need to assume a particular stance toward their partial attachments or employ particular forms of deliberation. What about individuals who do not have cosmopolitan dispositions or a belief in cosmopolitan principles? Could associations play a role in advancing cosmopolitan norms among them? Some approaches begin to allow for cosmopolitan dispositions to emerge among people with the right kind of relationship to their partial identities even if they do not describe their identity in terms of cosmopolitanism. Recognizing the potential of a broader range of associations requires an understanding of partial and indirect cosmopolitanism.

In order to meet the goal of evaluating a plurality of associational effects, none of the four categories of cosmopolitan theory can tell the whole story. However, each contributes in different ways to understanding what expressions of cosmopolitanism might look like. Rather than choosing among comprehensive theories of cosmopolitanism, defending particular principles, or creating one ideal cosmopolitan theory for associations, it is possible to see existing theories as representing partial expressions of cosmopolitanism. Let me briefly summarize the ways each category establishes potential content for criteria that could be used to evaluate the effects of an association.

Institutional Cosmopolitanism: These cosmopolitans argue that obligations arise due to relationships within coercive global institutions where some benefit at the expense of others. Theses theorists emphasize the global scope of institutional relations and the importance of institutionalizing fair standards and rules to condition behavior on the global level. To the extent that associations have a transnational scope to their institutional organization one can ask if they create new cosmopolitan obligations that bridge national boundaries. Even if they do not have extensive institutional organizations one can ask whether associations institutionalize standards that support cosmopolitan norms.

Natural Duties Cosmopolitanism: This approach focusing on individual moral development points to the possible educative role associations could play in recognizing and acting on cosmopolitan obligations. In assessing associations one might explore whether they help extend imaginations by drawing on commonalities or empower individuals by creating opportunities and teaching the skills to be a global actor.

Cultural Cosmopolitanism: Such cosmopolitans argue that we ought to cultivate local and transnational identities that embrace a desire to learn from others and a degree of humility about one's own identity. Openness to diversity is essential to respecting individual liberty and entails more than mere toleration. It demands engagement with others. Associations could be evaluated in terms of the type of transnational identities they construct. Do associations create self-reflective transnational identities that build a sense of community or solidarity across significant divisions among individuals (whether it be race, class, religion, or nationality, to name a few)? Furthermore, do these identities involve reciprocal relations that respect the individual dignity of members?

Deliberative Democratic Cosmopolitanism: Deliberative democratic theorists stress the powerful role deliberation can play in changing how individuals view the world. Cosmopolitanism requires a more inclusive global discussion on the issues that affect people across state borders. One can evaluate to what extent associations create spaces to cultivate practices of deliberative ethics even around questions of membership. Beyond the association itself, one can also ask to what extent deliberation among associations contributes to establishing public spheres or transforming global public opinion on issues more formal political institutions ignore.

Each of the theoretical categories of cosmopolitanism has implications for expressions of cosmopolitan ideals that associations could advance. Moreover, they can advance the expressions piecemeal. An association also need not fulfill all criteria. Associations can embody different aspects of cosmopolitanism to different degrees and in different ways. We live in an imperfectly cosmopolitan world. A middle-level theory of cosmopolitanism derived from existing theories can create a normative framework to evaluate the changes a broad array of associations could bring about in our world, even exclusive non-cosmopolitan associations. This entails the possibility that cosmopolitanism need not always be the result of direct reflective action of individual actors. Membership in associations could indirectly have an impact on those not already committed to cosmopolitanism. Recognizing the potential of a broader array of associations could also help bolster contemporary cosmopolitan theory's response to critiques that it cannot adequately respect diversity or partiality.

Can one stop here having established that different cosmopolitan theories could be used to evaluate the effects of associations? No, not if the goal is a nuanced middle-level theory of criteria. The categories of cosmopolitan theory need to be more directly connected to scholarship on associations in order to understand what it would look like for associations to satisfy partial expressions in each category of cosmopolitanism. The applications to associations so far have been quite general. What effects do associations have that could be relevant to cosmopolitanism? Can one generalize about the effects of associations to say they have effects that could advance the partial expressions of cosmopolitanism? Exploring these questions is the goal for the next two chapters.

NOTES

1. Darrel Moellendorf, *Cosmopolitan Justice* (Cambridge, MA: Westview Press, 2002), 32.
2. Charles Beitz, *Political Theory and International Relations* (Princeton, NJ: Princeton University Press, 1979), 166.
3. Thomas Pogge, "Cosmopolitanism and Sovereignty," *Ethics* 103, no. 1 (1992): 51.
4. A.J. Julius, "Nagel's Atlas," *Philosophy & Public Affairs* 34, no. 2 (2006): 187, 190.
5. Ibid., 188.
6. Beitz, *Political Theory and International Relations*, 166.
7. Thomas Pogge, *World Poverty and Human Rights: Cosmopolitan Responsibilities and Reforms* (Malden, MA: Polity, 2002).
8. Charles Beitz, "Social and Cosmopolitan Liberalism," *International Affairs* 75, no. 3 (1999): 519.
9. Theorists in this category of cosmopolitanism often draw on the work of John Rawls. What is particularly relevant here is the importance Rawls places on liberal institutions sustaining and perhaps even generating the dispositions or moral outlook that will maintain those institutions. One excerpt that Pogge references directly from Rawls has to do with the importance of institutions in sustaining the right kinds of moral values. Pogge quotes Rawls as arguing for the importance of "institutions that define the social background and . . . continually adjust and compensate for the inevitable tendencies away from background fairness" in "The Basic Structure as Subject" in *Values and Morals*, ed. A. I. Goldman and J. Kim (Dordrecht: Reidel, 1978), 54, quoted in Thomas Pogge, *Realizing Rawls* (Ithaca, NY: Cornell University Press, 1989), 255.
10. Pogge, *Realizing Rawls*, 229.
11. In making claims like this theorists such as Beitz and Pogge are drawing on the concept of a basic structure of society from John Rawls's theory. However differently the three theorists define the basic structure, they see it as, to use Rawls's words, having a "profound and pervasive influence on persons who live under its institutions." John Rawls, *Justice as Fairness: A Restatement*, ed. Erin Kelly (Cambridge, MA: The Belknap Press of Harvard University Press, 2001), 55.
12. Ibid., 56. In *Political Liberalism* John Rawls makes a similar point when discussing the basic structure institutions in society. He writes that "the institutions of the basic structure have deep and long-term social effects and in fundamental ways shape citizens' character and aims, the kinds of persons they are and aspire to be." John Rawls, *Political Liberalism* (New York: Columbia University Press, 1996), 68.
13. Pogge, *Realizing Rawls*, 229. Pogge draws an international conclusion from Rawls's reference to the principle of toleration emerging after the Reformation. In doing so Pogge draws from Rawls's article: "The Idea of the Overlapping Consensus," *Oxford Journal of Legal Studies* 7, no. 1 (Spring 1987): 18.
14. Pogge, "Cosmopolitan Sovereignty," 58 ft 19.
15. For an example of this see David Held, "The Transformation of Political Community: Rethinking Democracy in the Context of Globalization," in *Democracy's Edges,* ed. Ian Shapiro and Casiano Hacker-Cordon (Cambridge: Cambridge University Press, 1999), 84–111.
16. Darrel Moellendorf argues that obligations of justice are only generated if social practices or institutions "regularly affect the highest order moral interests of a person." *Cosmopolitan Justice*, 32.
17. Joshua Cohen and Charles Sabel, "Extra Rempublicam Nulla Justitia?" *Philosophy & Public Affairs* 34, no. 2 (2006): 147–175.

18. Ibid., 170.

19. Martha Nussbaum, *Frontiers of Justice: Disability, Nationality, Species Membership* (Cambridge, MA: Belknap Press of Harvard University Press, 2006), 258.

20. Ibid.

21. Catherine Lu, "The One and Many Faces of Cosmopolitanism," *The Journal of Political Philosophy* 8, no. 2 (2000): 235.

22. For a specific example, see Nussbaum, *Frontiers of Justice*, 410–412.

23. Ibid., 409–410.

24. Martha Nussbaum, "Introduction: Cosmopolitan Emotions?" in *For Love of Country?* ed. Joshua Cohen (Boston: Beacon Press, 2002), xiii.

25. Martha Nussbaum, "Patriotism and Cosmopolitanism" in Cohen, *For Love of Country?* 9–10.

26. Ibid., 9–10.

27. Ibid., 5.

28. Lu, "One and Many," 255.

29. Ibid., 265.

30. David A. Hollinger, "Not Universalists, Not Pluralists: The New Cosmopolitans Find Their Own Way" *Constellations* 8, no. 2 (2001): 239.

31. Nussbaum, "Patriotism and Cosmopolitanism," 13.

32. Nussbaum, *Frontiers of Justice*, 310.

33. Samuel Scheffler, "Conceptions of Cosmopolitanism," *Utilitas* 11, no. 3 (November 1999): 270.

34. Lu, "One and Many," 262 (italics in the original).

35. Ibid.

36. Ibid., 257.

37. Ibid., 265.

38. Ibid.

39. Amartya Sen, *Identity and Violence: The Illusion of Destiny* (New York: W.W. Norton & Company, 2006), 184.

40. Kwame Anthony Appiah focuses on art as a contribution to world culture in *Cosmopolitanism: Ethics in a World of Strangers* (New York: W.W. Norton & Company, 2006), chapter 8.

41. Jeremy Waldron, "What is Cosmopolitan?" *The Journal of Political Philosophy* 8, no. 2 (2000): 231. Italics in original.

42. Ibid., 232.

43. Ibid., 242.

44. Ibid.

45. Kwame Anthony Appiah, "Cosmopolitan Patriots" in Cohen, *For Love of Country?* 23.

46. Kwame Anthony Appiah, *The Ethics of Identity* (Princeton, NJ: Princeton University Press, 2005), 243.

47. Ibid., 236 (italics in the original).

48. Ibid., 267.

49. Ibid.

50. Appiah, *Cosmopolitanism*, 85.

51. Toni Erskine, *Embedded Cosmopolitanism: Duties to Strangers and Enemies in a World of "Dislocated Communities"* (New York: Oxford University Press, 2008), 3.

52. This and the next three quotes all derive from the same discussion found in Appiah, *Cosmopolitanism*, 166.

53. Appiah, *Ethics of Identity*, 256.

54. Ibid., 267.

55. Sen, *Identity and Violence*, 3.

56. Appiah, *Ethics of Identity*, 222–223.

57. Ibid., 229.

58. Ibid.

59. Anand Bertrand Commissiong, *Cosmopolitanism in Modernity: Human Dignity in a Global Age* (New York: Lexington Books, 2012), 7.

60. Jürgen Habermas, *Between Facts and Norms: Contributions to a Discourse Theory of Law and Democracy,* trans. William Rehg (Cambridge, MA: MIT Press, 1996), 352

61. Ibid., 365–356.

62. Ibid., 360. Italics in original.

63. Ibid., 341.

64. Ibid., 351–352, 381. Habermas argues that international non-governmental associations alone cannot serve as a solution to the dangers of globalization. Jürgen Habermas, *The Postnational Constellation: Political Essays,* trans. and ed. Max Pensky (Cambridge, MA: MIT Press, 2001), 82.

65. Seyla Benhabib, *The Rights of Others: Aliens, Residents, and Citizens* (New York: Cambridge University Press, 2004), 14. Italics in original.

66. James Bohman, "The Public Spheres of the World Citizen," in *Perpetual Peace: Essays on Kant's Cosmopolitan Ideal,* ed. James Bohman and Matthias Lutz-Bachmann (Cambridge, MA: MIT Press, 1997), 193.

67. Benhabib, *The Rights of Others,* 14.

68. Seyla Benhabib, "Democratic Iterations: The Local, the National, and the Global," in *Another Cosmopolitanism,* ed. Robert Post (New York: Oxford University Press, 2006), 58.

69. Ibid., 48.

70. James Bohman, "From *Demos* to *Demoi*: Democracy across Borders," *Ratio Juris* 18, no. 3 (September 2005): 297–298.

71. James Bohman, "Republican Cosmopolitanism," *Journal of Political Philosophy* 12, no. 3 (2004): 349.

72. Ibid., 349, 351.

73. Habermas, *Between Facts and Norms,* 360. What distinguishes public opinion (from individual or private opinion) is that it is socially constructed through communication in networks of sharing information.

THREE

The Lessons and Limits of a Global Civil Society Approach

Rather than choosing between cosmopolitan theories, the previous chapter categorized them in terms of different expressions of cosmopolitanism. This is the first step toward developing criteria to evaluate whether transnational voluntary associations are advancing cosmopolitanism. The second step in applying cosmopolitanism to associations requires exploring research on the effects of associations. Yet, the scholarship on transnational voluntary associations often references global civil society theories rather than cosmopolitanism. This is not all that surprising given that associations on the domestic level are often studied in the context of civil society. In fact, one might ask whether global civil society is not a more natural framework to employ when seeking ways to assess associations, especially if existing cosmopolitan theories need to be adapted in order to do so. As chapter 1 showed, some scholars specifically reject cosmopolitanism in favor of global civil society because it better respects pluralism. However, extending concepts of civil society to the global level meets with very different conditions than on the domestic level. Exploring domestic-level theories of associations can reveal lessons but also cautions about the limits of applying domestic approaches to understanding transnational associations. This chapter will briefly consider the lessons and limits of global civil society theory in order to better situate my middle-level theory of cosmopolitanism in terms of a significant alternative theoretical framework for assessing associations.

The most significant challenge of applying a theory of civil society to the world today is that there are crucial differences between domestic and global conditions such that a strict analogy would be "a mistake, a metaphor that misleads rather than illuminates."[1] However, a critique of global civil society does not have to result in rejecting the whole project of assessing associations from a global perspective. It is critical that the argument for rejecting global civil society does not miss lessons from middle-level theories of associations at the domestic level, which can help to inform a middle-level theory for transnational associations. Theorists of associations such as Nancy L. Rosenblum and Mark E. Warren emphasize the importance of recognizing the indirect effects of membership.[2] In order to fully understand the potential of associations it is helpful to give some attention to the lessons cosmopolitans can learn from normative theories of associations. After explaining in greater detail why global civil society is an inadequate framework for assessing associations, I will return to defending why cosmopolitanism, as understood in chapters 1 and 2, is a better source of normative criteria for associations.

WHAT IS *GLOBAL* CIVIL SOCIETY?

Global civil society scholars frequently distinguish themselves from cosmopolitan theorists, claiming cosmopolitan theories focus too much on universal law and global governance—exemplified by political cosmopolitan democrats such as David Held—at the expense of voluntary associations.[3] Global civil society is understood to be "a more genuinely pluralistic expression of global diversity (ranging from new social movements to indigenous rebellions and everything in between)."[4] However, a precise definition of global civil society, even among proponents of the term, remains far from settled. In general it seeks to rise above the nation-based theories of civil society to theorize a realm of transnational associations whose membership and missions transcend territory. Descriptively it can mean "the sphere of ideas, values, institutions, organizations, networks, and individuals located between the family, the state, and the market and operating beyond the confines of national societies, polities, and economies."[5] Among descriptive uses of the term there are some contexts in which it is understood to be an existing phenomenon. In other cases it is an emerging reality not fully realized. A purely descriptive approach that sees global civil society existing in international non-governmental organizations (NGOs) and social movements is the thinnest possible understanding of the term.

Often there is a more evaluative component delineating particular characteristics of actors that belong to global civil society. In this sense the term often includes "a normative aspiration" such as the establishment of a public sphere "to reach and include citizens everywhere and to enable them to think and act as global citizens," a kind of global consciousness.[6] Another normative view connects global civil society with "the notion of minimizing violence in social relations."[7] Rather than focusing only on the global scope of associations these views refer to the specific behavior of civil society actors.

The ideals of non-violent social interactions and a public conscience are discussed in global terms but the concept of civil society originally derives from domestic political theories. Debora Spini categorizes domestic civil society theories into two categories: civil society understood as a system of needs and civil society as a shared public culture.[8] As a system of needs, civil society is the place where individuals pursue their interests in cooperation with others. This is important to cohesive political communities because civil society reconciles individual self-interest and political life. Unorganized, atomized individuals can unite around shared interests in civil society thereby disciplining individual self-interest.[9] The other view emphasizes the power of civil society to develop and craft public opinion or create shared culture. Theorists differ over what is required for sustaining a public culture of shared values. Associations can play a role by bringing individuals together in ways that allow for discussion of values, cultivation of trust, development of democratic skills, and so on. In this way intermediary associations, those between the state and intimate relations of family, help to ensure the background conditions necessary to sustain democratic political institutions and a free society of cooperating individuals.

From these original theories there have been significant innovations in order to make the concept applicable to a global rather than national context. Certainly some differences between national and global associations are about accommodating differences in degree of complexity. It can be more costly to organize on the transnational level. There is also greater diversity in matters such as language, culture, and life experiences. In addition to these there are significant structural differences between the conditions under which civil society has been understood on the domestic level and the circumstances of associations on the global level. Mary Kaldor acknowledges differences between domestic and global interactions, but she also believes civil society can be adapted to the global realm. This can be accomplished if one recognizes that "by clothing the concept in historical garb, it is possible that the past has imposed a kind of straightjacket which obscures or even confines the more radical contemporary implications" of civil society.[10]

I will explore what expanding and adapting civil society to the global level entails by considering the two common understandings of civil society on the domestic level. Are the differences between the national and global context great enough that any extension requires too radical a transformation of civil society for it to be a useful global concept? Taking each view of civil society in turn, problems of extension become clear and benefits of cosmopolitanism are explored. Despite the efforts of Kaldor and others, the circumstances on the global level (the lack of a world state and a shared global public culture, in particular) ought to inhibit the extension of domestic understandings of civil society to the global realm.

Civil Society as a System of Needs

One common understanding of civil society sees it as a "system of needs" in which individuals join together in associations to seek their mutual interests.[11] In this approach, "civil society, intrinsically marked by conflict, needs the state" in order to mediate conflicts among individual interests.[12] Union in the state keeps civil society from becoming merely "the sum of individual egoisms."[13] It would not make sense to talk of civil society without a state.[14] Civil society actors are grouped in terms of their relation to the state whether supportive or oppositional. According to such a view, lack of a world state would require abandoning the concept of global civil society.

Why is the state so critical? In civil society understood as a system of needs or interests, the state creates background conditions of equality by placing individuals in relations of equality with each other—equal citizens. On the global level, there is no single world state to create at least some level of formal equality (equality before the law). There is no form of actual legal or political world citizenship and policing or regulating associations is not easily done. The United Nations (UN) regulates associations insofar as it establishes criteria associations need to meet in order to receive consultative status at the UN.[15] However, only those interested in consultative status would be affected by such requirements. As a result of the lack of a world state, freedom of association on the global level may simply reify existing power inequalities that could actually hamper realizing moral equality. If you feel all powerful then you may not think to consider the perspective of others or you may imagine you can get away with behavior that is morally questionable. Some even argue that the term *global* civil society is misleading since it really amounts to Northern Atlantic or Western civil society. The most powerful associations, in terms of financial as well as political influence, are often from those regions. Even a defender of global civil society, John Keane, believes that states are necessary to enforce an ethic for global civil society in order to ensure transnational actors do not employ violence.[16] Yet, states remain in very different relations of power with one another. Without a world state to create at least some relations of equality a concept of global civil society could mask massive inequalities in power.

Moral cosmopolitanism aims to provide a normative language that defends the moral equality of all individuals rather than depending on this as a background condition. As was discussed in chapter 2, institutional cosmopolitans specifically highlight the coercive relations of global economic and political institutions in order to demonstrate the obligation to reform those institutions. Inequalities of money, technology, and access to international organizations could impact the justice of global public spheres of deliberation as well. In the case of natural duties cosmopolitanism individuals have obligations to end suffering and exploitation even if no world state with a political form of world citizenship exists.[17] One way individuals could satisfy cosmopolitan obligations and advocate for reform is to develop transnational voluntary associations that aid in the redistribution of resources or that hold institutions accountable to just standards. Creating such cosmopolitan organizations must be accomplished in ways that are not patronizing but that respect the moral equality of all members and those that members interact with during their activities.

All this having been said, Kaldor's global civil society theory may not seem so different from the cosmopolitan approach just described. Her preferred normative vision of "activist civil society" involves associations working to oppose any form of unjust power whether it is state power or international political authorities or any other form of authority.[18] If free individuals had a real say in shaping global interactions they would choose to extend democratic participation and realize emancipation of individuals.[19] In this way global civil society actors need not be defined in terms of a global state or even primarily in terms of their relations toward global political authorities. Global civil society actors become those who advance their interests by opposing oppressive power whether from states, international government organizations, businesses, or other associations. The associations and social movements that make up "globalization from below" would constitute this form of civil society.[20] Can this shift, from defining civil society in terms of state power to power more generally, be smoothly extended to the global context where many entities are seen as sources of power? Extending an understanding of civil society as consisting of individuals organizing to protect their interests and needs considers powerful authorities as primarily dangerous. As a result it focuses on too narrow a scope of relevant effects of voluntary transnational associations. It makes the primary contribution of associations one of opposition. The Roman Catholic Church, for example, as well as other religious associations, "are in fact transnational NGOs of great size, resources, members, and energy. But for their politics, they surely would be included as part of 'global civil society' on any politically neutral interpretation of that term."[21] An activist view of global civil society has moved quite far from the idea of civil society as defined in relation to the state and society. Instead, it has come to represent progressive associations embodying particular ideals.

Kenneth Anderson and David Reiff, critics of the concept of global civil society, argue that placing progressive transnational associations under the umbrella of civil society (and all others outside it) makes global civil society associations into missionary movements. The international NGO movement "is self-sacrificing and altruistic. . . . It appeals to universal, transcendental, but ultimately mystical values—the values of the human rights movement and the 'innate' dignity of the person."[22] While a provocative alternative to global civil society, secularizing the idea of missionary activities only emphasizes the limited scope global civil society can take. Theorists studying domestic associations already recognize the problem with this type of civil society approach (or the missionary alternative). Even on the domestic level there is concern that theories of civil society cannot help understand the implications of associations if "the domains of civil society and association are not coextensive."[23] The missionary analogy may explain human rights or other advocacy NGOs as well as certain religious associations but it is not as clear a model for sports associations like the Olympics or transnational professional associations. Cosmopolitan theories can provide a more robust theoretical source for criteria that apply to a range of associations.

Even though cosmopolitanism could be susceptible to a similar problem of addressing only progressive associations that have self-conscious cosmopolitan purposes, as chapter 2 argued, cosmopolitan theory need not be limited in this way. If expanded to encompass different expressions of cosmopolitanism, it will be able to address associations beyond advocacy NGOs or progressive social movements. The next chapter, chapter 4, develops the cosmopolitan criteria using existing theories of cosmopolitanism and empirical studies of associations. At this point, it is important to emphasize that the benefits of cosmopolitan theory are twofold. First, it makes a sense of moral equality central. Second, it has the potential to evaluate a broad range of effects. Many contemporary cosmopolitans emphasize individual liberty and the importance of tolerating a diversity that includes non-cosmopolitan ways of being. (The only limits to toleration would be those associations that actively violate cosmopolitan ideals—such as terrorist organizations or other associations that aim to degrade humans rather than respect human dignity.) The theoretical goal has not been to cordon off a space for cosmopolitan associations. This is a benefit of cosmopolitanism. Doing so would hamper nuanced understandings of the potential of associations to advance certain norms and dispositions. In moving away from a presumption in favor of associations with a specific purpose, one can focus not only on the instrumental value of associations in advancing a particular ideal, but also on the broad range of indirect effects connected to membership and solidarity in transnational associations.

Civil Society as a Shared Public Culture

Another common theoretical understanding of civil society sees it as a space for creating shared values such as tolerance or a conception of property rights, or civil rights more generally.[24] This view sees civil society as encompassing "the groups where public opinion can be born."[25] Theorists differ over what shared values emerge and whether creating shared values needs to be the self-conscious intention of associations. One can group civil society theorists into two approaches to assessing associations as creators of public opinion: (1) convergence approach, and (2) compatibility approach.[26] As these approaches emerge in domestic analysis of civil society, convergence and compatibility are based on the context of democratic political institutions. Even though there is no global democracy, extensions to global civil society nevertheless show evidence of these approaches as well. In fact, democracy sometimes remains the critical standard. Therefore, it is not a great stretch to organize my discussion of this understanding of global civil society in terms of the categories of convergence and compatibility.

In the convergence approach associations are evaluated in terms of whether or not they embody certain values. On the domestic level, this can mean asking whether associations mirror democratic institutions or whether associations cultivate civic virtues. If an organization is organized hierarchically rather than holding democratic elections or deliberating freely it is not mirroring democratic institutions. Yet, the convergence approach does not require that associations strictly mirror institutional relations. What is critical is that they are seen as potential schools of democracy. Michael Sandel's cautionary tale of the dangers that come from ignoring the cultivation of an American political philosophy is one example of a convergence approach.[27] In his argument associations ought to help "cultivate a public spirit that the nation alone cannot command," because it is through associations outside of government that "the habit of attending to public things" is formed.[28] He gives the specific example of black churches during the civil rights era in the United States, arguing that "the civic education and social solidarity cultivated in black Baptist churches of the South were a crucial prerequisite for the civil rights movement." He continues by describing the civil rights movement as "more than a means of winning the vote" but also "a moment of self-government, an instance of empowerment." This was the case because it "offered an example of the civic engagement that can flow from local attachments and communal ties." Associations serve as places where individuals can practice the skills needed to be good democratic citizens.

Lack of global democratic institutions means that there are few if any established global institutional structures for associations to mirror or for which to develop specific virtues. On the domestic level, mirroring democratic principles has more obvious implications for evaluating associations. One recurring theme that emerges in references to civil society on the global level comes close to this convergence approach. Associations are evaluated in terms of whether or not they help to spread norms of democracy internationally. James Bohman's work on cosmopolitan deliberative democracy includes the need for "a vibrant transnational civil society" in order to help create "public spheres around various institutions with the goal of making their forms of inquiry more transparent, accessible, and open to a greater variety of actors and perspectives."[29] Bohman sees associations playing a supportive role to cosmopolitan democratic institutions. From such a perspective associations would be assessed in terms of traits like accountability or transparency that help to foster conditions and skills to support democratic political institutions.

In focusing on mirroring democratic values, the range of possible associational effects is lost. Cosmopolitanism, as chapters 1 and 2 pointed out, is not always or only about political institutions and democracy. Convergence around democracy need not be expected of associations for them to have effects that advance moral equality and a sense of transnational identity. Grassroots transnational voluntary associations play a role in resistance to rather than simply support for building or reforming international governmental and economic institutions.[30] The convergence approach also misses the potential indirect effects of associations in its attempt to evaluate associations as schools of democracy. If mirroring democracy were a critical effect then cosmopolitan associations would be the ones that adopt democratic organization and decision-making processes. This is too limited a view. In his theory of associations Warren also critiques the limits of a convergence approach even on the domestic level. Civic booster clubs, or other associations that emphasize our unity, cannot serve the purpose of emphasizing differences or bringing forth injustices that may be necessary for all voices in a democracy to be heard.[31] Even in advocacy associations democratic values are not always practiced internally within the associations. Dissenters are often encouraged to leave the association rather than compromising the association's stance. This may not mirror democratic behavior but it does leave associations with a clear and coherent public voice that can often more successfully engage in democratic political action for human or civil rights.[32] A criterion of mirroring or cultivating democratic virtues is therefore too limiting a view for evaluating effects associations have on any level—domestic or global.

A second way that scholars define civil society as shared public culture focuses more on the underlying dispositions associations cultivate in members, particularly those necessary to sustain democracy. In this compatibility view associations need not engage in democratic practices or be directed at realizing political change for them to advance norms compatible with democratic principles. One example of a compatibility view comes from domestic civil society arguments about the power of social capital. Associations with a range of different purposes (choirs, bowling leagues, book clubs . . .) bring strangers together in common activities. This can build trust, toleration, and reciprocity, or what is called social capital. Social capital built up through repeated interactions makes people willing to work together when it comes to more controversial political issues. Social capital spills beyond the association to create general conditions of trust necessary to sustain a flourishing democracy. This too is an evaluative theory because associations that build social capital ought to be encouraged. After all, not all associations build social capital.

Robert Putnam's famous metaphor of bowling alone is meant to illustrate the danger of a lack of social capital within a community.[33] He defines social capital as "features of social organizations such as networks, norms, and social trust that facilitate coordination and cooperation for mutual benefit."[34] Social capital helps by "developing the 'I' into the 'we.'"[35] However, Putnam is quite skeptical that transnational associations can cultivate social capital. Mass membership organizations should not even qualify as secondary associations according to him (which certainly removes them from the possibility of developing civil society). These members may identify with common symbols; they may contribute money to organizations, but their ties are "to common symbols, common leaders, and perhaps common ideals, but not to one another."[36] Putnam is not alone in this view. Other critics argue that shared social values are not present on the global level because there is too much fundamental diversity to support a claim of emerging social capital. Critics contend that groups may form but the idea that global communities of "we" are forming that could foster democratic cooperation is too optimistic. As one scholar puts it, people from different countries "tend to think differently even when attempting to think globally."[37] Although rejections of the potential for transnational associations to advance social capital are overstated, Putnam's approach does emphasize the need to study indirect effects of association rather than merely self-declared purposes.

There are scholars who challenge such pessimistic conclusions regarding transnational associations. Carol C. Gould says solidarity has to be redefined to ensure scholars can better recognize how it exhibits itself on the transnational level. In Gould's argument transnational solidarity is important but it is not necessarily solidarity around an identity, a "we." Instead individuals can unite around ideals of justice.[38] Global civil society scholars such as Jackie Smith directly reject Putnam's pessimistic view. She provides evidence of social capital emerging from transnational non-state actors. Smith provides countervailing empirical evidence based on international agreements and communication. She is particularly interested in extending the social capital approach to transnational social movements, organizations of activists working toward social change. She argues that international social movement organizations "serve as mediators between local interests and identities and global institutions. Their work, consequently, may be generating social capital relevant to groups that are marginalized in their own national polities, including political dissidents, the very poor, women, and religious minorities."[39] Through social movements local problems are linked to global sources and solutions. Common interests are crafted across seemingly unconnected or geographically distant issue areas. The generation of these common interests fits the ideal of civil society as constituting a space of shared public culture. Even without regular face-to-face meetings, Smith argues that it is social movements on the global level that are "the carriers and disseminators of global cultural reserves."[40] The social change they advocate is also aimed at democratizing the intrastate system. Smith's social change movements include those with a directly political purpose unlike Putnam's bowling leagues; however, it should be noted that Smith defines political change broadly to include social justice issues such as human rights, women's rights, or environmental causes.[41] Even though Smith focuses on associations that have a more directly cosmopolitan purpose of advocating for human rights, she is interested in evaluating the associations' effects, specifically whether they advance social capital. Smith's work does not preclude indirect effects despite her focus on effects of associations that self-consciously seek political or social change . A broader normative framework would not necessarily hinder the important contributions of her empirical research. Putnam's work on the domestic level, however, makes indirect effects more central.

How does all of this relate back to a comparison with cosmopolitanism? Moral cosmopolitanism does not necessarily require that associations be establishing one global culture or one world democracy. Cosmopolitanism also does not require that a global public culture exist before holding associations to certain standards of morality. In fact, it self-consciously presents itself as a theory of justice or identity that can be used to evaluate existing international relations. Yet, at the same time, many cosmopolitan theories seem to presume a self-conscious cosmopolitan attitude as necessary to realize cosmopolitanism. A concept of cosmopolitanism that allows for indirect expressions of cosmopolitan norms and attitudes could consider a broader range of associations. Focusing on effects (like social capital) should mean that the mission of an association becomes less central to evaluating it.

Even if some associations do indirectly build trust and reciprocity, focusing on social capital alone is too limiting. The compatibility view improves on the convergence approach by allowing for indirect effects but does not go far enough in accounting for diverse effects of associations. Critics of domestic versions of social capital point out such limitations.[42] What is missing from social capital theories, Rosenblum argues, is the mechanism. How do the actions of non-political associations translate into political forms of trust and cooperation? As she puts it, both the congruence and compatibility approach (she calls the later the mediating approach) "fail to offer a social or psychological dynamic capable of explaining whether and how trust, say, or cooperation, is transferrable from sphere to sphere, including democratic arenas. Virtues are not contagious."[43] Yet, for Rosenblum, none of this means associations do not have an impact on members. She simply rejects too specific a focus. All one can generalize about the effects of associations is that they provide conditions for individuals to experience pluralism.[44] This is important for a democracy but not as strong a connection to directly advancing specific democratic virtues. The criteria I establish for associations are narrower than

Rosenblum's broad conclusion about pluralism but broader than a narrow focus on the specific virtues of social capital.

Within the compatibility view there is another approach that does not make as robust a claim as social capital but argues instead for a more moderate view that there are some very thinly shared social values such as civility that define civil society on the global level.[45] What civility entails differs somewhat from theory to theory but by and large it entails a position on tolerance and non-violence. These standards define which associations are a part of a global civil society and set boundaries for what behavior ought to be supported and what ought to be prevented. If civility means simply non-violence, this would exclude non-violent uncivil associations from civil society. In this case the criteria of civility is overly broad. At this point, one would have arrived at the argument cosmopolitans make about the need to have a minimum threshold of toleration. It would not help us in assessing whether there are some associations that advance a particular ideal, whether it is democracy or cosmopolitanism. Surprisingly, given its aim at breadth, a position on civility could also be too narrowly interpreted if civility is connected to criteria beyond non-violence. The role of associations ought not to be understood as only mitigating conflict or generating trust. At times associations may challenge existing views or cause conflict—motivated by indignation at injustice—and in doing so advance moral equality. A notion of civility does not provide a strong enough basis for analyzing the variety of ways an association could impact norms and dispositions on the global level. It belies the complexity involved in considering how "the competing principles of individual rights and communal solidarity" interact on the global level.[46]

Scholarship on how associations could encourage civility or indirectly build social capital can provide very useful evidence for certain types of effects associations can have. However, a more nuanced theory is needed—one that can begin to help individuals and theorists alike understand the potential of a broader range of associations.

THE NEED FOR A MIDDLE-LEVEL
THEORY OF COSMOPOLITANISM

The overall conclusion drawn from assessing both approaches to civil society (as a system of needs and as a shared public culture) is well summarized by Warren's point from earlier that civil society and associations are not coextensive.[47] Studying the effects of associations cannot effectively be done from a civil society perspective alone. On top of that there appear to be significant differences between local and global contexts making it a stretch to extend civil society to the global realm. Moving from a global civil society framework to a middle-level cosmopolitan one makes clearer normative assessment of a broader range of associations possible even in the current conditions on the global level. The lack of a world state, for example, requires interpreting possible institutional effects of associations differently from how they might be assessed on the domestic level. The focus ought not simply be on mirroring existing institutional structures but rather advancing the creation of just transnational institutional relations and developing shared global rules and standards.

Taking Kaldor's claim that one should not be straightjacketed by the historical use of certain concepts, one can defend cosmopolitan theory from global civil society critics who argue it is not compatible with pluralism. It is important to acknowledge the problematic uses of cosmopolitan universalism but not dismiss all cosmopolitanism based on them. Historically cosmopolitanism has justified civilizing missions and imperialist colonial power. Yet, as I outlined in chapter 1, contemporary cosmopolitans work to ensure that cosmopolitan theory is based in a universalism that allows for diversity. The universalism found in cosmopolitanism need not be a threat. It can be a benefit. Respect for diversity can be achieved while maintaining some moral force to evaluate it. Moreover, the critiques of global civil society I have outlined show theories of civil society cannot be simply extended to the global level because of the significant differences between domestic and global conditions. If any theory is going to be adapted, it is better to adapt cosmopolitan theory, which begins from a global perspective. Instead of focusing on democratic civic virtues, social capital, or civility, it is necessary to focus on changing consciousness and developing dispositions that shift individuals' perspectives from a state-centric view to one that is more transnational. Lack of a global public culture means deliberation and common identities cannot simply be tied to political understandings of democracy. However, in the process of critiquing global civil society, the analysis of domestic theories of associations did reveal some lessons cosmopolitans could learn.

Associations ought to be assessed in terms of their transformative power. The compatibility approach emphasized the value of evaluating indirect effects of associations. Domestic theories of social capital illuminate the possibility for associations to have effects outside their self-conscious mission or purpose. How cosmopolitan norms are spread in the world can also be understood in terms of the effects associations have rather than focusing on the explicit purpose of an association. Cosmopolitans have not paid adequate attention to assessing the broad range of effects of associations.

Domestic theorists, who point out civil society's limits, including Warren and Rosenblum, construct theories of associations that move beyond typical civil society theories in order to address a wider variety of associational effects. Warren breaks democracy down into its core values in order to apply those to associations. Similarly, I break down cosmopolitan theories into core expressions in order to look for them in associations. Rather than defending cosmopolitan theory's fundamental principles anew, my project begins from existing cosmopolitanism and asks the question: If one is persuaded by cosmopolitan theories, how can one evaluate the plurality of associations that emerges from respecting the individual liberty of freedom of association? This requires drawing on empirical research such as that of global civil society scholars like Smith, who study the effects of associations. The effects are then evaluated using cosmopolitan theory. My goal is not to engage in a new kind of empirical research on the effects of associations myself. I draw on the scholarship of those who are already studying the effects of transnational associations. In order to answer the normative question of what ought cosmopolitans expect of associations it is necessary to bridge empirical and theoretical research.[48] This establishes a middle-level theory of cosmopolitanism.

Although middle-level theorizing as an approach is inspired by work on the domestic level, this kind of theorizing is even more important for cosmopolitanism. Cosmopolitanism is more abstract than domestic theories of democracy. It has not been institutionalized to as great an extent as democracy. Middle-level theorizing can connect abstract theories to empirical work on the effects of actual non-state actors. Before drawing on empirical scholarship (as I will do in chapter four), let me explain a bit more what makes this middle-level theory so important.

This approach differs from establishing ideal theory. In an ideal cosmopolitan theory of associations the standards would not depend on whether you could find them realized in the world. Even if no associations spread cosmopolitan norms or disposition that would not undermine the argument that associations could and should advance cosmopolitanism in certain ways. That having been said, the actual descriptive picture of the world is not so bleak. This is where the work of scholars on associations becomes helpful in developing and testing the criteria. The associations I have chosen as examples are meant to serve as illustrations of what indirect partial expressions of cosmopolitanism might look like. Because of the potential for tensions between cosmopolitan universal principles and partial associations to arise within actual examples that do not embrace or advocate cosmopolitan principles, it is important not to focus only on an ideal theory. A middle-level theory that can help navigate complex cases is needed. In describing the importance of his middle-level democratic theory Warren points to both the increasing complexity of politics (such that states can no longer solve problems alone) and the complex nature of democratic theory (with different theories focusing on different core elements of democracy) to justify his approach.[49] If states cannot solve problems alone, then associations become increasingly important, and because democratic theory is so complex, there are a variety of ways to evaluate the effects of associations. The same points can be applied to associations at the transnational level. Certainly politics and interactions at the global level are complex. Cosmopolitanism also consists of a variety of theoretical perspectives, as chapter 2 demonstrates. Therefore, the conditions seem to call out for a cosmopolitan middle-level theory.

Warren's middle-level theory goes one step further than my cosmopolitan argument. Once established, Warren feels a middle-level theory can help determine state policies toward associations. Because of the complexities in politics it is necessary to consider the effects of associations in relation to other agents in a democracy. Ecologies of effects flow "from a multiplicity of collective decisions and actions" by a series of agents: associations, states, and economic actors.[50] In this ecology, it is possible to aim for an optimal balance of democratic values and dispositions among the effects of different associations.[51] The state, he believes, can play a role in ensuring the right kind of balance by encouraging certain kinds of associations.[52] The implications Warren draws from his middle-level theory are a point of divergence between our two approaches. I make no argument about states or international governmental organizations regulating associations on the global level to realize an optimal balance of cosmopolitan associations. The complex and underdeveloped nature of political institutions on the global level makes it much more difficult to determine which agents should legitimately help achieve an appropriate balance and how.

What then are the implications of my middle-level theory? It is beyond the scope of my project to engage in the political implications for global governmental institutions. Yet, my criteria for associations could help to ensure associations are incorporated into theories of cosmopolitan political institutions in a more precise fashion. Human rights associations are not the sole source of support for the cosmopolitan dispositions necessary to support cosmopolitan institutions. There are potential implications of my argument beyond consideration of the relationship between associations and political institutions. In its current form, individuals who are members of associations or who are forming associations or funding associations could use my theory to guide them in evaluating the effects of their membership in associations. Scholars studying associations could also benefit from cosmopolitan criteria. The emphasis on indirect effects and the impact of these effects on those not previously committed to cosmopolitan principles or values is likely to be of interest to scholars who are trying to understand norm changes on the global level. Empirical analysis of different types of associations can help in understanding how associations shift norms but not how to justify that those advances are positive.[53] It is not enough merely to study the norm change and the mechanisms that lead to it. Kathryn Sikkink, a constructivist scholar of transnational advocacy networks, stresses that constructivists "can improve our discussions by being more explicit about our processes of ethical reasoning and by relating our research findings more explicitly to their normative implications."[54] Empirical research on associations needs to be combined with normative philosophical theories that make arguments for what norm changes ought to occur. One can use cosmopolitan normative ideals to evaluate the effects of a wide range of associations. Some scholars are already employing cosmopolitanism. The result is often specific forms of qualified cosmopolitanism, such as Christian cosmopolitanism or diasporic cosmopolitanism.[55] Rather than creating an endless series of qualified forms of cosmopolitanism it could be that some groups advance certain elements of cosmopolitanism and not others. It is vital to recognize the creative power associations have and helpful to be able to do this with standards that can apply to the complex ways associations might generate cosmopolitan norms and dispositions.

My middle-level theory of cosmopolitanism is not meant to set up an ideal type of association, nor it is supposed to simply describe different complex effects of associations. The normative exploration of transnational voluntary association in upcoming chapters does consider individual cases of associations. However, it is not intended to be "a kind of normative theory that mirrors the anthropologists' emphasis on individual cases, particularities, and differences."[56] Instead of engaging in a study of all the effects and intentions of each association, the goal is to draw out a few generalizable effects that illustrate how to advance cosmopolitan norms and dispositions. The criteria ought to be understood as establishing a set of core elements of cosmopolitanism that associations could partially and indirectly advance rather than a set of expectations that each and every association must meet in the same way. The associations explored in chapters 5 through 7 are therefore specifically chosen to highlight partial and indirect elements of cosmopolitanism. It is in these associations that lessons for cosmopolitanism can be overlooked.

Choosing associations without a cosmopolitan purpose can test the limits of a concept of partial cosmopolitanism. Choosing such examples does not mean a middle-level theory cannot account for those that threaten or those that aim to advance cosmopolitanism. The dangers of terrorist groups or transnational crime organizations are increasingly being studied. A minimum threshold of cosmopolitan toleration remains in place in a middle-level theory. My goal is also not to exclude associations with a self-consciously cosmopolitan purpose. In fact, a middle-level theory has interesting implications for this type of association. Human rights transnational voluntary associations are less problematic cases since their purpose is often to advance cosmopolitan principles of moral equality manifested in basic rights for all humans. Amnesty International, for example, seeks to advance civil and political rights, and Oxfam seeks to advance economic rights. They seem like perfect expressions of cosmopolitanism. Yet, these groups often have unintended consequences. A middle-level theory looks at effects. Scholars such as Makau Mutua argue that many human rights NGOs claiming to be non-ideological are, in fact, continuing a form of colonization by imposing their views on the communities they seek to help.[57] Even these associations might be partial expressions of cosmopolitanism because they do not advance every element of cosmopolitanism. Analyzing associations with a cosmopolitan purpose using a middle-level theory can provide greater insight into how they advance cosmopolitanism, even if it does not alter whether or not they are understood as associations that advance cosmopolitanism. The historical example of the British abolitionist Society for Effecting the Abolition of the Slave Trade will be used in chapter 4 to help illustrate the cosmopolitan criteria, because its purpose is less in tension with cosmopolitanism than applications of later associations. It too shows tensions remain as cosmopolitanism is only partially advanced.

The potential for associations to have a range of indirect and partial effects means one cannot fully understand the potential of associations from within the narrow bounds of civil society theories or from ideal cases of self-consciously cosmopolitan associations. The problem with convergence approaches that focus on associations mirroring certain values is that they do not allow for a broad array of associations on the global level with different effects. The problem with a compatibility approach that focuses on cultivating trust is that despite addressing indirect effects the focus remains either too narrow (social capital, trust building, civility) or too broad (non-violence) to develop a precise picture of the creative potential of associations. More nuanced criteria for associations are necessary to answer the question: What ought cosmopolitans expect of transnational voluntary associations? Scholarship on the effects of associations will be the focus of the next chapter, in which I seek to generalize about possible cosmopolitan effects of associations. This will be done with the goal of connecting associational effects to the partial expressions of cosmopolitanism developed in chapter 2. Unlike global civil society theories, cosmopolitan theories begin from a global normative perspective that can provide ways to evaluate a range of different transnational voluntary associations.

NOTES

1. Chris Brown, "Cosmopolitanism, World Citizenship and Global Civil Society," *Critical Review of International Social and Political Philosophy* 3, no. 1 (2000): 21.

2. Nancy L. Rosenblum, *Membership and Morals: The Personal Uses of Pluralism in America* (Princeton, NJ: Princeton University Press, 1998); Mark E. Warren, *Democracy and Association* (Princeton, NJ: Princeton University Press, 2001).

3. An example of David Held's arguments can be seen in his article "The Transformation of Political Community: Rethinking Democracy in the Context of Globalization," in *Democracy's Edges,* ed. Ian Shapiro and Casiano Hacker-Cordón (Cambridge: Cambridge University Press, 1999). Scholars who draw a distinction between cosmopolitan theory and global civil society include John Keane, *Global Civil Society?* (Cambridge: Cambridge University Press, 2003); Richard Falk, "Global Civil Society: Perspectives, Initiatives, Movements," *Oxford Development Studies* 26, no. 1 (1998): 99–104;

Gideon Baker, "Problems in the Theorisation of Global Civil Society," *Political Studies* 50 (2002): 928–943.

4. Gideon Baker, "Cosmopolitanism as Hospitality: Revisiting Identity and Difference in Cosmopolitanism," *Alternatives* 34 (2009): 108.

5. Helmut Anheier, Marlies Glasius, and Mary Kaldor, "Introducing Global Civil Society," in *Global Civil Society 2001,* ed. Helmut Anheier, Marlies Glasius, and Mary Kaldor (New York: Oxford University Press, 2002), 17.

6. Ibid., 17.

7. Mary Kaldor, *Global Civil Society: An Answer to War* (Malden, MA: Polity, 2003), 3.

8. Debora Spini draws a distinction between these two models of civil society in her article "The Double Face of Civil Society," in *The Search for a European Identity: Values, Policies and Legitimacy of the European Union,* ed. Furio Cerutti and Sonia Lucarelli (New York: Routledge, 2008), 143.

9. Rosenblum, *Membership and Morals,* 26–27. In this section she is discussing Hegel's *The Philosophy of Right* and how modern attempts to understand civil society often echo Hegel's "ethical project of integrating individuals into the life of public community."

10. Kaldor, *Global Civil Society: An Answer to War,* 3.

11. Spini, "Double Face,"143.

12. Ibid.

13. Ibid.

14. For such arguments, see Baker, "Problems in the Theorisation of Global Civil Society"; Brown, "Cosmopolitanism, World Citizenship and Global Civil Society"; Christopher Rootes, "Global Visions: Global Civil Society and the Lessons of European Environmentalism," *Voluntas: International Journal of Voluntary and Nonprofit Organizations* 13, no. 4 (December 2002): 411–429.

15. Some of the criteria include having a "democratically-adopted constitution," "appropriate mechanisms of accountability and democratic and transparent decision-making processes," and the majority of resources should come from non-governmental sources. In addition, "organizations established by governments or intergovernmental agreements are not considered NGOs." See, "Introduction to ECOCSOC Consultative Status," United Nations website for the NGO Branch of the Department of Economic and Social Affairs, accessed June 29, 2014, http://csonet.org/index.php?menu=30. See also "How to Apply for Consultative Status," NGOS Branch Department of Economic and Social Affairs, United Nations, accessed June 29, 2014, http://csonet.org/?menu=83.

16. Keane, *Global Civil Society?* 12, 87, 142, 145, and 206.

17. Famously, cosmopolitan theorist Immanuel Kant rejects the idea of a world state. He makes this point in the Second Definitive Article of Perpetual Peace: The Right of Nations shall be based on a Federation of Free States, in "Perpetual Peace: A Philosophical Sketch," in *Kant Political Writings,* ed. Hans Reiss, trans. H. B. Nisbet, 2nd ed. (New York: Cambridge University Press, 1991), 102–105.

18. Kaldor, *Global Civil Society: An Answer to War,* 8.

19. Ibid., 11–12.

20. Richard Falk, "Resisting 'Globalisation-from-above' through 'Globalisation-from-below,'" *New Political Economy* 2, no. 1 (1997).

21. Kenneth Anderson and David Rieff, "'Global Civil society': A Skeptical View," in *Global Civil Society 2004–2005,* ed. Helmut Anheier, Marlies Glasius, and Mary Kaldor (London: Sage, 2004), 29.

22. Ibid., 32.

23. Warren, *Democracy and* Association, 58.

24. Brown, "Cosmopolitanism, World Citizenship," 10, 19.

25. Spini, "Double Face," 142.

26. Rosenblum refers to two main approaches in understanding the role of associations: congruence and mediating. *Membership and Morals,* 36–41 and 41–45 respectively. My two categories are inspired by her distinctions.

27. Rosenblum uses Michael Sandel as an example in *Membership and Morals,* 38. She specifically references his book *Democracy's Discontents.*

28. Michael Sandel, *Democracy's Discontents: America in Search of a Public Philosophy* (Cambridge, MA: The Belknap Press of Harvard University Press, 1996), 314. All the quotes that follow in this paragraph come from the same page in Sandel's book.

29. James Bohman, "Republican Cosmopolitanism," *Journal of Political Philosophy* 12, no. 3 (2004): 349. For a similar argument, see Ronnie D. Lipschutz, "Reconstructing World Politics: The Emergence of Global Civil Society," *Millennium: Journal of International Studies* 21, no. 3 (1992): 389–420.

30. Richard Falk, "Global Civil Society and the Democratic Prospect," in *Global Democracy: Key Debates,* ed. Barry Holden (New York: Routledge, 2000), 164.

31. Warren, *Democracy and Association,* 27.

32. Ibid., 36.

33. Robert Putnam, *Bowling Alone: The Collapse and Revival of American Community* (New York: Touchstone Books by Simon & Schuster, 2001).

34. Robert Putnam, "Bowling Alone: America's Declining Social Capital," *Journal of Democracy* 6, no. 1 (1995): 67.

35. Ibid.

36. Ibid., 71.

37. Rootes, "Global Visions," 423.

38. Carol C. Gould, "Transnational Solidarities," *Journal of Social Philosophy* 38, no. 1 (2007): 156.

39. Jackie Smith, "Global Civil Society? Transnational Social Movement Organizations and Social Capital," *American Behavior Scientist* 42, no. 1 (1998): 100.

40. Ibid., 104.

41. Ibid., 94.

42. Warren, *Democracy and* Association, 31–36.

43. Rosenblum, *Membership and Morals,* 43.

44. Ibid., 17.

45. The work of Peter Berger and John Keane represents examples of emphasizing civility in discussing transnational associations. Peter Berger, "Religion and Global Civil Society," in *Religion and Global Civil Society,* ed. Mark Juergensmeyer (New York: Oxford University Press, 2005); John Keane *Global Civil Society?* A critic of depending on a shared culture of civility is Brown, "Cosmopolitanism, World Citizenship and Global Civil Society," 20.

46. Anand Bertrand Commissiong, *Cosmopolitanism in Modernity: Human Dignity in a Global Age* (New York: Lexington Books, 2012), 142.

47. Warren, *Democracy and Association,* 58.

48. In taking this approach I am following a method similar to the one Warren outlines for his democratic project. There are differences, and I do not claim to replicate his approach entirely. For his discussion of a middle-level theory see Warren, *Democracy and Association,* 13.

49. Ibid., 6, 8, 11.

50. Ibid., 207.

51. Ibid., 12–13.

52. Ibid., 13.

53. Empirical research has mapped the actions of a range of associations operating on the global level. An example of exploring this in the context of global civil society is the series *Global Civil Society* edited by Mary Kaldor, Martin Albrow, Helmut Anheier, and Marlies Glasius (most recently, London: Sage Publications). This is a series that presents work on different theoretical and empirical questions related to the theme of global civil society. Other examples include constructivist international relations scholars studying norm change, such as Margaret E. Keck and Kathryn Sikkink, *Acti-*

vists Beyond Borders: Advocacy Networks in International Politics (Ithaca, NY: Cornell University Press, 1998); Martha Finnemore and Kathryn Sikkink, "International Norm Dynamics and Political Change," *International Organization* 52, no. 4 (1998): 887–917. In addition it is worth noting that in taking a normative approach my argument differs from the work of scholars like Ulrich Beck. Beck seeks to create an understanding of cosmopolitanism that is objective and descriptive rather than normative and philosophical. Ulrich Beck, "Cosmopolitical Realism: On the Distinction between Cosmopolitanism in Philosophy and the Social Sciences" *Global Networks* 4, no. 2 (2004): 131–156.

54. Kathryn Sikkink, "The Role of Consequences, Comparison, and Counterfactuals in Constructivist Ethical Thought," in *Moral Limit and Possibility in World Politics*, ed. Richard Price (New York: Cambridge University Press, 2008), 111.

55. Maria Rovisco works on the cosmopolitanism of religious missionary groups and concludes that there are certain forms of Christian cosmopolitanism that emerge from such activities. "Religion and the Challenges of Cosmopolitanism: Young Portuguese Volunteers in Africa," in *Cosmopolitanism in Practice*, ed. Magdalena Nowicka and Maria Rovisco (Burlington, VT: Ashgate, 2009), 197. Tsypylma Darieva discusses a concept of diasporic cosmopolitanism in "Rethinking Homecoming: Diasporic Cosmopolitanism in Post-Soviet Armenia," *Ethnic and Racial Studies* 34 (2011): 490–508.

56. Jacob T. Levy, *The Multiculturalism of Fear* (New York: Oxford University Press, 2000), 13.

57. An example of this kind of argument can be found in Makua Mutua, "Human Rights International NGOs: A Critical Evaluation," in *NGOs and Human Rights: Promise and Performance*, ed. Claude E. Welch Jr. (Philadelphia: University of Pennsylvania Press, 2001), 151–161.

FOUR

Introducing Cosmopolitan Criteria through the Example of British Abolitionists

In 1787 a group of nine Quakers and three Anglicans formed the Society for Effecting the Abolition of the Slave Trade in London (sometimes referred to as the London Committee).[1] Its effects were far reaching. It advanced cosmopolitan norms of human equality by attacking the legitimacy of practices like the slave trade and later slavery itself as well as drawing into the public sphere a much more inclusive range of voices (women, some former slaves, as well as political and religious dissenters). Although the Society was not the only voice for abolition, historian Seymour Drescher uses it as a signal of when "organized abolitionism began."[2] Among the members of this association were powerful leaders of abolition in Britain, such as Thomas Clarkson and William Wilberforce. Thomas Clarkson, a founding member, became a professional abolitionist writing about the horrors of slavery, working to forge ties with other abolitionists, and spreading abolitionism internationally. William Wilberforce, a Member of Parliament, played a critical role in helping to achieve the Society's goal of passing a law to abolish the slave trade. One finally passed in 1807. The leaders' actions are important but the movement did not succeed merely due to the activities of elites. The London Society served as a kind of logistical headquarters for a national movement of provincial abolitionist committees and societies that provided a groundswell of popular support for ending the slave trade.[3] The shifts in social norms that delegitimized the slave trade checked governments and trading companies trafficking in slaves at a time when slave labor was actually very profitable.[4]

The abolitionist struggle also had a transnational scope. Slavery was part of a transnational trade. If Britain were to abolish the lucrative slave trade then France or Spain or Portugal would pick up the business. To end this trade, let alone slavery itself, abolitionists would have to do more than end it in the British Empire. Even if the petition campaigns, which included thousands of signatures, were domestic, the domestic support for the cause of abolition signaled so strong a public opinion that it influenced British foreign policy. The Marquis of Wellesley, British ambassador to Spain, warned a Spanish minister of "the hopelessness [of financial aid to Spain,] in the present temper of Parliament and the Nation on the subject of the Slave Trade . . . [without] a stipulation for the total and immediate abolition of the slave trade."[5] In fact, an 1814 British abolition petition of more than three-quarters of a million signatures had greater impact outside of Britain (influencing peace negotiations between Britain and France), than it did domestically where many of the core norms had already been adopted.[6]

Given its transnational effects, the London Society represents a good historical case for outlining criteria to assess the effects of associations. First of all, its purpose (getting a legal ban on the slave trade) is not threatening to cosmopolitanism. This makes it easier to focus on whether it helped to advance a range of different cosmopolitan effects. Since I am interested in exploring how associations can help to generate cosmopolitan norms and dispositions, it is also important to note that abolition was by no means a well-developed, internationally accepted norm before the formation of the London Society.[7] Second of all, the London Society's motives as well as its effects were not always straightforwardly cosmopolitan, making it possible to explore partial expressions of cosmopolitanism.

The Society did not explicitly employ the language of cosmopolitanism in championing its cause. In fact, one scholar argues that "many an act of self-interest has been dressed up in the garb of humanitarianism, abolition provides the very rare example of the tactic applied in reverse."[8] Members supported abolition for a variety of different reasons: advancing greater respect for the moral equality of those enslaved (cosmopolitan reasoning) but also protecting national security, economic interest, as well as British pride (non-cosmopolitan reasoning). Ending the slave trade transnationally could be couched in terms of national interest because it would prevent other countries from developing their colonies.[9] Beyond economic or security interests there were even religious reasons for ending slavery. Doing so was necessary to remove a source of moral corruption from British society and thereby save Britain from the wrath of God.[10] One reason constructivist international relations scholars discuss this society is that it serves as an example of moral issues winning over state and economic interests. Lives were lost in the navy as Britain tried to suppress the slave trade. Such actions put Britain in conflict with other international powers.[11] It seems as though a purely national-interest-based realist argument cannot explain the campaign to abolish slavery. Even with the mixed motives of its members and some non-cosmopolitan rhetoric, the London Society's purpose does not pose the more obvious challenges of the cases discussed in part II, which have fewer direct connections to cosmopolitan principles. Therefore, I will use British abolition as a starting point to help illustrate criteria for assessing the effects of associations. Doing so requires exploring what effects the London Society had and whether those effects were cosmopolitan in nature.

As I discussed in chapters 1, 2, and 3, judging the cosmopolitan nature of effects requires criteria that embody different core ideals of cosmopolitanism in order to create a framework applicable to the broad array of different associations on the global level. Scholars today have shown that the impact of transnational associations is significant. Some go so far as to argue that a global civil society already exists which can spread democratic norms on the global level and transform the world into a more just place.[12] When studying associations it is common to concentrate on the "self-conscious and dedicated efforts"[13] of those associations with goals such as advancing human rights. If ethical dilemmas are addressed it is in terms of dilemmas human rights or humanitarian associations face as they carry out their projects.[14] The case of the London Society makes it very clear that in order to evaluate the cosmopolitan effects of an association one ought not primarily focus on the motives of the association. (The goal of saving British souls and demonstrating British moral superiority are not particularly cosmopolitan.)

Developing criteria to account for indirect effects allows one to explore whether membership in associations fosters cosmopolitanism rather than simply determining the effectiveness of an association's self-conscious goals. In the case of the London Society, for example, the goal was ending the slave trade by passing a law in Parliament and influencing the laws of other countries through British foreign policy. Yet normative cosmopolitan moral theories can evaluate much more than the purposes of associations. Do associations bring individuals into transnational conversation, build transnational institutional or shared identity ties, establish more inclusive public spheres, or broaden imaginations to recognize common humanity? None of this is meant to undercut the importance of laws banning the slave trade. One can study how effective associations are at realizing their missions, but this could miss many other effects of membership in associations. I am interested in how cosmopolitan political theory might serve as a normative framework for evaluating the indirect effects of associations. Determining whether membership in associations affects how individuals see and relate to the world will enable cosmopolitan theorists to better understand how cosmopolitan norms might emerge in the world from motivations that are not necessarily cosmopolitan. For now the London Society serves as a historical example (lest one conclude from my later arguments that the influence of non-state actors is merely a more recent phenomenon) of how to evaluate whether an association has effects that change norms or dispositions in more cosmopolitan directions.

Engaging in this evaluation requires considering what cosmopolitans should expect from associations. In order to understand an association's cosmopolitan potential it is necessary to combine the cosmopolitan theories discussed in chapter 2 (institutional, natural duties, cultural, and deliberative democratic cosmopolitanism) with research on associational effects. In order to supplement the theoretical categories discussed in chapter 2 with research on associations, I rely on four categories of associations' effects: institutional, developmental, shared identity, and public sphere effects. Associations can have many effects beyond these four categories but the goal is to focus on effects that are relevant to cosmopolitans. After making the connection between theories of associations and cosmopolitan normative theories, I will use the British abolitionists and the London Society to consider the implications of this combination. How might the criteria from cosmopolitan theory apply to certain effects of the association? In particular, what could partial and indirect expressions of cosmopolitanism look like?

Since I have also previously argued that one should not see any one association as a perfect ideal that all others ought to mimic, a few contemporary examples of associations are also incorporated to flesh out elements of cosmopolitanism the London Society does not illuminate. Drawing on different examples serves as a reminder not to forget the complexity of associations' effects. This complexity is best acknowledged by bringing together categories of cosmopolitan theory and research on associations in order to establish a middle-level theory of cosmopolitan criteria. Let me now make this final critical connection to develop the criteria.

CONNECTING COSMOPOLITANISM AND THE EFFECTS OF ASSOCIATIONS

If, as I argued in chapter 2, no one existing type of comprehensive cosmopolitan theory has the tools needed to assess the plurality of different associations, then cosmopolitanism needs to be adapted in order to apply it to associations. One should see each type of cosmopolitan theory as representing certain core cosmopolitan values (such as empathy for fellow humans) or ideals (such as just transnational institutional relations). Yet, even with this adaptation, scholars are still left assessing each association individually to determine whether its effects advance cosmopolitan norms. Can one evaluate associations in a more effective manner? If one could establish categories of common effects relevant to cosmopolitanism, scholars interested in determining the cosmopolitan nature of an association could then assess specific effects to determine whether they are cosmopolitan in nature.

In taking this approach I rely, in part, on Mark E. Warren's work on democracy and associations. As I have already mentioned, Warren recognizes the challenge of generalizing about the effects of associations in a way that respects the diverse range of effects associations can have. He makes a case "against broad generalizations about plural associational landscapes, as well as against monocausal views of what a democracy needs to work."[15] This does not mean that all generalization should be rejected. Instead, theories offering one primary standard for judging associations or theories offering endless potential standards are not useful. It is possible to develop a few general categories of effects that respect diversity but allow for some comparison across associations. He outlines three categories of effects relevant to his focus on democracy: institutional, developmental, and public sphere effects.[16]

Warren's categories are a good place to begin since I too am interested in assessing associations. Connections between the way I categorized cosmopolitan theory and types of effects should also become clearer. In categorizing theories I was looking for types of cosmopolitan theories that were relevant to evaluating associations. The four categories—institutional, natural duties, and deliberative democratic cosmopolitanism—map on to three of Warren's categories of effects—institutional, developmental, and public sphere. Institutional effects connect directly to institutional cosmopolitanism. Developmental effects fit with natural duty cosmopolitanism's focus on the moral development of individuals. A category of public sphere effects connects well with deliberative democratic cosmopolitanism once theories are expanded to include associations, not only political institutions. Missing is a connection to cultural cosmopolitanism that is relevant for understanding how to balance diverse and partial identities in a cosmopolitan fashion. This theoretical approach seems very relevant to assessing membership in partial associations. Moreover, Jackie Smith's work on transnational social movements, referenced in my discussion of global civil society in chapter 3, emphasizes the important role that associations play in creating common transnational identities.[17] Therefore, I add a category of effect—shared identity effect—to Warren's list in order to account for the importance of cultural cosmopolitan theory's valuing of diverse cultures and identities. Once the categories of effects are established then the effects under each category need to be evaluated in terms of cosmopolitan theory rather than Warren's use of democratic theory. Cosmopolitanism understood as a thesis about responsibility and identity cannot be equated to democracy.

What would it mean for effects to be cosmopolitan in nature? For example, one can test whether or not an association generates a public sphere or a shared identity but this only speaks to the effects. It does not assess the effect. One ought also to ask whether the public sphere or the identity advances cosmopolitan norms or dispositions. In what follows the aim is to develop cosmopolitan criteria—questions one could ask about each effect—to determine if an association has effects that advance cosmopolitanism. Because the criteria do not establish a single whole or ideal type of association, they can be applied piecemeal. An association could exhibit partial expressions of cosmopolitanism by having some effects that satisfy cosmopolitan criteria. In order to help illustrate the criteria, I will assess the Society for Effecting the Abolition of the Slave Trade to determine its cosmopolitan potential in each category of associational effect.

Institutional Effects

What might it mean to evaluate the institutional effects of associations? This is where having an example like the London Society is helpful. How were British abolitionists organized? Did the Society have transnational institutional relations? If so, what were they like? These are some of the questions that one might raise to start investigating institutional effects.

As I already mentioned, the London Society was considered a logistical headquarters for the British movement to legally ban the slave trade. It played an important role in connecting different local abolitionist societies and committees with similar goals. (Parallel organizations did emerge but they offered more radical critiques of slavery or sought to adopt non-legislative tactics.[18]) The London Society did not usually initiate local societies but leaders from the London Society like Thomas Clarkson would often make connections with such local groups.[19] Many religious organizations, the Quakers in particular, that opposed abolition also assisted the London Society.[20] All this demonstrates, however, are the national connections not transnational ones. In fact constructivist scholars Chaim D. Kaufmann and Robert A. Pape argue that in order to understand the abolitionist campaign the first step is to recognize that "British anti-slavery was a national, not international enterprise."[21] Yet, in making this statement they mean that transnational pressure was not what lead to the domestic changes in British law. They are not claiming that there were no transnational ties or affiliations. If one is interested in whether the association had cosmopolitan effects in addition to legislative success, it is worth considering the ties formed in association with the Society.

The London Society certainly did not have the extent of transnational reach or organization that some associations have today. There were, however, some international connections. Thomas Clarkson, in particular, traveled to France in order to help coordinate efforts and build support for abolition in that country. In fact, he provided much of the information on the horrors of slavery used by the French organization Société des Amis des Noirs (Society of Friends of the Blacks) founded in 1788.[22] In addition, there was continual correspondence and even visits between British and United States abolitionists.[23] At the same time, transnational allegiances were not always smooth. Tensions emerged between forging international ties to assist other abolitionists and the concerns of abolitionists in countries such as the United States or France that the British were telling them what to do.[24]

The strong transnational ties among Quakers and religious missionary associations were another source of support for abolition on both sides of the Atlantic. In fact, around the same time as abolition was gaining force in Britain, "nonconformist sects became increasingly involved in missionary activity, especially in the West Indies."[25] (Missionary activity will once again emerge as relevant in my later discussion of the Anglican Communion in chapter 7.) Missionaries, who had not necessarily been sent with the purpose of freeing slaves, preached equality before God and often ended up playing a crucial role in the movement against slavery. As "a Jamaican slave, you were not a citizen, had no rights"; however, "in a mission chapel you could learn to read and write and could gain the status of a member, a deacon, a respected elder. Moreover, you were part of an international fellowship; Baptist and Methodist membership cards were printed in England."[26] The missionaries also spread firsthand information on the cruelties of slavery to congregations back home. Slave owners recognized the threat these missionaries posed, often harassing and even killing them. Despite little formal transnational institutional structure to the Society, it certainly drew on transnational ties of prominent leaders and existing transnational religious networks played a role in its self-understanding and advocacy efforts.

The international scope of abolitionist advocacy efforts shows attempts to transform norms and standards by institutionalizing a ban on the slave trade throughout the Atlantic. Even when the goal was focused on British law, there were necessarily transnational effects given that Britain controlled a colonial empire with a powerful navy. Abolitionists also attempted to use British foreign policy to change the laws and policies of other countries. For example, in 1814 there was a petition campaign in protest to the Treaty of Paris, which had been negotiated by the prestigious Foreign Secretary Castlereagh. The treaty included an article that allowed the French slave trade to continue for five more years. As a result of popular outcry, Britain entered the peace negotiations not from a position to make demands but rather granting loans and promises in return for other countries abolishing their slave trade. In fact, one scholar goes so far as to say that "the most dramatic impact of the 1814 petitions occurred outside the United Kingdom."[27] In this way the abolitionist movement certainly advanced a political agenda of changing British as well as other countries' laws in order to combat slavery.

What would it mean to evaluate these effects in terms of institutional cosmopolitanism? It seems as though the Society was interested in institutional change. Its leaders wanted to alter the legal institution of property, and they used international diplomacy to apply pressure to other countries to change their laws as well. In that sense, the institutional effects of this association do not seem to be in establishing new institutions but in realizing change through existing institutions.

Were these effects cosmopolitan? This can be determined by returning to institutional cosmopolitan theory. It argues that global economic and political institutions generate obligations due to the "deep and pervasive effects" those institutions have "on the welfare of people to whom they apply regardless of consent."[28] Cosmopolitan "duties of justice arise between persons when activities such as politics or commerce bring persons into association."[29] Abolishing the slave trade certainly deals with political and economic institutions that lack consent. The Society certainly sought to institutionalize new standards that better respected moral equality. It is not hard to imagine that this might be the case for other advocacy associations that seek to realize institutional change but do not always consist of a robust institutional structure connecting members in regularly structured activity. Members may support the association with donations or by signing petitions, without becoming professional abolitionists like Clarkson. Nevertheless, the association institutionalized standards or norms on the global level. The association helped achieve a law banning the slave trade. Although there had been groups advocating for abolition before the London Society, a norm against slavery had not become internationally or domestically powerful. Abolitionists even continued for decades after the ban on trading in slaves, pushing for the end of slavery itself. The attempt to influence laws in other countries also persisted after 1807. Even if countries were able to circumvent British attempts to stop the slave trade, it is worth noting that British abolitionists generated support for international pressure despite costs to the British.[30]

Scholars studying more recent associations also note the role they play in institutionalizing more cosmopolitan laws and norms. Associations advocate for establishing formal institutional structures such as the International Criminal Court as well as promote the need for changes in international and national legal norms.[31] The 1989 Convention on Rights of the Child is one example of an international legal convention that associations helped to shape. Another example is international women's groups that argued human rights ought to protect against domestic forms of violence. Shifts in international norms around what counts as a human rights violation put pressure on governments to take action in order to confront domestic violence.[32] These examples take an approach similar to the Society. They seek to change the norms of institutions outside the association itself. In addition to aiming at establishing new norms that delegitimize certain practices, associations also play a role in enforcing adherence to norms on the international level. "Compliance auditing by commercial firms and non-profits" is an example of this, and the Global Reporting Initiative is just such an association.[33] It has the goal of setting up "standardized social and environmental reporting systems to make them as routine as financial reporting."[34] This Dutch non-governmental organization (NGO) goes a step further than advocating for change in law. It seeks to enforce norms. Here the association itself serves to establish part of what cosmopolitan theorist David Held calls a "new institutional complex with global scope" that has the "character of government to the extent, and only to the extent, that is promulgates, implements and enforces this law."[35] In regulating governments, businesses, or other associations the institutions of NGOs can contribute to global governance.

So far the focus has been on associations consciously aiming to bring about institutional changes or support certain international norms, but now it is worth considering whether membership in an association's institutional relations may result in cosmopolitan obligations or norms. Do the institutions of a transnational voluntary association create relations among individuals that generate new cosmopolitan obligations? Although institutional cosmopolitan theorists usually focus on more coercive institutions rather than on voluntary associations, Joshua Cohen and Charles Sabel have argued that, over time, even voluntarily accepted obligations can gain force. The International Labor Organization, they argue, cannot suddenly refuse to represent certain sectors of the labor force even if those sectors were not part of the organization's original mission. Expectations have developed that give the International Labor Organization certain obligations.[36] Associations can bring individuals into institutional relations with each other that help them act on existing transnational obligations to reform unjust global political and economic institutions or that generate new obligations because of membership in that association. If an association's institutional relations exploit some members then cosmopolitan obligations require members to reform the institutions or rescind membership in the organization.

I have argued that applying institutional cosmopolitanism to associations means not only focusing on the purpose of an association but also evaluating the association's institutional structure and the obligations it generates. British abolitionists argued that because the British were benefiting from slavery they had special obligations to stop this practice, but these are not obligations generated by membership in the Society. Let me give a more recent example to illustrate how associations may generate obligations. The international labor movement against child labor in the textile industry, particularly in Bangladesh, initially failed to take into account the concerns of child laborers and their families leading to the unfortunate consequence that children were moved out of the textile industry into much less desirable and more dangerous areas of work (such as, prostitution).[37] Even though the result may be unintended, the association ought to bear some responsibility for aiding those it affected. Members of the association have special obligations to address any injustices. Obligations arising from an association's actions will also emerge in my later discussion of Médecins Sans Frontières (MSF), or Doctors Without Borders, which has struggled to address obligations it has to the local medical staff it hires.

In assessing the institutional structure of associations one might also ask whether there are ways of organizing the association that foster cosmopolitanism. There are no clearly cosmopolitan institutions to mirror so what would cosmopolitan institutions look like? It seems most obvious that such institutions would not be organized primarily in national terms. Carol C. Gould argues that transnational solidarity often means uniting around shared interests rather than around particular identities.[38] Of course some shared interests are more respectful of the moral equality of all humans than others. Class cleavages can form between associations or members based in wealthier countries (referred to as the global North) and those in less wealthy countries (referred to as the global South). Such divisions can result in paternalistic relationships between members or among associations. A purely transnational scope to the organization is not enough to conclude that the association is cosmopolitan. However, combining consideration of the association's institutional structure and evaluating the obligations it acts on can help to determine the cosmopolitan nature of institutional effects on membership.

Locating institutional effects therefore involves both evaluating the impact associations have on the institutionalization or enforcement of norms as well as assessing the association's own institutional relations. Associations like the Society that do not have a robust transnational structure of their own can nevertheless have cosmopolitan institutional effects if they institutionalize cosmopolitan norms or promote greater recognition of cosmopolitan obligations to establish more respectful international relations. In such cases the focus may involve the association's purpose, although as I will show later with the example of the Olympics, even transnational rules not directed at realizing cosmopolitan principles can have cosmopolitan effects. One can also evaluate the impact of membership. What effect do associations with more robust institutional structures have on members? Do they generate cosmopolitan obligations? The cases I draw on in chapters 5 through 7 have interesting ways of understanding how members are related through their institutional structure. Institutional relations in voluntary associations can generate obligations with real force despite being voluntary relations. Whether establishing new obligations across borders, reforming unjust institutional relations, or institutionalizing standards that better respect moral equality, associations can have institutional effects that advance cosmopolitanism.

Developmental Effects

Abolitionists were not great institution crafters but did have some institutional effects. Did they have any developmental effects? Associations ought to be evaluated in terms of their ability to impact the perspectives, attitudes, or dispositions of members. Do they help members recognize commonalities with fellow humans? Does that recognition help generate a sense of empathy and compassion for others? Dispositional shifts are critical for recognizing obligations that we have to fellow humans. In this section, I will explore what developmental effects might look like, especially in conjunction with natural duties cosmopolitan theory and its focus on the moral development of individuals. Did the Society have effects that fostered a more cosmopolitan disposition in members?

In addition to putting legislation before Parliament, the abolitionists campaigned to educate the British population about the inhumane nature of the slave trade.[39] Clarkson collected data on the number of sailors and slaves who died on slave ships. He measured slave berths and then published a poster showing a model of the cramped quarters. This information, combined with testimonials from doctors who had served aboard slave ships and from missionaries in the British West Indies, created vivid pictures that rallied support. The publication of slave testimonials was yet another way to "stir men and women to action . . . through the vivid unforgettable description of acts of great injustice done to their fellow human beings" and aimed to invoke "human empathy."[40] These elements of the abolitionist campaign recast slavery from a purely economic matter to one of moral relevance for all humans not simply those directly linked to the slave trade (slave traders and slave owners). Some abolitionists felt strongly that "the nature of the slave-trade needs only to be known to be detested."[41]

Some members of the Society even went a step further, cultivating empathy for the slaves by drawing analogies to forms of oppression the British faced. The goal was to invoke shared experiences of vulnerability to exploitation. Before banning the slave trade to the West Indies became a national topic of discussion, another form of slavery was on British minds. From 1600 to 1750, white slavery was a threat to at least twenty thousand people from Britain and Ireland enslaved in North Africa.[42] Naval impressment was another oppressive practice widely opposed. A backdrop of "more than a century of public anger at the press gangs strengthened the idea that violently capturing other human beings to put them to work was cruelly unjust—and could and should be fought against."[43] In addition, some elements of the abolitionist movement even cast harsh labor conditions in terms of slavery. In fact, "the climactic discussion of abolition in the winter of 1807 tended to draw attention towards, not away from, domestic poverty, and to encourage a linking of the two problems."[44] Broadening imaginations for abolition meant drawing on sentiments of anger or outrage toward existing practices the British faced but it also had implications beyond naval impressment and white slavery even extending to domestic labor conditions. This was the case despite leaders of the London Society not wanting to make connections to the conditions of domestic laborers.

At the same time that some elements of the abolitionist movement worked to cultivate empathy with slaves, others framed the struggle in terms of British beneficence and pity. This was certainly the view of some prominent members of the Society. Although Thomas Clarkson certainly wanted to end slavery, which he saw as "one of the greatest sources of suffering to the human race," he also considered reducing the suffering of slaves as "a minor benefit compared with Britain's liberation from a contagion that had poisoned 'the moral springs of the mind' and jeopardized Christian salvation."[45] William Wilberforce too espoused a view of abolition as "practical benevolence."[46] Trading humans was inhumane but once the barbaric trade stopped and former slaves were "taught by Christianity," he believed that they would accept the "sufferings of their actual lot . . . [and] will soon be regarded as a grateful peasantry" laboring in the sugar cane plantations.[47] Maintaining the support of certain members of the Society, especially powerful members like Wilberforce, required suppressing radical claims of equality. In fact, to win support for their cause, one member of the Society, James Stephan, "worked tirelessly as the abolitionists' professional watchdog, cautioning them to mute humanitarian arguments and to focus on questions of national security."[48] In fact, some scholars go so far as to argue that the reason British abolitionists succeeded was because supporters liked the idea of British moral superiority and could rally behind saving British society from corruption. In this case moral outcomes would not depend on moral motivations.[49] My argument concurs to the extent that cosmopolitan effects can emerge from actions not motivated by cosmopolitan ideals; yet, focusing only on the group's goals also misses effects that could interest cosmopolitans.

Looking beyond the specific goal of the association, one can find other possible developmental impacts. For example, new types of public leaders emerged through participation in the abolitionist movement. Religious dissenters, like the Quakers, who had been excluded from more formal political institutions were able to influence political action through the abolition campaigns. Women and some former slaves also gained access to public forums at a time when participation in more formal political institutions was not open to them. Although the Society was not interested in including many former slaves among its members, the public was very interested in hearing slave testimonials to the point that "African voices also rang out in the London debating societies."[50] Even more so than former slaves, women were active and engaged participants in the abolition movement. One of Wilberforce's campaign songs included lyrics calling on women to "muster your Charms on Humanity's Side" and ended with "Women and Wilberforce conquer again!"[51] Women participating in abolition events could learn skills and organizational techniques that were applied in the women's movement as well.[52] The broad range of tactics (including public debates, signing petitions, and boycotting goods) that the abolitionists employed enabled many different members of society to participate in the movement.

Having very briefly described some effects the abolitionist movement had on developing dispositions or skills in individuals, it is necessary to determine how to evaluate these effects in terms of cosmopolitanism. Natural duties cosmopolitanism, with its focus on expanding individuals' imaginations to recognize commonalities and the resulting obligations we have to fellow humans, is relevant to assessing these kinds of effects.[53]

How does natural duties cosmopolitanism apply to the Society? It had educative effects. Abolitionists broadened British sentiments by framing abolition in terms of shared experiences of vulnerability to exploitation. In fact, one author comments on how curious it is that, "the long public struggle against it [impressment]" has not been recognized as having "psychologically set the national stage for the much larger battle over slavery."[54] Drawing on common experiences of injustice can unite people and motivate them to seek change. Women's groups are a more contemporary example of drawing on common experiences. They were able to build transnational networks once they began to focus on common experiences of vulnerability to violence. Unlike issues such as veiling or suffrage, stopping violence addressed an issue that crossed cultural divides.[55] Yet, the Society also shows that common vulnerabilities do not automatically lead to a robust sense of moral equality. The focus could remain on members of the association, rather than on the individual who is being oppressed. Insofar as the rhetoric moved away from cultivating empathy and toward benevolence the cosmopolitan educative effect was weakened. Pity is not as cosmopolitan a sentiment as empathy because pity can take on a paternalistic attitude that references to empathy try to avoid. (For example, one does not empathize with non-human entities. You can pity an abused animal without empathizing with it.) Empathy is supposed to rest on fellow feeling. For an association to have cosmopolitan effects, it should generate a sense of obligation to fellow humans.

Despite some non-cosmopolitan motivations, abolitionists did make an important developmental impact on redirecting human imagination from thinking of slavery in economic terms to emphasizing the human element. In fact, abolition remained a popular movement even though it went against economic interests. "The true taproot of anti-slavery lay in

its successful mass political mobilization around a fundamentally uneco-
nomic proposition."[56] More recently other advocacy movements have
sought to shift the terms of certain debates to focus on the human implications of transnational problems. Environmental groups' campaigns to
stop deforestation have, in some cases, switched from describing the dangers of deforestation in scientific terms to providing testimony from humans who are directly affected.[57]

In addition to generating a sense of empathy based on shared experiences of vulnerability, developmental effects can also play an educative
role in terms of skill development. Cosmopolitans want us to act on, not
merely recognize, our obligations. Martha Nussbaum's cosmopolitanism
is based on a broader theory of justice that involves cultivating human
capabilities. All individuals have the right to lead flourishing human
lives, and this requires fostering capabilities rather than simply redistrib-
uting resources.[58] Therefore, developmental effects on individuals can
also to be evaluated in terms of empowerment and skill development.
The new opportunities to participate in public activities empowered
women and some former slaves, teaching them skills of political mobiliz-
ing as well as protest tactics such as petitioning and public speaking.
Although these opportunities did not always have a global scope, transnational pressure played a role in pushing British abolitionists to include
women more fully. Abolitionists from the United States like William
Lloyd Garrison objected to women delegates being seated in the balcony
with spectators during the 1840 Anti-Slavery International conference.[59]
In today's complex international world, it is often necessary to learn how
to operate within transnational networks particularly when those participating are not the ones who set up the institutions in the first place.
Associations may hold teach-ins or seminars in order to explain or exchange strategies for global action. The impact of international participation has been important to local groups in Taiwan, for example. A study
of Taiwanese associations showed that "those transnationally more engaged NGOs were also the groups most active in their own issue areas
inside Taiwan."[60] Through participation in international NGO meetings
Taiwanese activists learned how to frame issues as well as exchanged
resources and information with other activists.[61] Individuals can feel empowered if their actions result in having their voices recognized. These
can be confidence-building effects.[62] On the global level this might exhibit itself in the sense of being a global actor and being represented in
public dialogue.[63] Issues can be framed in terms of global concerns and
local actors can participate in bringing about international change.

It is crucial that cultivating a sense of empowerment should not be
done in a way that undermines the agency of others or dehumanizes
them. Organized crime may link individuals together but does not cultivate respect. Crime organizations that traffic in humans or transnational
terrorist organizations make this very clear in that they specifically target

innocent civilians. Any sense of global agency that develops at the expense of another's human rights is not compatible with cosmopolitanism.

Cosmopolitan developmental effects are about recognizing common vulnerabilities and the responsibilities we have as a result. Such recognition ought to be used as a way to empower individuals not to exploit them. What a study of associations shows is that issues, even ones that require global solutions, are not automatically conceived in global terms. Recognizing commonalities may mean recasting local issues in a transnational context. This process is not only about developing a new perspective but also about learning the relevant skills for acting as a global agent.[64] (I will discuss this more in the case of Anglican bishops from the global South and their changing role in the broader Anglican Communion, particularly as they navigate international conferences with greater ease.) Cosmopolitans can ask a series of questions to evaluate the developmental effects of associations. Do they expand the imaginations of members in order to recognize commonalities to fellow humans and the resulting obligations and responsibilities? Do they provide opportunities for individuals to cultivate skills and capabilities in order to be public actors and to perceive their local concerns from a broader perspective? All in all, developmental effects are the effects that associations have on individuals as opposed to institutions. These effects are educative rather than identity based, which will be the focus of the next category of effects. Acknowledging the implications of shared vulnerability is meant to get us to stop exploitation, not necessarily to form solidarity with others.

Shared Identity Effects

Institutional and developmental effects both involve recognizing and acting on obligations but the understanding of cosmopolitanism outlined in chapter 1 is not only about responsibility. Cosmopolitanism is also a thesis about identity. In order to truly live a cosmopolitan moral life one must consider one's relationship to one's country, to one's culture, and to other more particular identities. What would it look like for an association to contribute to a cosmopolitan way of life or cosmopolitan identity? In order to answer this question I add a category to Warren's list of effects, namely a shared identity effect. This reflects the challenge as well as the ideal of cultivating some degree of solidarity across borders.

Of course, not all forms of transnational solidarity are cosmopolitan (just as not all international institutions are cosmopolitan). Theorists discussing associations on the domestic level make it clear that determining the benefits of membership in associations must involve more than evaluations of solidarity and trust-building. Amy Gutmann describes how the Ku Klux Klan "may cultivate solidarity and trust, reduce incentives for opportunism, and develop some 'I's' into a 'we.'"[65] However, the "we" is based on solidarity in hatred and a desire to terrorize, which are not valuable to fostering a democratic or cosmopolitan community. There are, however, certain forms of association that generate identities helpful to cosmopolitanism. Cultural cosmopolitanism assesses how individuals relate to their identities and the forms of solidarity that shape their ways of life. Cultures are dynamic, not single pure authentic wholes. Individuals need to relate to their own partial identities in a way that does not involve "presenting oneself and one's cultural preferences *non-negotiably* to others in the present circumstances of the world" for that would hamper engagement with others.[66] Cosmopolitanism entails "engagement with the experience and idea of others" not only for purposes of satisfying obligations but also because it "helps people get used to one another."[67]

Evaluating solidarity on the international level is complex because it is often solidarity among distant others. Some, like Robert Putnam, who I discussed in chapter 3, question whether meaningful solidarity or trust can be built through transnational organizations.[68] Others, such as Gould, redefine transnational solidarity so that it is not "a matter of identity" but instead forged around shared values and a commitment to justice.[69] Cosmopolitan Kwame Anthony Appiah, however, keeps identity front and center in his cosmopolitan theory because universal principles exist in social contexts. The task for cosmopolitans is to find particular practices and interests around which individuals could form solidarities.[70] Appiah describes how cosmopolitan engagement with others means being open to "gaining insight from our interlocutors."[71] The process of learning that shapes our identity must be based on actual engagement with others on terms that accept our own fallibility. Transnational solidarity, even for Gould, who separates it from identity, is about mutual aid and reciprocal relations.[72] Not all relations, even those that aim to fulfill obligations to suffering others, foster reciprocal solidarity. Humanitarian aid may well fail this test because reciprocity presumes some form of return otherwise relations could exacerbate a sense of victimization.[73] A requirement of reciprocity may appear more feasible if one recognizes that reciprocity does not require an exchange of equal things. Relations can become reciprocal "to the degree that interlocutors are ready to learn from others."[74] How would one evaluate the effects of an association in terms of cosmopolitan shared identity? Did the London Society have any effects that built community or shaped identity?

I have already mentioned that the abolitionists drew on some shared experiences of vulnerability. These resulted in some developmental effects. Did they generate a sense of shared identity that was cosmopolitan? One of the movement's powerful images was the picture of a slave with the slogan: "Am I not a man and a brother?" It was replicated on campaign buttons and pins. Despite the language of common humanity, the slave is kneeling to plead for respect not demanding he be treated as an equal.[75] This is a very thin shared identity at best. It certainly goes to show that "alliances across groups do not automatically emerge from the existence of shared values or goals."[76] Both abolitionists and slaves wanted an end to the slave trade but this did not forge strong allegiances. Appiah would likely point to a lack of actual engagement with each other as a reason for this. There were a few exceptional cases of former slaves involved in the abolition movement. One famous example was Olaudah Equiano, who wrote a book about his life and took it on "the first great political book tour."[77] By and large slaves were seen as passive recipients rather than active members of the transnational society. The early abolitionist campaigns were also largely Eurocentric. Only later did abolitionists begin to target practices of slavery in Africa and other parts of the world. Even then there was no shared identity between slaves and Society members.

Whether partial identities were more cosmopolitan is a slightly more complex question. A concern with British identity indirectly played a role in advancing cosmopolitanism. British identity, defined as a standard bearer of liberty, was in conflict with British law that allowed slavery.[78] Pride in British national identity was seen as a way to motivate people to unite around abolition. The abolitionist movement was not merely driven by a small group of elites. Popular opinion played a large role in sustaining abolitionism through times when elites temporarily stopped pursuing the cause as avidly.[79] Solidarity and perhaps some shared identity developed among abolitionists from different parts of society (political leaders, religious dissenters, workers, women, even some former slaves) through participation in joint activities. This does remain a national identity but could connect with ideas of cosmopolitan patriotism.

Drawing on some contemporary associations may help to further flesh out the idea of shared identity effects. One interesting contemporary example of how even partial shared identities (that do not aim to encompass all humans) can generate a transnational perspective in members is the case of a labor campaign against the Coca Cola Company in Guatemala. Labor networks invoked the transnational identity of fellow Coca Cola employees over and above local or nationally defined labor communities. As a result British Coca Cola workers went on strike in support of their Guatemalan counterparts—without any of their own demands for the British branch of the company.[80] Transnational interaction can even lead to membership becoming more inclusive and reciprocal even if it does not start out that way. The business association Mujer a Mujer, which seeks to establish connections between businesswomen across the US–Mexico border, held seminars and hosted visits but did not at first include Latina women in the association's membership. Eventually it expanded to include them and their experiences as the group's own ideals seemed to demand.[81] These are examples from the business world. Shared identity is not limited to that sphere. Later cases of the Olympics and the Anglican Communion will show different types of associations that form common identities.

Generating a sense of community, solidarity, or shared identity requires attention to the role of symbols and shared practices, which can reiterate and reinforce transnational ties around a sense of shared community. The role of symbolism should become more relevant to cosmopolitans. British abolitionists used pins with their slogans to signal membership in the movement. Recognizing common vulnerabilities will not necessarily form solidarity based on identity because "the many interests that people have in virtue of our shared biology do not function outside their symbolic context."[82] Ties will more likely form through narrative construction of the world around particular, contingent practices and points of connection.[83] Participation in communal activities through a transnational association can help generate a sense of community among members. It need not entail similar roles for all members, but some kind of reciprocity or sharing of roles and duties is important to avoid undermining moral equality through paternalism. In this way, shared identity effects are not void of moral import. Members of transnational voluntary associations in North America or Western Europe ought not be patronizing in their attitudes toward those from other parts of the world. Membership based on reciprocal relations rather than only based on assistance might help to build communities in which members actually engage with each other in ways that involve learning from each other. Building those reciprocal relations may require paying attention to the role of tradition and symbolism. Creating shared identities does not necessarily result in new international laws or institutions, and such identities are not necessarily dangerous to cosmopolitanism. One should not conclude from this that the identities are morally irrelevant.

Cosmopolitans ought not only be interested in the scope of identities but also in whether they result in forms of solidarity that foster respect for human liberty and moral equality. When associations do bridge certain divides like state boundaries in order to establish a sense of solidarity it is quite an achievement, particularly if it creates ties of respect between members of the transnational community.

Public Sphere Effects

The final category of effects is public sphere effects. What might a public sphere effect look like? Deliberative democratic cosmopolitans argued for the importance of a particular kind of deliberative ethic and for cultivating global public spheres. These concerns can be linked to the scholarship on associations. Let me start with the example of the Society in order to see whether it cultivated spaces for discussion and deliberation.

The Society's work created a public dialogue on the issue of slavery that until then had primarily been discussed within fringe groups such as the Quakers. The change was quite marked. The number of public debates held on the issue of the slave trade or slavery rose dramatically, so that "abruptly, in February 1788, a Londoner would have been able to attend seven debates on the abolition of the slave trade, half of *all* public debates on record in the city's daily newspapers that month."[84] In addition to public debates, the abolitionists also published journals and newsletters that become forums for discussing slavery. These were made possible in part because the Society's Quaker founders were able to tap into already existing publishing and distribution networks within the Quaker community.[85] The abolitionists drew on the existing forums for debates as well as publishing networks but in the process they also transformed what was considered appropriate or worthy of public debate as well as who could legitimately speak in public. As already mentioned there was a significant public interest in hearing the testimony of former slaves. Abolitionists also affirmed the legitimacy of women's role in the public sphere by publishing petition lists that included the names of women signatories in their newspaper.[86] Eventually discussions even took place on a transnational level. In June 1840 Clarkson gave the opening address at the first World Antislavery Convention where "thirty-nine countries were represented, including Sierra Leone and Haiti."[87] Reports were shared on practices of slavery in various parts of the world.

Although institutional relations and skill development are certainly relevant effects, there seems to be more at stake when studying how the Society helped to transform language and create spaces for discussion. Evaluating networks of communication means turning to cosmopolitan theories of ethical communication. Such cosmopolitans consider public deliberation important because discussion among strangers is possible if individuals agree to present arguments in ways others could understand. Public spheres emerge through the coalescence of "bundles of topically specific public opinions."[88] Anyone affected by an issue ought to have the opportunity to participate in the decisions about that issue otherwise individuals are not respected as moral equals—one would effectively be saying that some are not worthy of being heard. "Discourse theory articulates a universalist moral standpoint," cosmopolitan Seyla Benhabib writes, because moral questions are not confined to state borders. They ought to be seen as "potentially extending to all of *humanity*."[89] Since many significant challenges today (environmental preservation, security threats, public health, to name just a few) extend beyond state borders, public discussion of solutions should not disregard consideration of those beyond one's borders.

What does all this mean for associations? Associations can cultivate norms of communicative power by employing persuasion rather than violence or money to effect change and gain influence.[90] John Dryzek sees great potential for transnational associations to advocate for human rights because defending national interest does not hamper them, as it does states or even international governmental organizations.[91] The transnational social movement against landmines is an example of how associations can even challenge the legitimacy of certain national defense tactics when it comes to indiscriminate weapons like landmines.[92] Dryzek recognizes the creative potential of associations to bring into public discussion new norms, making his theory particularly relevant to my argument. However, his focus remains on the self-conscious goals of associations to advance ideals like human rights. Associations that deal only with fellow group members cannot have the positive transformative effect that he desires. The example Dryzek gives of problematic transnational ties is a nationalist group that forms ties with its diaspora.[93] Focusing on group members rather than aiming to address humanity hampers the form of deliberation keeping it private rather than offering public reasons not contingent on particular identities. The Society is an interesting case because it did change the discourse on slavery from an economic issue to a legitimate topic of public moral and political concern. However, the discussions were often about British superiority and saving British souls (not common public concerns for all humanity).

Religious groups pose another interesting example. One scholar describes how striking it was that when speaking on issues of public morality Pope John Paul II did not only address "Catholics as faithful members of the church, obliged to follow specific particular rules of the Catholic moral tradition." Instead the pope spoke to "every individual qua member of humanity, obliged to follow universal human norms, which are derived from the universal human values of life and freedom."[94] What should interest cosmopolitans are the implications of speaking to a global community. Religious authorities like Catholic bishops "cannot enter the public sphere without necessarily exposing Catholic normative traditions and ecclesiastical institutional structures to public scrutiny."[95] Complex public sphere effects are possible. A group that advocates for its own interests may unintentionally end up engaging with or even creating a global audience.

Can there be other cosmopolitan effects tied to membership in the association? Benhabib believes that even discussions of membership can serve as potential places for cosmopolitan effects. Discussion and disagreement can allow for experimentation and transformation of the association. Benhabib's democratic iterations are about defining and justifying the boundaries of political membership—citizenship requirements.[96] Perhaps, deliberation internal to an exclusive voluntary association could have effects on members' dispositions. Conflict over membership criteria can be constructive if discussions involve offering justifications for exclusion that can be explained to moral equals. Explanations based on some group being inferior or subhuman would not count as ethical public reasons since they violate basic moral equality. The benefits of discussion are that it can remind members of internal differences rather than simply cloaking them with a claim of unity and consensus.[97] Local chapters of the abolitionist movement would sometimes develop more radical views and pressure other branches to abandon more gradual plans for abolition that compromised on key principles. This is clearest in the latter part of the movement when women's groups and some labor groups within the abolitionist movement argued for the immediate end to slavery itself, while the London Society defended a more politically viable option of starting with a ban on the trade in slaves.[98] Conflict does not always result in greater respect. It could also raise dangers of polarization or attempts to distinguish authentic forms of membership. Associations' deliberative effects should be evaluated rather than presumed to be progressive because they speak to humanity.

What the Society helps to demonstrate is that associations can cultivate public spheres not only by introducing topics into international discussion but also by creating spaces for deliberation among members in the association (as just discussed) as well as with non-members. The importance of arenas for public discussion is particularly significant on the global level because there are fewer ways for individuals to come together for common purposes than may be the case in a state. The London Society not only brought abolition into public debate but also established abolitionist newspapers and held international conferences. Today many associations including religious and professional associations hold international conferences. NGOs hold parallel summits to provide forums for discussing issues governments ignore. The World Social Forum is an example of a space in which associations can foster alternative visions of international economic and political cooperation.[99] To the extent that associations provide a space for the participation of individuals who do not have a place in current international institutions this could help to make global public spheres more inclusive, even if it is not the group's intent (a point that will become relevant when discussing the Olympics in chapter 6).

Considering the power of deliberation on the global level is critical but also challenging. Public deliberation is difficult to achieve on the global level. There are some associations where deliberation and persuasion are more paramount than in others. It would be particularly relevant to consider whether discussions over membership are handled in ways that respect the excluded by offering justifications compatible with respect for moral equality. There are, however, different ways to have public sphere effects. Associations need not be internally deliberative. Even Dryzek's examples of associations imply that public spheres of discussion and deliberation can arise from associations that are not themselves internally deliberative. Social movements and the media are two such sources.[100] Neither of these organizations is necessarily internally delib-

erative; yet, they might nonetheless contribute to public spheres of deliberation on the global level. In addition to this one needs to recognize that
public sphere effects ought to include more than formal deliberation but
also protests, awareness raising, and debate. Advocacy associations do
not limit themselves to deliberative methods but often seek to shock people or create provocative images that will trigger certain emotional reactions in order to get their issues into public dialogue.[101] The complexity
of public sphere effects becomes even greater when one asks if groups
that are promoting issues that do not advance cosmopolitanism (as long
as they do not harm cosmopolitanism) could nevertheless cultivate skills
of deliberation or create public dialogue that impacts global public opinion. Public sphere effects can involve raising issues that advance global
deliberation in public spheres beyond the association itself as well as
creating public spaces that generate transnational debate.

COSMOPOLITAN CRITERIA
FOR EFFECTS OF ASSOCIATIONS

The Society for Effecting the Abolition of the Slave Trade helps to illustrate different ways of exhibiting expressions of cosmopolitanism. Some
effects of the association advance cosmopolitanism more strongly than
others. The cosmopolitan institutional effects of this early transnational
movement were not as well developed as some associations today, but
institutionalizing new norms regarding the immorality of slavery in British as well as continental law was of critical significance. Although empathy for exploited slaves was cultivated through certain educational campaigns that emphasized shared expressions of vulnerability and exploitation, this association did not generate a robust sense of shared community with slaves. The association's cosmopolitan shared identity effect
was largely limited to partial ties among abolitionists. Even with its cosmopolitan goal of ending the slave trade, the Society is best understood
as embodying partial expressions of cosmopolitanism. Yet, concluding
that the Society has only partial expressions of cosmopolitanism does not
mean it is not worth studying or that its contribution was not significant.
History has shown that the Society had effects that advanced a cause
clearly compatible with cosmopolitan ideals of moral equality even if
cosmopolitan principles did not always motivate all of its members. The
effects of membership in the association even caused some members to
confront their motives in a new light. Wilberforce supported abolition
because it was incompatible with British moral superiority; yet, he was
confronted with the implications of his position when free laborers in
Britain demanded better working conditions. He almost lost an election
because of an unfavorable action that he had taken against cloth laborers.[102] If applying cosmopolitan criteria reveals a more nuanced picture

of British abolition, the implications will only be more significant for associations that do not actively advance cosmopolitanism.

Let me summarize how cosmopolitan criteria emerge from connecting categories of associational effects and the categories of cosmopolitan theory. When assessing associations there are two steps. First, one must ask: Does the association have any of the types of effects that could be cosmopolitan? If the answer is yes, then the second question becomes relevant: Do the transnational effects advance cosmopolitanism? Answering the second question requires drawing on cosmopolitan theories.

Institutional Effects: One can evaluate the institutional structure of an association or the institutions it helps to construct, as well as its impact on institutionalizing new practices or norms. Institutional cosmopolitans tell us to pay attention to how institutional structures and relations can generate obligations. This results in two critical questions. Does an association form transnational institutions that bring individuals into relations that recognize responsibilities beyond state borders (particularly any responsibilities generated by the association's own institutional relations)? Does an association institutionalize cosmopolitan norms by seeking to change international laws, norms, or institutions (including rules within its institutions)?

Developmental Effects: One can evaluate the educative effects of membership in associations. Natural duties cosmopolitans argued that one ought to educate individuals to ensure they have the moral dispositions to recognize their obligations to fellow humans. Therefore, how associations shape dispositions becomes central. Do associations expand imaginations to recognize the responsibility to reduce suffering and cultivate greater moral equality? Do they provide opportunities for individuals to see their local concerns in terms of global concerns and to develop the capacity for global action?

Shared Identity Effects: One can evaluate the identities and forms of solidarity associations forge among members. Cultural cosmopolitans tell us that evaluating shared identity effects means not merely studying the scope of identity but how transnational identities shape relations and solidarity. Do associations cultivate transnational identities around shared practices or common symbols of community in which solidarity entails reciprocal relations where all members are seen as contributing (even if in different ways)?

Public Sphere Effects: The role of discussion and deliberation becomes central to understanding how associations can contribute to generating spaces beyond states where global or transnational public opinion is crafted. Deliberative democratic cosmopolitans challenge us to consider whether the deliberation is ethical even if it is deliberation about terms of exclusion. Do associations contribute to global deliberation by changing the standards of legitimate language or transforming who is considered critical to the discussion? Do they introduce issues ignored by other actors? Do they craft forums for transnational discussion or encourage internal deliberation among members?

The London Society helps to illustrate these criteria, but now that they have been established applying them to more controversial associations will show the limits and potential of indirect and partial cosmopolitan effects. Médecins Sans Frontières, the Olympics, and the Anglican Communion all have greater tensions between cosmopolitan and non-cosmopolitan components than the Society. They also represent examples of associations cosmopolitan theorists do not commonly discuss: professional, sports, and religious associations. In such cases, focusing on the purpose of the association becomes less helpful in recognizing its cosmopolitan potential.

In order to anticipate the tensions that arise in exclusive associations let me acknowledge that in a middle-level theory of cosmopolitan criteria tensions actually come from two sources. They arise not only between effects of associations that are cosmopolitan and those that are not but also between expressions of cosmopolitan ideals. It should not be forgotten that the criteria draw on different comprehensive cosmopolitan theories that are not intended to be combined. If institutional effects and developmental effects are evaluated using competing conceptions of cosmopolitanism, how can they be combined into one middle-level theory for associations? Institutional cosmopolitanism considers cosmopolitan obligations to arise by virtue of our institutional relations with each other. Natural duties cosmopolitanism rests the source of moral obligation on our common humanity. According to the institutional approach, an individual who had not formed strong institutional ties through an association would have no obligation to create them. This would not be the case from a natural duties approach. Individuals have obligations to aid other humans prior to or irrespective of existing institutional relations. One can see the quandary: If associations do not have strong institutional connections, then is it even necessary to consider their cosmopolitan obligations? This question is made a bit less critical in my project since the goal is to focus on associations with some transnational connection (even if those are loose transnational ties). The question is whether or not transnational associations help foster cosmopolitan norms; therefore, traditional theoretical debates between different schools of cosmopolitanism are not as relevant to addressing the question posed here. More to the point, competing theories rarely completely reject what their rival theories have to say. If obligations arise through institutions, for example, the hope is often that moral dispositions will emerge from repeated patterns of institutional behavior. Natural duties theories usually hope that institutions will emerge or be adapted to help individuals fulfill obligations to fellow humans. Public sphere effects too seem to require certain views about the disposition of individuals participating in the deliberation as well as some institutional forums for such discussion. Shared identity effects may draw on shared institutional relations, or generate shared public spheres or cultivate transnational responsibilities.

The criteria focus on evaluating transnational associations and as such represent a middle-level theory of cosmopolitanism not a complete guide for individuals seeking to lead a cosmopolitan life and abide by cosmopolitan responsibilities. As I mentioned in earlier chapters, I am not presenting a comprehensive theory of cosmopolitanism. Individuals are not morally required, by any cosmopolitan theory I present or by my own argument, to join transnational voluntary associations. Associations are only one source for coordinated transnational action and my criteria for evaluating them is intended to supplement theories that focus on governmental institutions as well as more individual, personal moral development. Once an association exists one can evaluate whether it develops a sense of common humanity or establishes just institutional ties or shared identity effects. It is true that combining these views in a theory of cosmopolitanism for associations means that tensions will remain within cosmopolitanism.

Rather than evading tensions, I choose to explore applications of my criteria using associations without straightforwardly cosmopolitan missions in order to push the boundaries of what constitutes partial or indirect expressions of cosmopolitanism. Cosmopolitan theory must grapple with how best to assess partial associations without losing its critical edge. In the words of Bruce Robbins, "situating cosmopolitanism means taking a risk. Until now, only the enemies of cosmopolitanism have been eager to situate it. Cosmopolitanism's advocates, on the other hand, have most often felt obliged to keep it unlocated in order to preserve its sharp critical edge, as well as its privileges."[103] One step in the direction of situating cosmopolitanism involves paying attention to actual associations rather than only ideal hypothetical examples but it also means ensuring cosmopolitan moral ideals remain in order to evaluate (not only to describe) the effects of associations. The cases discussed in part II have been ordered in terms of an increasing degree of tension between cosmopolitan and non-cosmopolitan components to see the potential of finding cosmopolitanism in unlikely places. They will not only demonstrate how one could apply the criteria but also continue to help clarify what partial or indirect expressions of cosmopolitanism might look like. One case may highlight certain effects more clearly than another but they are not meant to stand as sole examples of a particular cosmopolitan effect. They represent the complex ways associations could express different elements of cosmopolitanism. Acknowledging the creative potential of associations needs a strong normative framework but also one flexible enough to respect diversity. A middle-level theory of cosmopolitan criteria aims to realize both goals.

NOTES

1. Although I present the historical case of British abolition of the slave trade, the goal of abolishing slavery continued. After Parliament passed a law abolishing the slave trade in 1807, Thomas Clarkson played a role in advocating for Parliament to pass a bill for slave emancipation within Britain—which it did in 1833. The Anti-Slavery Society continues today in an association called Anti-Slavery International, which traces its history back to Clarkson on its website (www.antislavery.org).

2. Seymour Drescher, *Abolition: A History of Slavery and Antislavery* (New York: Cambridge University Press, 2009), 213.

3. Ibid., 214, 217. Not all abolitionist groups in Britain were affiliated with the Society. As I will discuss later, some took more radical positions. Drescher, *Abolition*, 221. Drescher also discusses the role of popular support and public opinion in "Whose Abolition? Popular Pressure and the Ending of the British Slave Trade," *Past and Present* 143 (1994): 138, 140.

4. Working to abolish the slave trade was a costly enterprise in terms of money and lives. Some argue that the cost of abolitionist campaigns was "more than five thousand lives as well as an average nearly 2 percent of national income annually for sixty years." Chaim D. Kaufmann and Robert A. Pape, "Explaining Costly International Moral Action: Britain's Sixty-year Campaign against the Atlantic Slave Trade," *International Organization* 53, no. 4 (1999): 631.

5. Drescher, "Whose Abolition?" 162.

6. Ibid., 160.

7. Kaufmann and Pape, "Explaining Costly International Moral Action," 640.

8. Ian Clark, *International Legitimacy and World Society* (Oxford: Oxford University Press, 2007), 49.

9. Ibid., 49. See also David Brion Davis, *Slavery and Human Progress* (New York: Oxford University Press, 1984), Chapter 5 "British Emancipation: A Deception Model, Part One."

10. Davis, *Slavery and Human Progress,* 117, and 138–143. Kaufmann and Pape, "Explaining Costly International Moral Action," 646.

11. See Kaufmann and Pape, "Explaining Costly International Moral Action," 1–5. Margaret E. Keck and Kathryn Sikkink also discuss international pressure applied in order to end the slave trade. *Activists beyond Borders: Advocacy Networks in International Politics* (Ithaca, NY: Cornell University Press, 1998), 41–51. Ian Clark discusses the abolition of the slave trade in terms of world society theory in *International Legitimacy,* Chapter 2 "Vienna and the Slave Trade, 1815."

12. For examples of this type of argument see Richard Falk, *On Humane Governance: Toward a New Global Politics* (University Park, PA: Pennsylvania State University, 1995), 205; as well as Paul Wapner, "Politics Beyond the State: Environmental Activism and World Civic Politics," *World Politics* 47, no. 3 (1995): 311–340. David Held is also optimistic about civil society in "The Transformation of Political Community: Rethinking Democracy in the Context of Globalization," in *Democracy's Edges,* ed. Ian Shapiro and Casiano Hacker-Cordon (Cambridge: Cambridge University Press, 1999), 84–111.

13. Falk, *On Humane Governance,* 181.

14. Examples include David A. Bell and Jean-Marc Coicaud, eds., *Ethics in Action: The Ethical Challenges of International Human Rights Nongovernmental Organizations* (New York: Cambridge University Press, 2007); or Alexander de Waal, *Famine Crimes: Politics & the Disaster of Relief Industry in Africa* (London: African Rights & the International African Institute, 1997); or John Eade and Darren O'Byrne, eds., *Global Ethics and Civil Society* (Burlington, VT: Ashgate, 2005).

15. Mark E. Warren, *Democracy and Association* (Princeton, NJ: Princeton University Press, 2001), 21.

16. Ibid., Chapter 4 "The Democratic Effects of Associations."

17. Jackie Smith, "Global Civil Society? Transnational Social Movement Organizations and Social Capital," *American Behavior Scientist* 42, no. 1 (1998): 93–107.

18. Drescher discusses one parallel group—the antisaccharite movement—that opposed the consumption of slave-grown sugar. *Abolition*, 221.

19. Ibid., 214.

20. Ibid. See also Davis, *Slavery and Human Progress*, 139.

21. Kaufmann and Pape, "Explaining Costly International Moral Action," 661.

22. Drescher, *Abolition*, 151.

23. Fredrick Douglas even paid a visit to Thomas Clarkson. Adam Hochschild, *Bury the Chains: Prophets and Rebels in the Fight to Free an Empire's Slaves* (Boston: Houghton Mifflin Company, 2005), 354.

24. Transnational ties might even become counterproductive in certain circumstances. Keck and Sikkink talk about moments of American resentment at the intervention from British abolitionists. *Activists Beyond Borders*, 42. Kaufmann and Pape talk about how French support for abolitionists was not always helpful during periods such as the French Revolution when the British feared any connection to revolutionary activity even if it supported abolition. "Explaining Costly Moral Action," 662.

25. Kaufmann and Pape, "Explaining Costly Moral Action," 647.

26. Hochschild, *Bury the Chains*, 338.

27. Drescher, "Whose Abolition?" 162. For a general discussion of foreign policy see 150–164.

28. Charles Beitz, *Political Theory and International Relations* (Princeton, NJ: Princeton University Press, 1979), 166.

29. Darrel Moellendorf, *Cosmopolitan Justice* (Cambridge, MA: Westview Press, 2002), 32.

30. Kaufmann and Pape, "Explaining Costly Moral Action," 659.

31. For examples see Robert McCorquodale, "An Inclusive International Legal System," *Leiden Journal of International Law* 17 (2004): 493–494.

32. Keck and Sikkink, *Activists beyond Borders*, Chapter 5 "Transnational Networks of Violence Against Women."

33. John Gerard Ruggie, "Reconstituting the Global Public Domain—Issues, Actors and Practices," *European Journal or International Relations* 10 (2004): 512.

34. Ibid.

35. David Held, *Democracy and the Global Order: From the Modern State to Cosmopolitan Governance* (Stanford, CA: Stanford University Press, 1995), 237.

36. Joshua Cohen and Charles Sabel, "Extra Rempublicam Nulla Justitia?" *Philosophy & Public Affairs* 34, no. 2 (2006): 147–175.

37. Ethel Brooks, "Transnational Campaigns against Child Labor: The Garment Industry in Bangladesh," in *Coalitions Across Borders: Transnational Protest and the Neoliberal Order,* ed. Joe Bandy and Jackie Smith (Lanham, MD: Rowman & Littlefield, 2005), 129.

38. Carol C. Gould, "Transnational Solidarities," *Journal of Social Philosophy* 38, no. 1 (Spring 2007): 148–164.

39. This kind of activity would satisfy Warren's discussion of development effects on the domestic level because he addresses the importance of gathering and sharing information. *Democracy and Association*, 71.

40. Hochschild, *Bury the Chains*, 366.

41. Granville Sharp quoted in Hochschild, *Bury the Chains*, 366. Thomas Clarkson also wrote in a similar vein "that it was only necessary for the inhabitants of this favoured island to know it, to feel a just indignations against" slavery. Quoted in Hochschild, *Bury the Chains*, 366.

42. David Brion Davis, "The Universal Attractions of Slavery," review of *Abolition: A History of Slavery and Antislavery*, by Seymour Drescher, *New York Review of Books*, 56, no. 20 (2009): 72.

43. Hochschild, *Bury the Chains*, 225.

44. Drescher, "Whose Abolition?" 153.

45. Thomas Clarkson's *History of the Rise, Progress and Accomplishment of the Abolition of the African Slave Trade by the British Parliament* published in 1808, quoted in Davis, *Slavery and Human Progress*, 117. Clarkson hoped that revitalizing religion could be achieved if people shifted their focus from economic self-interest to moral concerns.

46. Davis, *Slavery and Human Progress*, 140.

47. William Wilberforce quoted in Hochschild, *Bury the Chains*, 314.

48. Davis, *Slavery and Human Progress*, 172–173.

49. Kaufmann and Pape, "Explaining Costly International Moral Action," 664.

50. Hochschild, *Bury the Chains*, 136. For a similar point see Seymour Drescher, "History's Engines: British Mobilization in the Age of Revolution," *The William and Mary Quarterly* 66, no. 4 (2009): 740.

51. A campaign song quoted from the *Leed Mercury* 14, November 1806, in Drescher "Whose Abolition?" 146.

52. Keck and Sikkink argue this was common in the United States. *Activists Beyond Borders*, 52.

53. Martha Nussbaum, *Frontiers of Justice: Disability, Nationality, Species Membership* (Cambridge, MA: Belknap Press of Harvard University Press, 2006), 258, 410–412. Catherine Lu makes a similar point in "The One and Many Faces of Cosmopolitanism" *The Journal of Political Philosophy* 8, no. 2 (2000): 257.

54. Hochschild, *Bury the Chains*, 225.

55. Keck and Sikkink, *Activists Beyond Borders*, 166, 176–178, 192.

56. Seymour Drescher, *The Mighty Experiment: Free Labor versus Slavery in British Emancipation* (New York: Oxford University Press, 2004), 236.

57. Keck and Sikkink, *Activists Beyond Borders*, 141.

58. For more discussion of her capabilities approach, see Martha Nussbaum's *Frontiers of Justice*.

59. Keck and Sikkink, *Activists Beyond Borders*, 46.

60. Chen Jie, "Burgeoning Transnationalism of Taiwan's Social Movement NGOs," *Journal of Contemporary China* 10 (2001): 619.

61. Ibid., 621–623, 629. Note that the actual description of the Taiwanese NGOs in Jie's article is much more complex then the brief references here.

62. Warren raises this point in his analysis of domestic associations in *Democracy and Association*, 71.

63. Because of his focus on democracy, Warren places consideration of representation under institutional effects. Warren, *Democracy and Association*, 83, 84. My cosmopolitan theory lacks the focus on a democratic government to mirror institutionally. As a result I do not limit considerations of representation to institutional effects. Representation can also enable confidence-building and a sense that one's local issues are connected to (or represented in) discussions about solutions to international problems.

64. Warren talks of opportunities to learn political skills in his discussion of associations and democracy. *Democracy and Association*, 72. His focus is not on the global level where the challenges of agency are not necessarily only about mastering political agency.

65. Amy Gutmann, "Freedom of Associations: An Introductory Essay," in *Freedom of Association*, ed. Amy Gutmann (Princeton, NJ: Princeton University Press, 1998), 6.

66. Jeremy Waldron, "What is Cosmopolitan?" *The Journal of Political Philosophy* 8 (2000): 231.

67. Kwame Anthony Appiah, *Cosmopolitanism: Ethics in a World of Strangers* (Princeton, NJ: W.W. Norton & Company, 2006), 85.

68. Robert Putnam, "Bowling Alone: America's Declining Social Capital," *Journal of Democracy* 6 (1995): 65–78. See my discussion of this in chapter 3.

69. Gould, "Transnational Solidarities," 156.

70. Kwame Anthony Appiah, *The Ethics of Identity* (Princeton, NJ: Princeton University Press, 2005), 253

71. Ibid., 264.

72. Gould, "Transnational Solidarities," 150–154.

73. Ibid., 157. See also Betty Plewes and Rieky Stuart, "The Pornography of Poverty: A Cautionary Fundraising Tale," in *Ethics in Action,* ed. Daniel A. Bell and Jean-Marc Coicaud (New York: Cambridge University Press, 2007); and Valerie Sperling, Myra Marx Ferree, and Barbara Risman, "Constructing Global Feminism: Transnational Advocacy Networks and Russian Women's Activism," *Signs* 26, no. 4 (2001): 1115–1186. Both of these articles make arguments about the dangers of exacerbating a sense of victimization.

74. Gould, "Transnational Solidarities," 158.

75. Hochshild, *Bury the Chains,* 133.

76. Audie Klotz, "Transnational Activism and Global Transformations: The Anti-Apartheid and Abolitionist Experiences, "*European Journal of International Relations* 8, no. 1 (2002): 59.

77. Hochshild, *Bury the Chains,* 168.

78. Drescher, "Whose Abolition?" 165.

79. Drescher, *Abolition,* 139–140.

80. Thalia G. Kidder, "Networks in Transnational Labor Organizing," in *Restructuring World Politics: Transnational Social Movements, Networks, and Norms,* ed. Sanjeev Khagram, James V. Riker, and Kathryn Sikkink (Minneapolis: University of Minnesota Press, 2002). See also Mike Gatehouse and Miguel Angel Reyes, *Soft Drink/Hard Labor: Guatemalan Workers Take on Coca-Cola,* ed. James Painter (London: Latin American Bureau, 1987).

81. Kidder, "Networks," discusses this example as well.

82. Appiah, *The Ethics of Identity*, 252.

83. Ibid., 253, 257.

84. Hochschild, *Bury the* Chains, 129.

85. Drescher, *Abolition*, 214.

86. Ibid., 217.

87. Ibid., 267.

88. As discussed in chapter 2, the concept of the public sphere is drawn from the work of Jürgen Habermas in *Between Facts and Norms: Contributions to a Discourse Theory of Law and Democracy,* trans. William Rehg (Cambridge, MA: MIT Press, 1996), 360. Although associations cannot serve as the sole creators of political public spheres they contribute to certain forms of public discourse and can raise issues ignored by states. John Dryzek stresses the later point in *Deliberative Global Politics: Discourse and Democracy in a Divided World* (Malden, MA: Polity, 2006).

89. Seyla Benhabib, *The Rights of Others: Aliens, Residents, and Citizens* (New York: Cambridge University Press, 2004), 14.

90. Warren, *Democracy and Association,* 80. He too references Habermas's work for his discussion of communicative power.

91. Dryzek, *Deliberative Global Politics*, 113. Dryzek does not consider himself a cosmopolitan. However, the kind of informal political actors he describes are precisely the kind of actors I believe ought to be incorporated into a cosmopolitan framework. Therefore, I do not believe I am misconstruing his theory if it is seen as contributing to my adapted version of cosmopolitanism.

92. Ibid., 47, 57.

93. Ibid., 59–60.

94. José Casanova "Global Catholicism and the Politics of Civil Society," *Sociological Inquiry* 66, no. 3 (1996): 367.

95. Ibid., 368.

96. Seyla Benhabib, "Democratic Iterations: The Local, the National, and the Global," in *Another Cosmopolitanism,* ed. Robert Post (New York: Oxford University Press, 2006), 48, 58.

97. Anna Snyder, "Fostering Transnational Dialogue: Lessons Learned from Women Peace Activists," *Globalizations* 3, no. 1 (2006): 36.

98. Hochschild, *Bury the Chains,* 108. On women's groups in particular, see page 324.

99. For an example of a discussion about the World Social Forum see Günter Schönleitner, "World Social Forum: Making Another World Possible," in *Globalizing Civic Engagement: Civil Society and Transnational Action*, ed. John D. Clark (Sterling, VA: Earthscan, 2003).

100. Dryzek, *Deliberative Global Politics*, 154.

101. Warren, *Democracy and Association*, 81.

102. Drescher, "Whose Abolition?" 153.

103. Bruce Robbins, "Actually Existing Cosmopolitanism," in *Cosmopolitics: Thinking and Feeling Beyond the Nation*, ed. Pheng Cheah and Bruce Robbins (Minneapolis: University of Minnesota Press, 1998), 2.

Part II

Applying Cosmopolitan Criteria to Exclusive Associations

FIVE

Cosmopolitan Professional Ethics

Experts without Borders in Médecins Sans Frontières

Médecins Sans Frontières (MSF), Doctors Without Borders, invokes a responsibility to act in the face of human need. If you have the skills to provide emergency medical care, then you have a duty to do so even if the emergency is in another country. In the words of Dr. James Orbinski, former president of the International Council of MSF, "our action is to help people in situations of crisis. And ours is not a contended action. Bringing medical aid to people in distress is an attempt to defend them against what is aggressive to them as human beings."[1] An obligation for medical professionals to provide emergency medical care irrespective of national borders or political ideology supports cosmopolitanism's core principle of the moral equality of all humans. Unlike thin versions of moral equality that simply condemn the mistreatment of fellow humans, MSF fits the more robust version in which moral equality requires some form of equal treatment. It serves as an example of how an exclusive, elite, professional association can establish obligations on the international level by interpreting professional codes of conduct from a cosmopolitan perspective. However, the goal in studying MSF is not simply to reinforce its classification as part of the "narrow type of cosmopolitan space"[2] consisting of professional non-governmental organizations (NGOs). Applying cosmopolitan criteria demonstrates that even a humanitarian organization like MSF does not embody all elements of cosmopolitan ideals. Instead, I explore the effects of membership in MSF to determine which partial expressions of cosmopolitanism it advances and how it can help us understand what cosmopolitan effects of associations could look like.

Members of MSF, expatriates as well as national staff, work to administer humanitarian aid in more than seventy different countries in conflict zones, refugee camps, areas hit by natural disasters, and the slums of developed countries. In the course of providing medical aid they give witness to human rights violations that the world is ignoring. As a result of its work, MSF actually can serve as an example of two important types of transnational non-state associations: professional and humanitarian relief associations. The professional element of MSF is less commonly explored than its humanitarian relief mission, yet the exclusive professional side of this association holds lessons on potential sources for cosmopolitan ideals. As a relief organization it may at first seem obviously cosmopolitan with its goals of treating any human in need and witnessing to human rights violations. However, even here, MSF's cosmopolitan effects are partial. Despite its name, MSF only becomes a critic of respecting state borders if a state rejects aid and assistance. It is also the case that the broad understanding of cosmopolitanism I explored in chapter 1 includes not only a claim about responsibility but also a goal of fostering transnational community or cosmopolitanism as an identity and a way of life. MSF's role in advancing cosmopolitan identities is only incidental when it occurs at all. This association serves as evidence of my broader claim that one ought not only assess the purpose of an association in order to determine its potential to advance cosmopolitanism.

Analyzing MSF in terms of its effects rather than its goals quickly results in acknowledging tensions that may emerge between cosmopolitanism understood as a thesis of obligations and as a thesis of ethical identity. Since part of my larger argument is that cosmopolitan theory must embrace rather than resolve such tensions, MSF can be explored for lessons about negotiating tensions. Addressing challenges humanitarian relief associations face is not new but the challenges I draw out have implications for cosmopolitan theory not commonly recognized. Usually analysis of MSF focuses on how to reconcile the goal of the association (which could be understood as cosmopolitan since all humans are entitled to emergency medical care) with the resources to realize these goals (which are often quite limited) and the effects (which may result in the unanticipated outcomes). What this amounts to is the question: How can one realize ethical ideals in a non-ideal world? Another approach to assessing MSF explores the tensions inherent in the mission of the association between a universal concept of humanitarian aid and the particular expertise it uses to provide aid "essentially prioritiz[ing] Western knowledge."[3] This raises the question: What should the goals of MSF be? Using these two questions to assess MSF may seem similar to my purposes since they address tensions; however, there are limits to both approaches. In the second approach focusing on motives misses the potential unintended effects of the association's actions—positive or negative. The first approach addresses the fact that "humanitarian action is always defined by ethical dilemmas"[4] but assumes a normative framework without addressing why humanitarianism or human rights ought to be the appropriate standards for evaluating associations. As chapter 2 showed, cosmopolitan political theory can provide a robust normative framework that ensures effects not merely self-proclaimed purposes are evaluated. One might also ask whether an association primarily provides a forum for those already committed to its principles and ideals or whether it actually contributes to the spread of cosmopolitanism.

In order to help locate the spread of cosmopolitan norms and dispositions, my middle-level theory adapts cosmopolitan normative theories to better apply them to the effects of actual associations. This theoretical approach bridges the gap between comprehensive theories of cosmopolitanism that provide a robust moral framework and scholarship on the effects of associations. I consider not merely whether an association's effects are compatible with cosmopolitanism but whether the effects actually advance or promote elements of cosmopolitanism. Evaluating the effects can help reveal the potential of exclusive associations, such as MSF.

Applying the criteria I have developed in chapter 4, one can evaluate the institutional, developmental, shared identity, and public sphere effects of MSF. Analysis of MSF reveals that there are some expressions of cosmopolitanism in each category of effects, although the criteria highlight places in which MSF could better satisfy cosmopolitan obligations. Because MSF is quite self-conscious in its recognition of the tensions between its goals and effects this association might learn from an application of cosmopolitan theory to its effects. It also means that this case will address indirect unself-conscious cosmopolitanism less than the next two cases of the Olympics and the Anglican Communion. The idea of partial cosmopolitanism, however, is critical to painting a more nuanced picture of this association's cosmopolitan impact. In particular it helps to illustrate the potential tensions between developmental effects of cultivating a sense of impartial responsibility through adherence to professional ethics and shared identity effects of fostering a sense of transnational solidarity. The relevance of humanitarian associations to cosmopolitanism may not be a big surprise but the relevance of specific professional associations may be more surprising.

THE CASE OF MSF IN BRIEF

A group of French doctors formed Médecins Sans Frontières in 1971 after returning from volunteering on a French Red Cross mission in Biafra. Bernard Kouchner, one of the founders, was frustrated to find that the media overlooked political sources of the crisis in Biafra. At the same time he was not supposed to speak about what he had seen because the

Red Cross's neutrality position required that doctors "abstain from all communications and comments on the mission."[5] Silence was seen as the way to ensure access to patients since political authorities would feel less threatened by the presence of silent doctors and allow them to complete their work. MSF was founded in order to allow doctors serving in humanitarian crisis situations to speak out if violations of human rights were being ignored. This makes MSF a particularly interesting case for cosmopolitans because it was founded in order to challenge concepts of neutrality understood as respecting state sovereignty. The humanitarian as well as advocacy goals of MSF were emphasized in the 1999 Nobel Peace Prize Lecture James Orbinski delivered on behalf of MSF. He began by describing MSF's goals as "to help people in situations of crisis" and continued that crises do not occur "in a vacuum" so it requires speaking out "with a clear intent to assist, to provoke change, or to reveal injustice. Our action and our voice is an act of indignation, a refusal to accept an active or passive assault on the other."[6] In fact, if MSF feels its aid is being misused or hampered it may speak out even if this results in being expelled from the country where it is trying to provide aid.

Witnessing human rights violations is important, but MSF's primary mission is to administer medical aid "to populations in distress, to victims of natural or man-made disasters and to victims of armed conflicts."[7] Addressing emergencies is "more than simply generosity, simply charity."[8] It is an obligation, a duty. This obligation stems not from adherence to a philosophical tradition of cosmopolitanism but rather from a reinterpretation of the professional code of doctors. In the Hippocratic Oath a doctor promises: "I will remember that I remain a member of society, with special obligations to all my fellow human beings, those sound of mind and body as well as the infirm."[9] This is commonly understood to mean that doctors do not only have responsibilities to their patients. In an emergency a doctor has an obligation to assist the injured or sick in any way he or she can. This is why in situations of emergency one can call out, "is there a doctor in the room?" For MSF this obligation is not fulfilled through helping those in one's immediate location. If there is a greater emergency elsewhere doctors have an obligation to lend their expertise to the process of healing there.

Expertise is a critical criterion for membership in this organization. In fact, the first MSF charter made the exclusive professional nature of the association clear stating that membership in the association should consist "exclusively of doctors and members of the health sector."[10] Today membership in the association has expanded to the point that the name, particularly its English version—Doctors Without Borders—is a bit misleading. MSF volunteers include doctors and nurses but also logisticians, who organize resources for setting up and running a mission, as well as engineers, who set up clinics, latrines, and fresh water sources to create the conditions necessary for combating certain diseases. In addition to expatriate volunteers, MSF also hires local or national staff. In 2012 MSF had 2,592 international staff working in the field in over seventy different countries. An even larger number of around 29,228 (or 86 percent of MSF's staff in the field) were national staff hired or volunteering to work with MSF in their home countries or regions.[11] All of these individuals are vital to the process of providing medical care. Therefore, the professional code has broader implications.

I have chosen this case to exemplify the cosmopolitan potential of a transnational voluntary professional and humanitarian relief association; however, it should be noted that this means recognizing tensions between voluntarism and professionalism. As discussed in chapter 1, transnational voluntary associations are often referred to as voluntary in order to distinguish their relations from state or family ties, but the image of volunteers does not always help in understanding membership. The "myth of voluntarism," as Lester M. Salamon calls it, imagines associations based on informal ties among philanthropic individuals that give associations their "special character" based in the ability to "reach outlying communities, promote participation, innovate and operate at low cost."[12] At the same time, in order for the effects of associations to be long lasting it is often necessary to have a reliable set of participants, who have "technical capacity" and an awareness of "broader policy considerations."[13] Technical capacity is even more critical when dealing with medical emergencies. Debates over professionalization *vs.* voluntarism are very much alive in MSF, but this kind of professionalism is a bit different from the focus I take in exploring MSF as a professional association. Rather than a focus on the class of human rights professionals, I explore the impact of self-consciously embracing particular professional duties based on professions such as medicine. There are certainly limits to what professional associations can realize but this does not mean overlooking how they can, in certain cases, advance cosmopolitanism. If different associations contribute different elements of cosmopolitanism, as I argued in chapter 4, then what might a professional association like MSF advance? Is professional ethics one path to becoming more cosmopolitan?

Applying the criteria I have developed to MSF can teach cosmopolitans about the potential of associations to effect expressions of cosmopolitanism at the same time that they struggle with the challenges of navigating tensions involved in realizing cosmopolitanism.

DETERMINING COSMOPOLITAN EFFECTS

Institutional Effects

An association can be assessed in terms of its institutional effects by exploring the institutional structure of the association. Scholars studying associations on the domestic level often ask whether associations mirror or support democratic institutions. There is no comparable democratic structure on the global level; however, institutional cosmopolitan theorists such as Charles Beitz, Darrel Moellendorf, or Thomas Pogge argue that even without a world state international institutional relations can generate obligations by tying people together across borders in economic and political relationships that should be justifiable to all those participating in them. Adapting institutional cosmopolitan theory for application to associations, I derived criteria that sought to evaluate whether associations generate or help fulfill cosmopolitan obligations through institutional relations. This leads to two questions when assessing institutional effects. First of all, does the institutional structure of an association generate new cosmopolitan obligations through connections formed across the globe? Second of all, does the association institutionalize common standards or rules of a cosmopolitan nature that are meant to apply universally or at least transnationally in a way that reinforces cosmopolitan obligations? The second criterion can account for associations without much formal organization that may advocate for the establishment of international institutions (for example, the International Criminal Court) or the institutionalization of international laws (for example, bans against landmines). Using the two criteria I will assess MSF's institutional effects.

First, what is the nature of MSF's organizational structure, and does it generate respect for cosmopolitan obligations? MSF serves as an interesting example of what more cosmopolitan institutions could look like. However, at first glance MSF appears wedded to a state-based organization because it consists of different national branches. The five operational branches that organize and send out missions are located in Belgium, France, Holland, Spain, and Switzerland. There are also delegate offices in charge of recruiting, fundraising, and raising awareness located in Australia, Austria, Canada, Denmark, Germany, Greece, Hong Kong, Italy, Japan, Luxemburg, Norway, Sweden, the United Kingdom, and the United States. In December 2011, MSF Brazil, MSF East Africa, MSF Latin America, and MSF South Africa officially became associations within MSF's international organization. There is also a South Asia Regional association based in India. Although these are all connected under MSF International with its headquarters located in Geneva, the different national and regional associations have a great deal of autonomy from MSF International and from each other. "All are independent legal entities, and each elects its own board of directors and president. Most associations have an executive office that raises funds and recruits staff for MSF's operation."[14] In fact, sometimes "MSF's structure appears inefficient," when, in cases like Afghanistan, five MSF sections may be operating in the same location.[15] The level of branch autonomy is also anecdotally revealed in Dr. James Maskalyk's recounting of his experiences with MSF in Sudan. He was a Canadian working on a MSF Swiss mission. Upon arriving at the airport in Sudan he finds that the only MSF contact there is waiting for a member of the MSF Spain mission. Dr. Maskalyk has to wait for his MSF Swiss contact.[16]

Despite the national autonomy, one cannot see branches as only organized in terms of geographic location or nationality. Branches may emphasize particular types of expertise or types of missions. MSF Holland, for example, focuses on conflict zones, while MSF Belgium specializes in setting up AIDS programs.[17] National attachments are further deemphasized because "MSFers are no more bound to serve their own nation's section than a member of the Blue Jays baseball team must be 'from' Toronto."[18] Dr. Maskalyk's experience demonstrates this, as he is a Canadian working on a MSF Swiss mission. Individuals may choose to join the branch doing the most interesting work or organizing missions where their expertise best contributes. The same person can even participate in different branches at different times. There are MSF volunteers who have worked for multiple operational branches.

Nevertheless, nationalist oriented disagreements do occur. Historically, MSF France struggled with the inclusion of other national branches because it saw itself as central to the association because of its historical prominence as the founding section.[19] Another reason is that some countries continue to be more highly represented on missions. Although MSF does not emphasize the nationality of its expatriate staff, some general patterns in membership do emerge. France usually sends the largest number of volunteers but countries with smaller populations such as Belgium send very large numbers proportionate to their population.[20] Citizens of the United States usually represent about 10 percent of the total international staff.[21] Not all members feel patriotic loyalties to a branch. In the words of one logistician from the United States, "I didn't grow up in France, or Belgium, or Holland. . . . For me, it was just a dismay seeing all this wasted energy; The French are this, the Dutch are that, the Belgians are this. Who gives a shit?"[22] Fluidity of membership can help to maintain at least some transnational perspective.

Emphasizing the flexibility and autonomy among branches (as opposed to a more rigid hierarchical structure) is central to MSF's self-conception as an international movement. In his Nobel Prize Lecture, Orbinski declared that MSF is "not a formal institution, and with any luck at all, it never will be."[23] However, there is an international structure to this association. MSF International, with the help of the International Generally Assembly (IGA), works to "safeguard MSF's medical humanitarian mission, and provides strategic orientation to all MSF entities."[24] The IGA meets annually and includes representatives from all the associations. This is the body that elects the International President, and the International Board fulfills the work delegated to it by the IGA. The IGA usually deals with issues concerning MSF as a whole such as financial appropriations or other general strategic plans rather than issuing specific decrees.[25]

At times MSF International has taken more drastic action to sanction branches that it did not deem in compliance with the overall mission. In June 1999 MSF Greece was expelled in order to "protect the independent humanitarian character of the organization."[26] The Greek section, responding to popular pressure in Greece, had agreed to work in Kosovo and Belgrade conflict zones only under Serbian government approval. This opposed MSF's position, which was demanding Serbian leadership admit a non-partisan international team that could assess human rights violations on all sides of the conflict. The expulsion of MSF Greece is one example of how membership in the MSF's international structure can generate cosmopolitan obligations by placing individuals in new institutional relations. Greek doctors or Greek relief organizations could make whatever agreement they chose with Serbian officials. Members of the Greek section of MSF, however, were supposed to be constrained by principles of impartiality. MSF Greece's actions "had broken the trust vital to membership in any organization [by refusing] to acknowledge the position of the rest of the MSF movement."[27] MSF demands that members from different states respect obligations they have as members of the broader transnational organization. Christophe Fournier, a former International President, commented that the Greek case demonstrates how "internationalism in the movement may work for impartiality but it doesn't provide a lot of independence for each section's culture and society."[28]

As MSF becomes more diverse there are actually increasing calls for MSF to embrace internationalism more fully. MSF South Africa has self-consciously sought to be regional rather than national as evidenced by its multinational board, for example. It sees one of its contributions to MSF as new ideas for how to make institutional structures more international.[29] The internationalism of MSF is only acceptable if it is truly international rather than functioning like a Western European association. In the words of two leaders from MSF South Africa, "being of Western origin is not the problem, but functioning in the current world as a Western organization is."[30] Renée Fox, who completed a lengthy sociological study of MSF, points out that the inclusion of associations from non-European regions does not always entail a status that grants the association actual or significant decision-making power within the international organization.[31] Attempts to be more inclusive are also hampered by the lack of clear criteria for new associations to be fully admitted, something MSF South Africa confronted.[32]

The relations between branches of the associations are not the only parts of the international structure that can be evaluated in cosmopolitan terms. MSF also enters into relationships with those it encounters and works with on missions. Former president of MSF France, Rony Brauman, makes it clear that "the use and abuse of the presence of NGOs and their operations can sometimes cause a lot of damage. NGOs then acquire a responsibility, a fact which they all too often fail to recognize."[33] Institutional cosmopolitans would agree that institutional relations with "deep and pervasive effects on the welfare of people to whom they apply regardless of consent"[34] ought to be based on relations individuals could consent to because double standards and exploitation undermine moral equality.

The transnational institutional relations formed with local workers hired or affiliated with MSF connect those workers to other members of MSF. Do these relations result in new cosmopolitan obligations? Yes, although MSF does not always fully live up to those obligations. Nicholas de Torrente of MSF USA, for example, remarked that the pattern has been to extricate expatriates if security conditions on a mission become too dangerous, but national personnel have to remain behind.[35] In individual cases MSF workers have sometimes been able to sneak local workers into a neighboring country. When Wouter Van Empelen and his MSF team fled Rwanda, he managed to get patients and national staff over the border into Burundi by "throwing handfuls of money at the Interahamwe killing squads while leading his convoy of vehicles at full speed to the border. Once there, a priest traveling with them threatened the border guards with eternal damnation if they didn't let the convoy pass. The convoy—and the border guards—were saved."[36] This is not always the case. Members of a MSF France team fleeing into Tanzania "were forced to abandon their national staff at the border. At least seventeen were massacred. The fate of the remaining twenty-three was likely the same; they were never heard from again."[37] Informally it seems MSF expatriates seek to protect local workers. The need to adjust policies and practices in order to better acknowledge obligations to the local personnel it hires has become a large topic for discussion and action in MSF. Sudanese workers in Darfur were evacuated to other parts of Sudan when MSF determined conditions in Darfur had become too dangerous for its staff to remain. However, they could not be evacuated out of Sudan.[38] Borders cannot be so easily overcome for these national staff. The principle of *sans frontières* at the core of the association's understanding of responsibility requires calling attention to MSF's cosmopolitan obligations toward local MSF workers.

A second way to assess MSF's institutional effects is to consider whether this association institutionalizes practices and norms that help realize cosmopolitanism. As a professional organization, MSF lends its expertise to institutionalizing new standards and norms within the medical and pharmaceutical fields. MSF challenges unjust medical research priorities. The way patents work, for example, creates incentives for making small adjustments to existing drugs in order to continue profiting off the patent, rather than spending money on the research and design of new drugs particularly for those neglected diseases (like African sleeping sickness) affecting mainly people in poor countries. Patents can increase prices on drugs. In South Africa in 2001, MSF publicly flaunted international patent laws and assisted local groups in illegally importing generic antiretroviral drugs for AIDS patients. [39] In other cases research is needed to develop treatments that are efficient to administer in conditions where individuals cannot stay around for follow-up inoculations or to fulfill drug regimens that must be taken over long periods of time. MSF advocates for changes in medical standards that advance greater respect for those made vulnerable through international institutions of patent law beyond their control or those ignored by medical research. These effects certainly are compatible with a cosmopolitan obligation to reform unjust international institutions. The actual institutionalization is expected to occur through more formal organizations like the World Health Organization (WHO) or in international law rather than through MSF, which is limited to the mission of providing medical relief aid. Nevertheless, through its work "MSF and organizations like it are leading the global health policy process that the WHO is essentially following." [40]

In summary, MSF's institutional structure does generate cosmopolitan obligations for members, who become responsible for abiding by the ideals of the international organization above national loyalties. Members could have joined for many different reasons but now have similar obligations. The mixed international membership of branches also prevents a merely national based organization. Where MSF struggles to live up to cosmopolitan obligations is in the institutional ties forged with local workers—although MSF is increasingly cognizant of the need to address the challenge in some way. MSF is also shaping global health policy as it works to overcome unjust institutional structures that hamper its work of providing emergency medical care.

Developmental Effects

The potential cosmopolitan effects of this association can also be assessed in terms of the developmental impact the association has on shaping how members see the world and what skills they develop. In studies of domestic associations, the focus is on studying whether individuals learn skills relevant to being good democratic citizens. What would it mean for developmental effects to be cosmopolitan? The category I labeled natural duties cosmopolitanism emphasized the importance of cultivating respect for moral obligations by educating people about commonalities across borders. Since "compassion contains thought," Martha Nussbaum argues, it is possible to train it.[41] Applying these ideas to the effects of associations means creating criteria for assessing educative effects. First of all, one can ask whether associations help expand the imagination of members to see commonalities across borders. Second, one can ask whether associations create opportunities for individuals to be global actors who see the challenges they confront as transnational problems. With these two questions in mind let me now explore the developmental effects of MSF.

In associations where members are expected to travel to dangerous places with few if any comforts, one might assume that those who join already have cosmopolitan views and that membership in the association is an expression of this. If that were the case it would make the question of developmental effects on members less central to how the association spreads cosmopolitan norms. However, expatriate members seem to join MSF out of a wide variety of reasons including a desire to help others, unhappiness in previous occupations, religious inspiration, unemployment, and even adventure.[42] Since my criteria address effects not motivation they allow one to evaluate the impact of membership in MSF even on individuals who join for non-cosmopolitan reasons. Are such members transformed through the educative effects of the association?

First, does MSF expand the imaginations of its members in order to recognize commonalities or build empathy across national borders? Let me begin with the implications of the concept *sans frontières,* which sounds decidedly cosmopolitan. The translation of the French *"frontières"* to the English "borders" loses some of the breadth in the original meaning of *sans frontières.* "Without borders" is meant to connote a range of stances including not only a relation to state sovereignty, but also a position of neutrality or impartiality in the face of political, cultural, and social differences. MSF does challenge state sovereignty, if it hampers dealing effectively with what are now commonly transnational public health concerns. It has even lead clandestine missions on occasion rather than wait for state authorization.[43] When it comes to providing emergency medical care doctors have an obligation to consider all individuals as worthy of treatment, as moral equals "irrespective of race, religion, creed or political convictions."[44] This position continues the International Committee of the Red Cross's (ICRC) tradition of understanding that "blood always and everywhere has the same color."[45] The core ideals of MSF too stress biological commonalities across many other differences.

In order to evaluate the effects of the association one must consider how these ideals of common humanity are conveyed to and cultivated in members. How are members educated into these principles and is the training transformative? MSF aims to train expatriates to perceive challenges they face from a more cosmopolitan perspective drawing on biological similarities and medical responsibilities rather than focusing on differences. Recounting what he learned in his time spent with MSF Orbinski described developing "a way of seeing that requires humility, so that one can recognize the sameness of self in the other. It is about the mutuality that can exist between us, if we so choose."[46] MSF expatriates certainly come to recognize certain commonalities and the vulnerability of those they help in field experiences. Recently MSF workers in the field have begun blogging about their experiences to bring the field experiences home to donors, friends, and family as well as to help make sense of their experiences. Writing a blog in order to stay connected to friends and family, one doctor working in Sudan ended up concluding that "mostly, though, it was where I told a story about humans: the people from Abyei who suffered its hardships because it was their home, and those of us who left ours with tools to make it easier for them to endure."[47] Canadian nurse Leanne Olson points out that in the work MSF does: "you end up seeing people at their most vulnerable."[48] Learning to recognize vulnerabilities is one of the ways natural duty cosmopolitan Martha Nussbaum thinks it is possible to cultivate empathy across vast differences. The quote from nurse Olsen certainly indicates recognition of the vulnerability of others. MSF volunteers are placed in circumstances to recognize vulnerabilities but not necessarily common vulnerabilities. Does work with this association build compassion or pity? Exploring whether MSF workers also experience a new recognition of their own vulnerability is needed to fully explicate this developmental effect.

Commonalities can also be tested in the face of cultural differences. Before sending them on missions, MSF tries to train expatriates in the association's philosophy as well as some basic skills needed for working with patients and other expatriates from different cultures. Nurse Kathleen Bochsler recalled the value of training people "to solve problems with people who have totally different ideas."[49] Field missions place MSF expatriates into situations where they confront different cultures and perspectives. Richard Bedell, advisor on medical ethics for MSF Holland, recalls a project in Afghanistan where a man was refusing to let male doctors treat his wife. Bedell had to remind himself that a "man does not want to see his wife die, even in Afghanistan. He simply doesn't see the choice. That's what we can't forget. We can't forget to respect people, even if we don't understand."[50] Training MSF expatriates to adopt cosmopolitan attitudes is critical but difficult. There are limits to MSF's developmental educative effect because its goal of emergency medical relief demands quick action cutting down on the ability to provide lengthy training or long-term field mission placement. Rather than training its staff in how to handle the specific cultural differences of a mission, MSF leaders rely "heavily on what they assume to be the idealism of most of their volunteers, their youthful adventuresomeness, courage and resiliency . . . and on the power of those qualities to help the volunteers cope with the unknown."[51] This is not enough, Bedell argues. While "there is some general exposure to the phenomenon of cultural difference during the preparatory course" before the first mission, he believes, "even with our best efforts, one would find situations that one didn't expect. So what you need to do is equip people with a certain attitude for learning, a certain readiness to observe, listen and learn."[52] In the end it seems that MSF trains individuals in the importance and need for working with others but needs to better cultivate particular attitudes or dispositions that shape how individuals react to unexpected challenges in a respectful manner. Training people in how to respond to emergencies may foster cosmopolitan dispositions. MSF helps to demonstrate how cultivating a cosmopolitan disposition of compassion and empathy may require not just learning about the other but training the imagination to react compassionately in unknown or unexpected circumstances.

Being empowered on a transnational level is the second possible developmental effect. It can account for individuals with different motivations—those who already recognize common humanity but come to be empowered global actors as well as those who only develop cosmopolitan dispositions through empowered global action. When it comes to assessing MSF in this way the fact that it is a professional association once again becomes significant. MSF reinterprets the Hippocratic Oath so that doctors have global duties and demonstrates through its missions that such global action is possible. One doctor described a sense of achievement that can occur through working on a MSF mission. Unlike in a big hospital where you do not always see the fruits of your labor, for MSF expatriates there can be real gratification from the job.[53]

Despite opportunities for doctors to become global actors, experiences of empowerment are coupled with experiences of deep frustration and powerlessness when workers are unable to make a significant difference given the enormity of many problems MSF faces. In the words of one expatriate: "I felt beaten by the waves of suffering, of killing, of screams, of silent stares, of terror, and waves of not just political indifference but malfeasance."[54] The association has to ensure that new members are included on field missions in order help combat cynicism and keep the association strong. Missions can take a huge toll on volunteers, leading one MSF volunteer to exclaim about MSF: "they could give a shit about me, man—they squeeze me like a lemon . . . then come begging me to work. . . . They don't actually try and work on people, and try to develop them."[55] Some of those who criticize MSF also recognize that MSF is trying to respond to overwhelming need. One nurse commented: "I think a lot of people go on their next mission too quickly, without having had a chance to decompress at home. . . ."[56] Once one recognizes the duty to act and has the ability to act it can be hard to balance a feeling of duty to others with meeting one's own needs.

Increasingly MSF and other humanitarian organizations are recognizing the psychological toll on their workers. In a term that ought to serve as a serious reminder of the challenges of moral cosmopolitan obligations, psychology research indicates that relief workers dealing with traumatic experiences in conflict zones can experience "compassion fatigue."[57] One possible criticism of cosmopolitanism has to do with the potentially overwhelming nature of vast international obligations coupled with a lack of capacity to make a significant difference. This can lead to moral apathy rather than consistent, compassionate moral action. However, inaction is not necessarily an inevitable outcome. In the words of one volunteer, Heidi Postlewait: "I never went into this [humanitarian relief work] with these grand ideas of changing the world. . . . I think I was more patient and realistic."[58] Because of this it was difficult for her to hear others talk as though "in the one- or two-year mandate of a mission, that everything could come about and be peaceful and democratic. I just thought that was foolish." As a result of her less idealistic perspective "I wasn't let down as much as them at the end of the missions." The idealist, who enters humanitarian work with the goal of changing the world, can end up disillusioned and despising the whole endeavor, while the individual who goes in not expecting to live up to all the ideals of humanitarian work is able to navigate the world of moral dilemmas and ethical compromises. An idealistic motivation for helping in conflict zones may not necessarily always lead to a sense of obligation or a sense of empowerment and global agency. Despite some of these important cautions, it also seems to be the case that those who experience compassion satisfaction while working in conflict zones have developed coping techniques.[59] Training and mentoring can help individuals to learn these techniques. Such skills may end up being critical to realizing cosmopolitan developmental effects.

The complex combination of deeply depressing as well as incredibly uplifting moments that expatriates describe are not necessarily the same experiences of national workers. Their experiences can be just as complex and in many cases even more so because they are often among those traumatized by the conflict or health crisis.[60] One danger is that instead of empowerment MSF's assistance constructs "a space of victimhood"[61] in which individuals feel like passive recipients of foreign benevolence. In fact, the local staff MSF hires sometimes consists of medical professionals, who are far from passive victims. Other times individuals are trained in medical or other skills needed to serve their community. In the Community Care Initiative in Sierra Leone, for example, MSF trained individuals in the basics of diagnostics and treatment of malaria so that they could assist in rural villages far from MSF centers. "I wanted to be a community volunteer for the sake of my own people," one local worker stated.[62] In Khayelitsha, South Africa, MSF trained workers to treat infections and administer treatments in the AIDS program. One such worker "laughingly described herself as 'a half-doctor.'"[63] Other programs bring individuals with HIV together and train them to educate and support others with HIV/AIDS.[64] This may be empowerment on local not global levels, but MSF has such effects all over the world. Morris of MSF Holland, administrator of the East African headquarters in Nairobi, argued, "aid agencies play a real role in developing a local sense of civic and social responsibility."[65] These local actions can have broader implications through transnational associations. Those who worked hard to form MSF South Africa showed the ability of individuals to connect their local health concerns to global organizations as they sought to form their own independent association in MSF International.

There are, of course, limits to MSF's ability to empower. This association aims to empower within a particular field—medicine—and this form of empowerment will not be available to all. Rather than seeing this as a weakness one can recognize how a profession interpreted in more cosmopolitan terms may result in advancing a sense of dignity through the cultivation of skills practiced in a respected field.

As a whole, developmental effects from MSF are varied. Expatriate volunteers are trained to focus on basic biological commonalities among all individuals despite cultural differences. They also have a chance to act in communities beyond their home country borders. In addition to cultivating a sense of obligation some very general sense of global perspective toward local problems arises in communities where MSF works due to the presence of MSF expatriates who are giving the problem transnational attention. When it comes to local MSF workers there seems to be some evidence that practical training can have empowering effects at local levels. Newly forming MSF associations like MSF South Africa show the potential for international implications of local empowerment as well. At the same time, this association points out the potential challenges of widening imaginations without training and mentoring individuals in how to cope with the overwhelming nature of transnational obligations.[66] MSF also demonstrates the importance of assessing effects rather than focusing primarily on motivation. It turns out that idealistic cosmopolitan motivations do not necessarily ensure a sense of global agency or a strong sense of obligation. Considering the developmental effects of MSF shows the challenges of realizing cosmopolitan goals like providing impartial medical relief aid.

Shared Identity Effects

The category of shared identity effects entails exploring the ways in which an association cultivates a sense of fellow feeling or solidarity. Identities and solidarities can be assessed in terms of cosmopolitanism if one believes cosmopolitanism should entail not merely a search for commonality but respectful engagement with particular individuals from different cultures and ways of life.[67] Understanding cosmopolitanism as a way of life does not mean ignoring moral obligations because a normative definition of solidarity entails not only fellow feeling but also respectful relations toward other members of the group. In assessing an association's shared identity effects one needs to ask whether an association cultivates a sense of transnational community as well as whether an association cultivates a particularly cosmopolitan way of relating to partial, exclusive transnational identities and communities. For example, do the transnational identities value curiosity and openness to others and are relations among members reciprocal rather than paternalistic? In asking such questions, the category of shared identity effects shifts attention more directly to evaluating ties formed between expatriates and the communities where they work. Does MSF form a sense of solidarity or transnational community? What are the identities MSF helps form and how might one evaluate them?

MSF does aim to cultivate a more transnational sense of community. Not all humanitarian organizations use expatriate volunteers, whereas "we [MSF] wanted to promote the relationship between societies."[68] Furthermore, as I have already mentioned, this relationship is not meant to be one of paternalistic benevolence but rather one of duty and respect—giving individuals what is owed to them as fellow humans and moral equals. By labeling certain conditions as inhumane MSF is recognizing that people are worthy of being treated better.[69] There are connections between expatriates and the communities in which they work but the effects seem better understood in developmental terms than as crafting shared identities or global communities. Duty and obligation (developmental effects) do not always translate into a sense of shared identity or community. The comments of MSF expatriates reveal some personal bonds with people in the cities, villages, and camps where they work. "It is very easy to fall in love with these people," remarks one MSF volunteer working in the Sudan.[70] In the words of another: "Do you feel any solidarity with an African who is in shit up to his eyeballs, or not? It's a very simple question, and I answer yes, one hundred percent."[71] The impetus for forming an AIDS treatment program in South Africa arose in part through MSF expatriates watching friends and co-workers in the field dying of AIDS.[72] Another story that relates evidence of some sense of affective ties comes from a MSF field blog in which an expatriate describes getting lost but at "every dead end I encountered, I was greeted with a family who would say 'Fautall' (Sit and be welcome). The community I had originally thought of [as] having nothing was hosting me as a guest—offering me tea, beans and bread. . . . Perhaps stripping away the materialism of life gives people a sense of belonging and 'self.'"[73]

At the same time, activities of this association work against cultivating a truly broad sense of world community. The common experience of working in traumatic or difficult situations may build the developmental effect of empathy but also creates distance: "there's absolutely nothing that links these people to your way of life."[74] Fiona Terry, the research director at Foundation Médecins Sans Frontières, MSF's think tank, questions whether solidarity is the appropriate term for relations with local communities. She delineates the many ways distance is created between the experiences of expatriates and local communities. "We don't live by their side, we go back to our comfortable houses at night, we drive in our nice four-wheel drives, we have all the modern conveniences of email, we can talk with our friends and family. Can we really say we're in solidarity with them? It sounds nice, it makes us feel better, but it might be naïve to think that victims in the field feel this."[75] The association does send expatriates into local communities but does not aim to create common experiences, which could generate a sense of common identity. Distances between expatriates and the community are not obviously overcome simply by being present in a community. After having lived in Abyei for five or six weeks, James Maskalyk found that he "couldn't tell you one particular thing about the place, one custom, one habit of its people" and while some of this was due to his self-described tendency "to retreat when I need respite," it was also due to the very large difference between life in Canada and in Abyei, where "I see the poorest, the ones with no mosquito nets, or no access to clean water. Not only does our language seem irreconcilable, so do our worlds."[76]

Merely stopping at the conclusion that MSF does not cultivate much of a sense of world solidarity or global identity would miss the question of whether partial identities are cosmopolitan in nature. Exclusive transnational identities can be more or less cosmopolitan depending on whether the ties bridging borders are based on respect and reciprocity. James Maskalyk and Fiona Terry, who drew our attention to big differences in the quotes above, do not address the potential cosmopolitan nature of an identity as member of MSF. Since I am making an argument about partial cosmopolitanism, it is worth considering if there are cosmopolitan identity effects among members of MSF. Members can vote or serve on the international board of the association, unlike many charities where the board is made up of those who contribute money. The goal is to generate a sense of personal investment in the operation of the association.[77] Even if they do not join the administrative ranks of the association, they work together in the field. They gather together at conferences. Then they often return to the field for other missions where they meet again.

Expatriates also often indicate a shared experience of being transformed in a way that makes it difficult for them to fit in back home. This feeling of placelessness they describe may seem to fit with cosmopolitanism's ideal of rising above national allegiances. However, viewed from the perspective of shared identity criteria, the effect of placelessness is problematic as it destroys a sense of community.[78] Expatriates do not gain a new home in part because MSF has a policy of rotating workers to different geographic regions and missions often in order to prevent burnout. As a result of this rotation "just when a home is becoming comfortable and familiar, it is time to leave," leading to sense of disorientation.[79] However, these shared experiences of placelessness can connect MSF workers with each other even as it distances them from others. In the words of one MSF doctor who was traveling outside of his mission site: "it is a strange but certain phenomenon that when you identify a stranger as someone who works for MSF, you welcome them into your fold of friends, perhaps family might be more apt."[80]

When it comes to asking if the relationships formed are reciprocal and respectful, there are once again different ways to view the association. MSF is sometimes accused of seeing those it aids as "'beneficiaries'— passive recipients of humanitarian aid—and not as active agents capable of changing the conditions that lead to their vulnerability or at least participating in the process."[81] This is certainly a danger humanitarian relief organizations face. Among MSF workers the association aims to cultivate relationships of equality not often found in the medical profession. Doctors, nurses, logisticians, and administrators all operate on a first name basis without titles in order to underscore the fact that doctors cannot perform their work without the help of many others. Medical aid to fight cholera is ineffective without engineers, for example, to construct latrines and safe water taps. It is a communal endeavor where each different expertise plays its central role. This constructs relationships of respect for the contribution of different members.

International relationships of respect and reciprocity among members of MSF are also improving with the creation of new MSF associations from Africa, South Asia, and Latin America. This begins to transform the MSF identity from a Western European one to a more international one.[82] It is worth noting that medical workers in South Africa, particularly national workers, could have formed their own organization rather than join MSF. Sharon Ekambaram, founding director-general of MSF South Africa, objected to its overly Western identity, yet felt it was nevertheless "worth being a part of a battle to change it [MSF]."[83] Her sense of being part of the change in MSF fits with at least some sense of reciprocity as different members learn from each other.

It seems clear that MSF has some thin shared identity effects. MSF expatriate aid workers may form a kind of exclusive fellow feeling around a shared experience of placelessness and through working together on missions or in the institutions of the association. Also, a sense of reciprocal transnational relations is forming among members in the original branches and those in newer associations outside of Europe. It is questionable how strong a sense of solidarity or transnational community is formed with those MSF aims to aid—its patients. Individual personal ties are certainly formed in the communities where expatriates work, something cosmopolitans should not overlook, but MSF rotates expatriates regularly making it hard to form any lasting sense of community or solidarity.

Public Sphere Effects

MSF's primary mission of providing medical aid at times requires giving witness to overlooked human rights violations that hamper its work. Particularly because MSF takes a role in speaking out, it can be analyzed in terms of its public sphere effects. What is a public sphere? As I explained in previous chapters a public sphere is a "social phenomenon" that can "best be described as a network for communicating information and points of view . . . in such a way that they coalesce into bundles of topically specified *public* opinions."[84] Deliberative democratic cosmopolitan theorists take public spheres global arguing that if one is really to respect others as potential rational co-deliberators one "cannot limit the scope of the *moral conversation* only to those who reside within nationally recognized boundaries."[85] It is possible to communicate between strangers in complex relationships if one uses public language rather than the language of intimate relations among those who know each other well. Cross-border public conversation, John Dryzek argues, is what transnational NGOs do well.[86] They do not have to adhere to national interests, and so they can initiate discussion on issues states ignore. From these theories I derived two criteria. First, one can ask whether associations generate discussion around issues ignored in other international forums, making existing public spheres more inclusive. Second one can ask whether associations foster a culture of deliberation and discussion that creates public spheres by establishing spaces for public dialogue.

Satisfying the first criterion would fit with MSF's mission. It aims to break the silence in small ways through "the whispered single syllables acknowledging the doctor has found the source of the pain" as well as through international advocacy campaigns.[87] MSF uses its well-respected, Nobel Prize–winning, transnational organization to grab media attention for ignored issues of injustice. The professional aspect of the association helps MSF to serve as a respected witness because of the prestige of the medical profession.[88] For example, MSF spoke out against global double standards of healthy nutrition. Food aid that does not include milk products is missing nutrients essential for the healthy development of children under the age of two years. In most cases donors would not deny their own children milk, de Torrente pointed out.[89] The touring exhibit "A Refugee Camp in the Heart of the City," in which a mock refugee camp is set up in a city park, is another example of an attempt to raise awareness of the conditions MSF witnesses refugees having to endure.[90]

MSF does not only raise policy issues, it shapes public spheres by transforming language. One example of this re-purposing of language is MSF's use of the concept of neutrality. It is different from how states invoke the term. When applied to states, neutrality means not getting involved. The "impartiality of universal medical ethics," as MSF understands it, entails speaking out not simply remaining silent.[91] In arguing for this interpretation MSF is also directly challenging the claims of other humanitarian organizations, which may believe remaining impartial means remaining silent. One controversial example of the latter is the International Committee of the Red Cross. In the past, the "Red Cross has not made public the details of its activities, so that it will be acceptable to states in future conflicts."[92] MSF's actions have actually led to reforms in an understanding of the obligations of humanitarian actors like the ICRC have to speak out in order to condemn violations of human rights.[93] MSF does not maintain complete control over language or even spaces of deliberation, both of which can be exploited. Recently, MSF condemned attempts by the United States to legitimize its military actions through incorporating NGOs and humanitarian aid workers into its military strategy in Iraq and Afghanistan.[94] Challenging the United States' appropriation of humanitarian language, MSF ensured that this strategy was not without some public debate.

Through its relief work MSF contributes to creating spaces for discussions about humanitarianism leading to considerations of the second public sphere effect. Does MSF create spaces for discussion? There is some internal culture of dialogue that exists in meetings and to a limited extent in the field. Commonly discussions in the field tend to be about practical concerns given the urgent circumstances. Situations in conflict zones, in particular, require strict adherence to rules for the safety of those involved, limiting the scope for deliberation. On a mission in Burundi, a MSF doctor picked up a weapon to help a village defend itself against approaching enemy troops, violating MSF's mandate not to take sides or bear weapons. Patrick, MSF's manager in Burundi, removed the doctor from the mission. The doctor protested, "this is not an army; this is not a hierarchy. Let's negotiate!" Patrick responded "Surprise! . . . This is a hierarchy and I'm in charge. You're out on the next plane."[95] Some principles are beyond discussion. At the same time, MSF is working to incorporate blogging in field missions creating some space for discussion between those in the field and people in other parts of the world who read and comment on the blogs. MSF is still figuring out what ethics is required for blogging about fieldwork given that doctors are supposed to respect patient privacy.[96]

Outside the field, internal debates often take the form of public meetings or articles and collected editions, some of which I have used as sources. Furthermore, MSF seeks to cultivate a practice of participatory democracy when it comes to discussing the direction it should take on a particular crisis or how to best live up to the association's principles. [97] These debates deal with questions such as: Where ought MSF seek funding? What are its responsibilities to local staff when security conditions deteriorate? "How can we judge whether a compromise [with the association's principles] is acceptable?" [98] In her study of MSF, Fox often comments on the remarkable willingness of MSF to be self-critical and to encourage debate. [99] Nevertheless, at the end of the day decisions must be made and some members of MSF believe that there is an unnecessary "embarrassment about voting" since consensus is the goal. [100] While reaching consensus may seem like something cosmopolitans would approve of, the desire for ideological coherence can place stress on diversity. The more viewpoints outside of Europe are included, the more new ideas and perspectives might come to the table. This need not preclude consensus but may at times require voting if association principles are interpreted in different ways. At the moment the international board consists mostly of Western Europeans and new associations are not always given the same decision-making powers within the organization's structures. The cosmopolitan potential of international deliberation could certainly grow but that depends on how MSF incorporates new branches.

Influencing the public is critical to achieving its goal of easing suffering in medical emergencies. MSF aims to be "both a humanitarian actor and an agent of change." [101] While MSF the association does not represent or seek to create many new international forums for deliberation, it does have public sphere effects by raising awareness, shaping and defending the language of humanitarianism, as well as fostering some spaces for cultivating the skills of transnational deliberation among members.

CONCLUSION: IMPLICATIONS OF THIS CASE

Applying the cosmopolitan criteria to MSF's effects shows that some are more likely to advance cosmopolitanism than others. This may seem an obvious conclusion—one that will likely fit many associations. What is it that the criteria have added to our understanding of cosmopolitanism or of MSF? When studying MSF the criteria bring greater precision and organization to understanding the mixed potential of MSF. This can illustrate areas for reform but also draw lessons from what is working well. There are also larger implications of this case for cosmopolitanism. This association reveals how cosmopolitan effects may come into tension. Recognizing these tensions and acknowledging that there may be no solutions is critical to my theoretical claim that one needs to develop a concept of partial cosmopolitanism. The particular tension that emerges in MSF is that between developmental effects and shared identity effects.

The educative effects of an exclusive professional organization that emphasizes transnational moral obligations and biological commonalities help to bridge borders for expatriates, transforming them in the process. In the words of one MSF expatriate working in Pakistan: "I will soon leave Pakistan, it will never leave me as I find myself profoundly changed by being here. . . . I will be forever grateful for the perspective I have gained, for the things I have learned."[102] MSF emphasizes the special cosmopolitan obligations of medical professionals to treat all individuals equally because we are all humans who bleed red. Impartial equal medical treatment means that doctors should not take up arms to aid one side of a conflict. It means that they ought to look through cultural differences and recognize a husband's goal is to care for his wife despite different cultural expectations for that care. In fact, Rony Brauman, of MSF France, concludes that MSF can best protect against imperialistic and paternalistic attitudes if it emphasizes its professional codes. MSF workers, he writes, must "consider their own professional practices, and demonstrate that what they are doing is founded on principles more solidly based, and hence more demanding, than the appeals to the emotions which are so tempting to exploit."[103] Bonds that do form are stretched as expatriates are rotated around the globe to where care is most needed. Earlier quotes from MSF workers point to ways participation in the association cultivates a sense of obligation that can form from seeing the urgent need for their skills. (At times this can become an overwhelming pressure.) They have the skills needed and the capability to help. How can they not act? The fact that this is a professional association plays a role in cultivating a sense of cosmopolitan obligations in members even if members join for a variety of reasons and even if the association does not specifically invoke cosmopolitan philosophy.

At the same time, the professional nature of this association prevents the cultivation of a shared sense of global identity or community. The way common humanity is lodged in a common biology does not necessarily lead to solidarity. As Kwame Anthony Appiah cautions us, "the many interests that people have in virtue of our shared biology do not function outside their symbolic context."[104] Because of this, "a shared biology, a natural human essence, does not give us in the relevant sense, a shared ethical nature."[105] MSF consciously adopts a limited mandate to avoid creating a sense of permanent dependency that would undermine the agency and independence of local communities but this may also come at the expense of a robust shared identity around a reciprocal form of solidarity between MSF and the local communities it aids. This can result in a paradox where "the more successful MSF is at protecting existence in the name of a politics of rights and dignity, the more this temporary response threatens to become the norm."[106] One might argue that generating a shared identity is not feasible for an emergency-based humanitarian association of a professional nature. Emergency medical aid seems to create such different conditions and roles for aid workers and local communities that it is difficult to build a sense of transnational shared identity. Moreover, conditions expatriates face require rotation in order to prevent burnout. The intent may be to prevent compassion fatigue but the result is also to hamper constructing transnational community.

Membership in MSF may foster stronger developmental than shared identity effects. Among MSF members a professional code of conduct gives MSF grounds for demanding members rise above pity and act on a sense of professional obligation. Yet, codes of professional conduct and humanitarian norms have their limits for creating ties of solidarity beyond an abstract conception of a moral community of equals. A broad definition of cosmopolitanism says that some sense of cosmopolitanism as a way of life remains critical to fully realizing cosmopolitanism. Respectfully interacting with the local population in order to create solidarity might require including them in some ways in the association—or at least better including local staff MSF hires. The partial identity formed among members of MSF is starting to become more transnational as new MSF associations like MSF South Africa join MSF International. Here too attitudes of reciprocity and fallibility are critical.

The case indicates the need for categories of partial expressions of cosmopolitanism at the same time it emphasizes the potential of such partial forms. Professional associations can advance elements of cosmopolitanism. MSF actually inspired a broader movement of "without border" professional associations—including veterinarians, reporters, engineers, and even clowns without borders. All of these associations are based on the principle that their professional duties and codes of conduct extend beyond local communities. Moreover, the impact of professional associations may not be limited to their effects on professionals. The professional nature of an association can lend respectability to an organization's public sphere effects, as MSF demonstrates. If other associations have similar effects the diffusion of professional norms could be a way in which membership in a transnational association leads individuals, for a variety of reasons, to voluntarily abide by norms that support cosmopolitanism.

In addition to the partial cosmopolitanism of professional associations the idea of indirect cosmopolitanism also comes through by shifting from a focus on the motives of an association to its effects. The motivation for joining MSF does not necessarily align with the principles or ideals of the association. Nevertheless, MSF volunteers can realize cosmopolitan effects through membership in the association. They are confronted with new obligations and requirements that they abide by MSF's principles. MSF workers are transformed by their experiences. They find it difficult to return home once their worldview is altered. But, as Orbinski writes: "why would I want to see the world any other way than the way it is?"[107] Members may find themselves educating other people as they try to explain and justify their actions.

The categories of effects also reveal some ways MSF could move in more cosmopolitan directions without fundamentally altering its mission or giving up its professional membership. As the first institutional criterion indicated, members of an association can gain obligations from institutional relations they establish. MSF needs to accept more responsibility for local workers. In addition, ties with new branches need to be on fair terms. Inclusion without reciprocity is not real inclusion; however, reciprocity need not mean the same expectations apply to every member. MSF associations forming in countries with less money and fewer resources should have other ways of contributing to the MSF International. If MSF were to acknowledge the moral implications of its partial effects, it might also come to recognize the need to work more cooperatively with other NGOs. MSF considers its independence as critical for gaining access to patients but also as critical for building the trust needed to speak out about violations of human rights on all sides of a conflict. However, MSF might consider giving up some of that independence in order to work with NGOs that fulfill other needs from food, to shelter, to education, to advocacy that MSF does not consider part of its mandate. Coordination across different associations is not always easy as associations are not all organized the same way and often compete for resources from the same pool. Still, a public sphere that includes different actors can provide a stronger voice and more nuanced picture of individuals' needs. The presence of different voluntary associations might also lead to reforms in associations, as it did in the case of the ICRC, which developed a willingness to break its silence about human rights abuses in the face of the increasing competition from associations such as MSF. [108]

Rather than requiring MSF fully promote each criteria, one can see the association as an example of how cosmopolitanism can come about piecemeal. Recognizing where the association is less cosmopolitan should not necessarily undercut the cosmopolitan effects it has in other areas. Rony Braumann goes so far as to conclude that one ought to recognize "that humanitarian aid could have perverse effects" such as lengthening conflict but that this does not mean one should stop humanitarian aid to victims of a conflict. [109] Instead it ought to lead "one to at least ask the right questions on the type of program to design, on the control to exercise, and on the level of aid to channel." [110] William Schulz with Amnesty International makes a similar point that, "the perils inherent in witnessing on behalf of others . . . require constant vigilance" not halting all such work. [111] Considering the effects of an exclusive association like MSF can be more useful than imagining an ideal type of cosmopolitan association because it helps explore how to negotiate rather than resolve the tensions with and within cosmopolitanism. Recognizing partiality and fallibility is vital to ensuring cosmopolitanism does not become imperialistic. [112] Recognizing partiality can also help cosmopolitans better understand the impact of associations. A middle-level theory of cosmopolitanism can locate expressions of cosmopolitanism in associations without requiring the entire association serve as an example of cosmopolitan principles. The criteria can indicate where associations fail to advance cosmopolitanism at the same time they can indicate overlooked sites or sources of cosmopolitan potential. A partial concept of cosmopolitan can recognize that the professional aspect of MSF, although exclusive, has significant benefits even at the expense of robust forms of global solidarity. The goal of employing cosmopolitan criteria to evaluate associations should not be to resolve all tensions between elements of cosmopolitanism. In some cases an association may be successful precisely because of its exclusivity and the resulting tensions.

NOTES

1. James Orbinski, "Médecins Sans Frontières—Nobel Lecture," (The Nobel Foundation, 1999). Accessed on *Nobelprize.org*. Nobel Web AB 2014, http://www.nobel prize.org/nobel_prizes/peace/laureates/1999/msf-lecture.html.

2. Matt Baillie Smith and Katy Jenkins, "Disconnections and Exclusions: Professionalization, Cosmopolitanism and (Global?) Civil Society," *Global Networks* 11, no. 2 (2011): 170.

3. Ibid.

4. James Dawes, *That the World May Know: Bearing Witness to Atrocity* (Cambridge, MA: Harvard University Press, 2007), 18.

5. Patrick Aeberhard, "A Historical Survey of Humanitarian Action," *Health and Human Rights* 2, no. 1 (1996): 38.

6. Orbinski, "Nobel Lecture."

7. "The MSF Charter," available on the MSF-USA website, accessed May 22, 2008, hppt://www.doctorswithoutborders.orgaboutus/chater.cfm.

8. Orbinski, "Nobel Lecture."

9. Hippocratic Oath: Modern Version, by Louis Lasagna, Academic Dean of the School of Medicine at Tufts University (1964).

10. MSF's first charter, drafted in 1971, quoted by Jean-Hervé Bardol, "Caring for Health" in *Humanitarian Negotiations Revealed: The MSF Experience*, ed. Claire Magone, Michael Neuman, and Fabrice Weissman (New York: Columbia University Press, 2011), 199. The current charter adopts broader language, reading instead: "the association is made up mainly of doctors and health sector workers and is also open to all other professions which might help in achieving its aims," accessed July 12, 2013 from MSF's website, http://www.doctorswithoutborders.org/aboutus/charter.cfm.

11. These figures are drawn from MSF's *International Activity Report 2012*, "Facts and Figures" section, HR Statistics, page 99. This report is available at www.msf.org. The managing editor for the English edition of this report is Jane Linekar. At the time of writing, this was the most recent detailed activity report available.

12. Lester M. Salamon, "The Rise of the Nonprofit Sector," *Foreign Affairs* 73, no. 4 (1994): 120, 122.

13. Salamon, "The Rise," 122. Shamima Ahmed and David Potter make a similar point about the advantages of professionalism, understood in terms of professional NGO workers. See Shamima Ahmed and David Potter, *NGOs in International Politics* (Bloomfield, CT: Kumarian Press, 2006), 29.

14. "The MSF Movement," accessed December 9, 2013, http://www.msf.org/msf-movement.

15. Dan Bortolotti, *Hope in Hell: Inside the World of Doctors Without Borders* (Buffalo, NY: Firefly Books, 2004), 65.

16. James Maskalyk, *Six Months in Sudan: A Young Doctor in a War-torn Village* (New York: Spiegel & Grau, 2009), 24.

17. Ibid., 24. See also Bortolotti, *Hope in Hell,* 65.

18. Elliott Leyton, *Touched by Fire: Doctors Without Borders in a Third World Crisis,* photographs by Greg Locke (Toronto: M&S, 1998), 50.

19. Renée C. Fox, *Doctors Without Borders: Humanitarian Quests, Impossible Dreams of Médecins Sans Frontières* (Baltimore: Johns Hopkins University Press, 2014), 40–51, 64–65.

20. For more specific numbers see Bortolotti, *Hope in Hell,* 64.

21. MSF sends about 2,000 to 3,000 international staff on missions. In 2009 the United States had about 200 aid workers participating and in 2010 around 340. From MSF/Doctors Without Borders website under "About Us: History and Principles," accessed January 26, 2014, http://www.doctorswithoutborders.org/aboutus/?ref=main-menu#sthash.MYd0meVD.dpuf.

22. MSF volunteer quoted in Bortolotti, *Hope in Hell,* 65.

23. Orbinski, "Nobel Lecture."

24. "The MSF Movement." See also "How does the Association work?" accessed July 26, 2014, http://association.msf.org/how-does-the-association-work.

25. "Assemblies/IGA," accessed July 26, 2014, http://association.msf.org/assemblies-iga.

26. James Orbinski, *An Imperfect Offering: Humanitarian Action in the Twenty-First Century* (New York: Walter & Company, 2008), 332.

27. Ibid., 332. For an extensive discussion of MSF Greece's expulsion and their re-admissions see Fox, *Doctors Without Borders,* chapters 4 and 5.

28. Christophe Fournier, quoted in Fox, *Doctors Without Borders,* 91.

29. Fox, *Doctors Without Borders,* 189, 197.

30. Jonathan Whittall and Sharon Ekambaram, "Genuine Reform: Adapting to a Changing Global Environment" quoted in Fox, *Doctors Without Borders,* 193.

31. Fox, *Doctors Without Borders,* 252.

32. Ibid., 185–186.

33. Rony Brauman, foreword to *The World in Crisis: The Politics of Survival at the End of the Twentieth Century,* ed. Médecins Sans Frontières, MSF project coordinator aJulia Groenwold, and Associate Editor Eve Porter (New York: Routledge, 1997), xxv.

34. Darrel Moellendorf, *Cosmopolitan Justice* (Cambridge, MA: Westview Press, 2002), 32.

35. Nicholas de Torrente of MSF USA speaking at "On the Medical Frontlines: Richard Knox in Conversation with Doctors Without Borders," public lecture attended by the author at the Boston Public Library on Thursday, June 5, 2008.

36. Orbinski, *Imperfect Offering,* 174–175.

37. Ibid.

38. "On the Medical Frontlines."

39. Orbinski, *Imperfect Offering,* 360.

40. Richard Horton wrote this in a 2002 article in *Lancet,* one of the world's leading medical journals. Orbinski quotes Horton in *Imperfect Offering,* 370.

41. Martha Nussbaum, "Patriotism and Cosmopolitanism," in *For Love of Country?* ed. Joshua Cohen (Boston: Beacon Press, 2002), xxiii.

42. Especially in its early years, MSF cultivated an image of adventure and excitement. As a result it gained the reputation as a group that would go where others feared to tread. For a discussion of this see Fox, *Doctors Without Borders,* 259 as well as Bortolotti, *Hope in Hell,* 56. Dawes makes a similar point about humanitarian aid workers when he discusses how the risks of humanitarian aid, far from dissuading participation, actually encourage some to join associations that seem to offer opportunities for excitement. Once a member, the work of saving others can become addictive due to the power rush of saving others as well as satisfying one's own "moral craving," Dawes, *That the World May Know,* 116, 118–119.

43. Clandestine missions were carried out in Afghanistan, Kurdistan, El Salvador, and Eritrea. Rony Brauman, "Médecines Sans Frontières Experience," in *A Framework for Survival: Health, Human Rights, and Humanitarian Assistance in Conflicts and Disaster*, ed. Kevin M. Cahill, M.D. (New York: BasicBooks and Council on Foreign Affairs, 1993), 218.

44. "The MSF Charter," accessed July 12, 2013, http://www.doctorswithout borders.org/aboutus/charter.cfm.

45. Jean Pictet quoted in David P. Forsythe, "The Red Cross as Transnational Movement: Conserving and Changing the Nation-State System," *International Organization* 30, no. 4 (1976): 613.

46. Orbinski, *Imperfect Offering*, 4.

47. Maskalyk, *Six Months in Sudan*, 5.

48. Quoted by Bortolotti, *Hope in Hell*, 86.

49. Quoted by ibid.

50. Quoted in ibid., 248, 257.

51. Renée C. Fox, "Medical Humanitarianism and Human Rights: Reflections on Doctors Without Borders and Doctors of the World," *Social Sciences & Medicine* 41, no. 12 (1995): 1613.

52. Quoted in Bortolotti, *Hope in Hell*, 257.

53. Hansel, M.D., "On the Medical Frontlines," public lecture, 2008.

54. Orbinski, *Imperfect Offering*, 234.

55. Quoted in Bortolotti, *Hope in Hell*, 230.

56. Quoted in ibid., 230.

57. Saif Ali Musa and Abdalla A.R. M. Hamid, "Psychological Problems among Aid Workers Operating in Darfur," *Social Behavior and Personality* 36, no. 3 (2008): 408.

58. This quote and the next two come from Heidi Postlewait quoted in Dawes, *That the World may Know*, 144.

59. Cynthia B. Ericksson et al., "Social Support, Organizational Support, and Religious Support in Relation to Burnout in Expatriate Humanitarian Aid Workers," *Mental Health, Religion & Culture* 12, no. 7 (2009): 681.

60. Musa and Hamid, "Psychological Problems," 415.

61. Francois Debrix, "Deterritorialised Territories, Borderless Borders: The New Geography of International Medical Assistance," *Third World Quarterly* 19, no. 5 (1998): 838.

62. "Training health workers to respond to malaria in Sierra Leone," video clip available on MSF-USA website, accessed April 25, 2008, http://www.doctorswithout borders.org/news/article.cfm?id=2631.

63. Fox, *Doctors Without Borders*, 138.

64. Ibid., 139.

65. Quoted in Leyton, *Touched by Fire*, 181.

66. Ericksson et al., "Social Support," 681.

67. See Kwame Anthony Appiah, *Cosmopolitanism: Ethics in a World of Strangers* (Princeton, NJ: W.W. Norton & Company, 2006).

68. Jean-Marie Kindermans of MSF Belgium quoted in Bortolotti, *Hope in Hell*, 257–258.

69. Mike Toole, "Frontline Medicine: The Role of International Medical Groups in Emergency Relief," in *The World in Crisis: The Politics of Survival at the End of the Twentieth Century*, ed. Médecins Sans Frontières, MSF project coordinator Julia Groenwold, and Associate Editor Eve Porter (New York: Routledge, 1997), 18.

70. A MSF volunteer working in the Sudan quoted in Bortolotti, *Hope in Hell*, 259.

71. Quoted in ibid., 259–260.

72. Fox, *Doctors Without Borders*, 123.

73. Kevin Barlow, "Dear Darfur" February 14, 2008 MSF field blog entry "The Farchana Sky," quoted in Fox, *Doctors Without Borders*, 31.

74. Quoted in Bortolotti, *Hope in Hell*, 259–260.

75. Fiona Terry quoted in ibid., 257.

76. Maskalyk, *Six Months in Sudan*, 112.

77. Bortolotti, *Hope in Hell*, 76.

78. Kenneth Cain, a former humanitarian aid worker, talks about a sense of place-lessness and how destabilizing it is in many aspects of life. He is quoted in Dawes, *That the World may Know*, 156.

79. Dawes, *That the World may Know*, 89.

80. Maskalyk, *Six Months in Sudan*, 105.

81. Jonathan Whittall and Ekambaram, "Genuine Reform: Adapting to a Changing Global Environment" quoted in Fox, *Doctors Without Borders*, 194.

82. Fox, *Doctors Without Borders*, 189, 197.

83. Discussed in ibid., 188.

84. Jürgen Habermas, *Between Facts and Norms: Contributions to a Discourse Theory of Law and Democracy*, trans. William Rehg (Cambridge, MA: MIT Press, 1996), 360. Italics in original.

85. Seyla Benhabib, *The Rights of Others: Aliens, Residents, and Citizens* (New York: Cambridge University Press, 2004), 14. Italics in original.

86. John Dryzek, *Deliberative Global Politics: Discourse and Democracy in a Divided World* (Malden, MA: Polity, 2006).

87. Orbinski, *Imperfect Offering*, 9.

88. Claudine Herzlich, "Comments: Professionals, Intellectuals, Visible Practitioners? The Case of 'Medical Humanitarianism,'" *Social Sciences & Medicine* 41, no. 12 (1995): 1618.

89. "On the Medical Frontlines," public lecture, 2008.

90. Layla Merrit, "Doctors Without Borders Brings Refugees' Plight to U.S.," *The New York Amsterdam News* (October 5–October 31: 2006).

91. Debrix, "Deterritorialised Territories," 835. Joelle Tanguy and Fiona Terry put it this way: "Often the sole witness to these violations, MSF volunteers consider themselves accountable to international civil society and humanitarian principles, rather than to governmental or multilateral financial backers of aid. As a consequence, MSF's testimony (*témoignage*) is raised in public rather than in closed diplomatic circles." Tanguy and Terry, "Humanitarian Responsibility and Committed Action: Response to 'Principles, Politics, and Humanitarian Action,'" *Ethics & International Affairs* 13, no. 1 (1999): 32.

92. Forsythe, "The Red Cross," 613.

93. Aeberhard concludes, "ultimately, the complex relations between these NGOs and the ICRC has enhanced the effectiveness of these largely complementary organizations" in "A Historical Survey," 39.

94. Nicolas de Torrente, "Challenges to Humanitarian Action," *Ethics & International Affairs* 16, no. 2 (2002): 2–8. The military must leave open a realm for the free independent humanitarian aid of NGOs. This is not to say that the US military should not provide care for the populations in Afghanistan and Iraq, but de Torrente makes it clear that this is not humanitarian aid. It is a requirement of the Geneva Conventions.

95. Leyton relates this story. *Touched by Fire*, 136.

96. Fox, *Doctors Without Borders*, 15, 17.

97. Two important meetings that helped to shape key association policies occurred in 1996 in Chantilly, France (MSF discussed what it meant to witness) and in 2004 at the La Mancha Conference (MSF discussed the increasing role of national staff). For more discussions on these meetings see Fox, *Doctors Without Borders*.

98. Marie-Pierre Allié, "Introduction: Acting at Any Price?" in *Humanitarian Negotiations Revealed: The MSF Experience*, ed. Claire Magone, Michael Neuman, and Fabrice Weissman (New York: Columbia University Press, 2011), 3.

99. Fox, *Doctors Without Borders*, 5, 257.

100. A member of MSF quoted in ibid., 107.

101. Tanguy and Terry, "Humanitarian Responsibility and Committed Action," 33.

102. Joe Starke, "Medicine at the Frontier," December 22, 2009, MSF blog entry "Closing Snapshots of Life and Work in NWEP." Quoted in Fox, *Doctors Without Borders*, 34.

103. Rony Braumann, "When Suffering Makes a Good Story," in *Life and Death and Aid: The Medécins Sans Frontiéres Report on World Crisis Intervention*, ed. Francois Jean (New York: Routledge, 1993), 158.

104. Kwame Anthony Appiah, *The Ethics of Identity* (Princeton, NJ: Princeton University Press, 2005), 252.

105. Ibid.

106. Peter Redfield, "Doctors, Borders, and Life in Crisis," *Cultural Anthropology* 20, no. 3 (2005): 343.

107. Orbinski, *Imperfect Offering*, 258.

108. Aeberhard, "A Historical Survey," 39.

109. Rony Braumann in *Humanitaire: Le Dilemme* (Paris: Les Editions Textual, 1996) quoted in Tanguy and Terry, "Humanitarian Responsibility and Committed Action," 34.

110. Brauman continues from previous source, quoted in Tanguy and Terry, "Humanitarian Responsibility and Committed Action," 34.

111. Quoting William Schulz from Amnesty International USA in Dawes, *That the World May Know*, 217.

112. Appiah, *Cosmopolitanism*, Chapter 9, "The Counter-Cosmopolitans."

SIX

Advancing Cosmopolitanism through International Competition

At first glance, world championship sports competitions such as the Olympic Games may seem like nothing more than sublimated war fought by national teams of athletes. As essayist George Orwell puts it, "even if one didn't know from the concrete examples (the 1936 Olympic Games, for instance) that international sporting contests lead to orgies of hatred, one could deduce it from general principles."[1] Understood as sublimated war, the Olympic Games are a threat to cosmopolitan ideals of mutual respect and transnational community. However, former International Olympic Committee President Jacques Rogge describes the "the essence of the Olympics [as] athletic competition and world unity."[2] The founder of the modern Olympic Games, Pierre de Coubertin, believed that "we shall not have peace until the prejudices which now separate the different races shall have been outlived. To attain this end, what better means than to bring the youth of all the countries periodically together for amicable trials of muscular strength and agility?"[3] Understood in terms of peaceful world unity, the Games become a quintessentially cosmopolitan activity. Neither view is nuanced enough. Significant tensions exist between the goal of advancing mutual understanding and the staging of competitions that pit national teams against each other.

If the self-declared purpose of organizing sports competitions cannot fully reflect the cosmopolitan potential of the Olympics, then how ought one evaluate its effects? Cosmopolitan political theories do not adequately address how to assess whether transnational non-governmental associations advance cosmopolitan norms. When non-governmental associations are addressed it is usually associations like Amnesty International or Human Rights Watch that self-consciously aim to advance cosmopolitan ideals of moral equality through advocating for human rights norms.

145

Associations, however, often have purposes that are not self-consciously cosmopolitan (like staging world championships). Even when looking beyond the purpose of the association to its effects complexities arise. Non-governmental associations behave in ways that make it difficult to completely separate their aims or effects from governmental and economic forces. John Keane, a theorist of global civil society, calls this the overdetermined nature of transnational associations.[4] The Olympics is a prime example of how "the signs of commerce are now a prominent feature of global sports events."[5] Given such complex purposes and effects cosmopolitans ought to consider what it means for associations to advance cosmopolitanism in some ways but not others. Rather than imagining some purely cosmopolitan sports association, the Olympics is used to consider how one might assess the effects of a non-governmental association without a cosmopolitan purpose.

Assessing indirect effects of associations is how scholars studying domestic civil society have sometimes addressed the effects of associations with a variety of purposes. In order to determine whether an association advances democratic norms Mark E. Warren, for example, establishes criteria for three types of effects—institutional, developmental, and public sphere effects.[6] These are helpful categories, but cosmopolitanism is not simply global democracy. Assessing the indirect effects of transnational associations, with membership from more than one country, requires developing cosmopolitan rather than democratic criteria. What would constitute cosmopolitan criteria?

Although political and economic effects are discussed the main focuses will be on advancing moral norms of cosmopolitanism and a sense of transnational community. Cosmopolitanism as employed here means belief in the moral equality of all humans across national borders and a sense of transnational community based on such respect. This understanding does not engage the traditional debate between the strong versions of cosmopolitanism (that consider universal moral equality to require impartiality and "the ability to stand outside of having one's life written and scripted by any one community") and the weak versions of cosmopolitanism found in nationalist theories like that of David Miller (that "states that every human being has equal moral worth" but rejects the idea that this requires equal treatment across national borders).[7] What both views share is a moral conception of cosmopolitanism that rejects the idea of cosmopolitanism as consumer capitalist globalization.[8] Even from the stronger version of moral cosmopolitanism it is possible to argue that respect for moral equality must be informed by respect for a diversity of associations. As long as individuals are free to leave an association and an association does not violate human rights, it ought to be tolerated.[9] What cosmopolitanism still needs is a clearer way of assessing whether the transnational non-governmental associations that can be tolerated are also actually advancing norms or dispositions that foster a sense of transnational community that respects the moral equality of all humans.

In order to encompass the range of possible cosmopolitan effects of associations, one can draw on four main approaches to cosmopolitan theory. All four fall closer to the strong cosmopolitan view on a spectrum of strong to weak versions of cosmopolitanism. These more robust theories of cosmopolitanism provide the answers to how one could evaluate whether associations are advancing cosmopolitan norms. The goal is not to debate the merits of strong versus weak cosmopolitanism. Instead, each approach will be explored in terms of what it can say about cosmopolitan implications for transnational associations.

The four approaches are as follows: the first approach focuses on establishing fair rules for institutional relations on the global level, the second on developing individual moral capacity, the third on fostering a cosmopolitan identity, and the fourth on creating public spheres of discussion. On their own none of these approaches is adequate for understanding cosmopolitan effects of associations. Taken together they help to fill in what cosmopolitan theory requires in the context of Warren's three types of effects and adds a fourth category of shared identity effect. Rather than using a hypothetical association to illustrate what cosmopolitan effects would entail, evidence from historical and social scientific analysis of the Olympics will be employed to explore institutional, developmental, shared identity, and public sphere effects.

Evaluating the effects of associations in terms of whether they advance cosmopolitanism adopts a normative stance. Advancing cosmopolitanism is considered a positive goal. This normative stance does not, however, entail the additional implication that an association must be in full compliance with all cosmopolitan criteria or else be considered a threat to cosmopolitanism. In other words, it is possible to consider how the Olympics might better advance cosmopolitanism without arguing that it should not be tolerated unless it does. It may remain only a partial expression of cosmopolitanism. Nevertheless, associations like the Olympics without explicit cosmopolitan goals have the potential to indirectly advance cosmopolitan norms among those who do not already embrace cosmopolitan principles. Sports organizations ought to receive greater attention from cosmopolitan theorists interested in how cosmopolitanism might be advanced in the world.

THE CASE OF THE OLYMPICS IN BRIEF

Some brief background on the Olympics demonstrates why it lacks a straightforwardly cosmopolitan purpose despite Rogge's rhetoric on global unity.

Combining "nationalist impulses" and "cosmopolitan vocabularies,"[10] Pierre de Coubertin, founder of the modern Olympics, established world championships in order to motivate greater cultivation of physical strength. He saw physical strength as crucial to the national security of his home country of France.[11] An athlete "should shape his body through sport and glorify his country, his masculinity and his flag through this action."[12] At the same time, international standards and norms of sports, such as fair play and respect for fellow competitors, create an arena of rule-bound interaction on the global level where "there were supposed to be no national rivalries, but peace in the competition areas."[13]

The Games were also part of a transnational civilizing mission for Coubertin. "It was [Coubertin's] view that sport must be theatre and conceivably even 'cult' or 'religion,' (he also used these words). All this Coubertin succeeded in implanting among cosmopolitan bureaucrats of international Olympism."[14] Ceremonies and symbols of the Olympics are meant to create a sense of transnational Olympic community among elite athletes as well as the audience. When the first Olympic Games opened in Athens, Greece, on April 5, 1896, the audience was one of the largest to be assembled for peaceful purposes since ancient times (about seventy thousand in the stadium and another estimated fifty thousand on the surrounding hills).[15] The Olympic flag with its logo of five interlocking rings has become one of the most recognized logos in the world.[16] The Games continue to develop rituals and ceremonies: the 1936 Olympics added the torch relay. Like states with their flags, patriotic symbols, and ceremonies, the Olympics creates spaces and symbols in order to generate a sense of communal feeling.

Despite the aim of creating an international Olympic community, nationalist aspects of the Olympic Games have historically vied with more international goals. After Hitler came to power and restricted the participation of Jewish athletes in the Berlin Games, the International Olympic Committee did not take the Games away from Berlin. Instead, Hitler turned the Games into a massive propaganda exhibition for his regime. Governments are not the only ones that use the Olympic stage to gain attention. During the 1972 Munich Games Israeli athletes were killed after terrorists kidnapped them from the Olympic Village. Since the 1980s some corporations have also seen the Olympics as "a platform for the penetration . . . into global markets and global consciousness."[17] This commercialization sometimes takes national forms as countries seek to brand themselves through sanitized images of national cultural history.

Cosmopolitans need standards beyond the purpose of the association to understand how transnational non-governmental associations like the Olympics help spread cosmopolitan norms and attitudes in some ways but not others. The criteria outlined next allow for partial or indirect forms of cosmopolitanism creating a more balanced picture of the cosmopolitan impact of the Olympics.

DETERMINING COSMOPOLITAN EFFECTS

Institutional Effects

One tradition of cosmopolitan theory focuses on cosmopolitan obligations that arise due to the transnational nature of institutional relations. In this view, cosmopolitanism entails obligations that emerge not "simply by virtue of the nature of [an individual's] personhood. On the contrary, duties of justice arise between persons when activities such as politics or commerce bring persons into association."[18] What is at stake is usually the coercive character of international political and economic institutions that exploit some people for the benefit of others.[19] Theorists like Darrel Moellendorf, Charles Beitz, and Thomas Pogge argue that institutions ought to be structured according to fair rules so that all individuals affected by the institutional relations could consent to the rules. The focus of an institutional cosmopolitan approach is usually economic and political organizations of globalization because of their "deep and pervasive effects on the welfare of people to whom they apply regardless of consent."[20] There is not the same strict moral imperative to reform transnational non-governmental associations precisely because membership is often voluntary. Individuals consent to join and are free to exit. Nevertheless, one can evaluate whether an association's institutional structure generates cosmopolitan norms even if that is not a requirement of traditional versions of institutional cosmopolitan theory.

The Olympics highlights how to explore the institutional effects of an association. An association's organizational structure could build ties that bridge national allegiances or other global cleavages by establishing institutional relations. It took a while before the Games developed into what they are today, but already by the 1930s competitors from more nations were entering the Games. The International Olympic Committee seeks to expand beyond European and North American cities when determining locations for the Games. But universal relations are not necessarily cosmopolitan. Therefore, one must also ask whether an association institutionalizes universal rules or standards that cultivated greater respect for the moral equality of all those participating in the organization. Usually this is understood to mean institutionalizing human rights norms into international law or the rules of international governmental organizations like the United Nations. The universal rules of sports serve as an under-explored example of a cosmopolitan institutional effect.

The International Olympic Committee (IOC) that Coubertin founded in 1894 is still at the core of the Olympic organizational structure. The IOC is organized internationally; however, unlike other international organizations where representatives to the organization represent their specific countries, members of the IOC are representatives of the IOC to their home country not *vice versa*. Avery Brundage, a former IOC president, conveyed this perspective, in the following words: "in the International Olympic Committee I am not a representative of the US. . . . As a member of the committee, my first allegiance is to a principle—the principles of the Olympic movement. . . . Members of the committee cannot be pre-instructed by their countries."[21] This shows a cosmopolitan priority to the institutional structure of the IOC. Yet, a global scope is not enough for an association to be cosmopolitan. This becomes clear when one considers that Brundage was also an active proponent of keeping the 1936 Olympics in Berlin despite the exclusion of Jewish athletes and other racist policies.

Despite transnational institutional relations, national attachments still play a significant role in the Olympics. It might appear that the Olympics increases negative forms of nationalism by structuring the competitions as between individuals representing different nations. Individual athletes must all be attached to a national team. This limits those individuals from countries such as Taiwan that are not recognized as independent. Countries also use national medal counts as a mark of prestige despite the IOC's rejection of tabulating medal counts by country. As a result athletes may be seen as fighting for national glory, subsuming the individual into the national unit. This is unacceptable from a cosmopolitan view that sees individuals rather than nations as the fundamental moral unit. Extreme examples of this danger include organized programs of steroids administered to athletes in order to increase performance during the Games. If a win signals national success then a loss can be held against athletes. Cultivating such perspectives can also hamper athletes developing a cosmopolitan disposition if they see themselves solely as representatives of a particular state.

If the institutional organization is nevertheless to have cosmopolitan effects it is necessary to evaluate the universal rules and requirements necessary for staging global games. The technical rules of Olympic sport may not seem obviously relevant to cosmopolitanism. However, they create a framework to organize peaceful, rule-governed international interaction beyond the nation even if the nation is still present. Coubertin made competitive sports the core of the Olympic Games. This differs from Turnen, another philosophy of sport less compatible with international ambitions, that was flourishing at the time Coubertin revived the modern Olympics. Turnen involved group calisthenics with individuals moving together as one. Friedrich Ludwig Jahn, the founder of Turnen, believed that "the purpose of their exercise was to strengthen the body in preparation for the fight against the enemies of the fatherland as well as to fill the mind with glowing enthusiasm for the fatherland and hate for the foe."[22] Coubertin and Jahn were both patriots but Coubertin sought to establish world championships for "enlarging the acquaintance of nations, for stretching, without, of course, breaking, their respective hermeneutic circles so that they might intersect in novel and interesting ways."[23] After the initial international impetus of Coubertin and others who helped to revive the Games, standardization and internationalization of sports was further promoted because of the commercial benefits of spectator sports. Multinational companies like Coca Cola see sporting events as an avenue for reaching global markets.[24]

The aims of IOC members and of others who want to use the international reach of the Games are certainly mixed; however, internationalization of competitive sports was made possible through standardization of the unique rules of sports. These rules have universal scope. In order to play each sport individuals must abide by the same rules. As people play in stadiums or fields with the same design and according to the same rules not only can individuals from different nations compete against each other but also achievements can be compared across the world. Excellence in sports became connected with breaking records of great human achievement. The community of competitors is therefore ultimately global—fellow humans.[25] In fact, "among elements of mass culture, where cross-national exchanges are typically informal, sport is unique in having a powerful system of transnational governance, mirroring the international political structures that have sprung up along side national governments in the twentieth century."[26]

The IOC, National Olympic Committees, and International Sports Federations establish and enforce the rules as well as standard technical requirements of each sport to which participants must abide. In slightly hyperbolic terms, one scholar describes the IOC as acting like national leaders challenging "the 'primacy of the state' worldview, especially as . . . IOC executives receive diplomatic immunity around the world."[27] In addition to diplomatic relations the IOC even has official observer status at the United Nations, meaning an IOC representative can speak (although not vote) in the General Assembly. Despite the IOC's behaving like a state in these ways, the rules of sports are actually distinct from traditional rules of international power politics, warfare, or economics. Each sport in the Olympics is "bound by rules and structured by values that are its own autonomous creation" and their aim is "victories and pleasure."[28] They are, after all, games. It is "precisely because of their arbitrariness (which renders them value-neutral) [that] they are readily accepted and understood across cultures, nations, communities, and classes—human collectives that often do not want to understand each other otherwise."[29] For a cosmopolitanism that is informed by diversity, it should be noted that the universal nature of sports rules does not eliminate all difference. A competitive view of sports is privileged. Competitive sports may come into tension with certain cultural practices particularly in cases where "sport associated with self-awareness or rivalry can be at variance with an education system following certain cultural patterns" particularly one like Turnen that stresses cooperation or the group rather than the individual.[30]

Tensions certainly remain within the Olympics between the transnational standards that measure human excellence at particular sports and nation-based organizational components—such as national teams—or the meaning sports can have in different cultural and temporal contexts.[31] The Olympics is not a perfectly cosmopolitan organization but rather helps to show how one might locate certain cosmopolitan elements in an association. The Olympics holds individuals and states to the shared expectations of common transnational activity around rules of a game. What is particularly interesting about this case is that unlike other more advocacy-oriented associations that seek to establish international laws, rules of sports are not meant to contribute to global governance or international law. Membership and participation in the association's activities are crucial to realizing the cosmopolitan effects of these rules. This is a non-governmental association but institutional rules can still help to understand how an association might spread cosmopolitan norms indirectly among those interested in sports but not previously committed to cosmopolitan principles. In the end, institutional effects can be assessed in terms of whether an association establishes transnational organizational structures based on cosmopolitan rules and standards that help to advance norms of moral equality and transnational community.

Developmental Effects

Analyzing institutional relations addresses only one facet of associations and one approach to cosmopolitanism. Another strand of cosmopolitan theory considers cosmopolitan duties to arise not through institutional relations but through membership in the moral community of all humans. For cosmopolitan theorists of this tradition, like Martha Nussbaum, it is necessary to teach individuals to recognize the basic commonalities they share with strangers in order to generate a sense of empathy for others.[32] This leads Nussbaum, for example, to argue that cosmopolitans ought to be interested in shaping an appropriate early childhood education. Cosmopolitanism requires individual moral development: in exploring developmental effects the focus shifts from establishing institutional ties and rules to affecting individuals' attitudes.

How could this approach help one to understand cosmopolitan effects of associations? Assessing an association according to cosmopolitan developmental standards can involve asking whether an association expands the imaginations of members to recognize commonalities across borders in a way that bridges differences. Locating points of commonality can help empower individuals by connecting local action to global action. People can come to see themselves as more than merely passive recipients or victims of global forces.

What opportunities does the Olympics provide to broaden imaginations better to recognize the moral equality of all humans and see local matters from a global perspective? The rules mentioned earlier under institutional effects not only ensure cooperation in a common activity, but also have a developmental effect by shaping the dispositions of individuals that discipline themselves to the rules. Although competitive sports entail winning and losing, they do not merely sublimate the virtues necessary for war. The Olympic Games are just games and as games acknowledging the rule of law—following the rules of the game—is essential to the glory achieved through victory in sports.[33] A key virtue is fair play—good sportsmanship.

Coubertin self-consciously saw the Games as a means of moral cultivation. The self-discipline and self-control necessary for training and achieving excellence in sports could shape individuals' dispositions. "Sports may not make angels of brutes," he wrote, "but there is a great possibility that they will temper that brutality, giving the individual a bit of self-control. That, at least, is something!"[34] He grafted his ideals onto older norms of chivalry, arguing that mutual respect and recognition of commonalities could rise above national division if athletes came to "appreciate the performances of their rivals."[35]

Jettisoning the more elitist overtones of an emphasis on chivalry, contemporary scholars of the Olympics still describe the potential for competitors to see each other as fellow athletes and in so doing recognize a commonality that crosses national borders. Moreover, it is a commonality that is based on a form of mutual respect. "Sport arguably provides for cross-cultural encounters with the other, forcing us into bodily and normative dialogue with those that we might find irrational or culturally abominable. Playing sport competitively forces us to think ourselves into the shoes of the opponent."[36] Sports can achieve this because the virtues are measured in "performance, output and results."[37] Most sports do not by nature exclude particular groups of people. Inclusive games can help to undermine the notion that certain groups of people are not worthy of competing against (although the case of excluding women will be discussed later). "Simply to play the same game on the same field according to the same rules is to acknowledge an essential equality, a common humanity, among competitors."[38] Sports have been one social arena in which color barriers and inclusion of immigrants have on occasion "enhanced the social acceptance of diversity while at the same time remaining a battle ground for primordial identities, exclusive nationalism and localism."[39] The cosmopolitan effect is partial. Overcoming prejudice may not extend far beyond the sports arena and/or may be limited to particular celebrity athletes. Still, it does show some potential to move toward recognition of equality and forms of inclusion.

Mutual respect cannot be reinforced merely through rules of sports or remonstrations from the IOC. The IOC's insular secretive nature seems to have effects that oppose the ideas of fairness the Olympics embodies. It has been rocked by scandals of vote buying and misuse of funding. There is, however, some motivation to maintain the values associated with the Olympics if for no other reason than that they are crucial for marketing purposes. [40] This could be understood as an indirect reason for supporting particular values.

Another aspect of the Games, namely their ambulatory nature, can help to expand the imaginations of not only athletes but also audiences who might not otherwise learn about a particular country or culture. Each city that hosts the Games is required to organize a cultural program to "promote harmonious relations, mutual understanding and friendship among the participants and others attending the Olympic Games." [41] In this way the Olympics functions as a crude form of "the peoples' ethnography." [42] These cultural expressions occur most visibly in the opening ceremonies, which showcase aspects of the host city's culture.

Hosting the Olympics is a way for countries to attempt to enhance their public appeal. [43] This is certainly not an opportunity for all countries. Few cities have the infrastructure necessary to host world championships. For those who are able and willing to host:

> people are said to feel empowered by the successful staging of such monumental events and by succeeding in the eyes of the world. They are argued to develop a sense of common purpose with their fellow citizens and to feel a greater sense of ownership of both the event itself, and the community of which they are a part. . . . That positive feelings of empowerment and civic pride are often associated with the staging of major Games is beyond doubt. [44]

The range of ways to participate in the Olympics allows different groups of people—athletes, volunteers, and audiences—the chance to become part of a global endeavor. Volunteers, who assist in staging the Games, for example, may receive language training or lessons in multiculturalism so that they can provide a welcoming environment and assist the many international visitors to the Games. The Games can be a chance to showcase the best of a country's culture and demonstrate hospitality to visitors by welcoming those who come for the Games.

A cosmopolitan developmental effect based on locating commonalities and equality must not overlook inequalities that continue to exist. Claims of world unity could result in blindness to "the fact that a nation's sportive stature often does not correspond to its political stature." [45] Even considering more countries as potential places for hosting the Games does not necessarily mean that domestic inequalities will be addressed. When the IOC announced that Beijing would host the 2008 Olympics, there were protests that China should not have been given the Games because of its history of human rights violations (including violations connected to sports, such as using sport stadiums for mass executions). [46] In such cases cosmopolitan developmental effects that cultivate respect for moral equality may be partial at best or non-existent. Yet, as will be addressed later, public protest can generate another kind of cosmopolitan effect, namely a public sphere effect.

Although equality may not always extend beyond the sports arena (and may not be complete there either), virtues of good sportsmanship could emerge based on some basic equality among fellow competitors. This can cultivate a degree of moral equality that crosses national boundaries. Hosting the Games can lead to the empowerment of individuals as they become actors in the staging of global events. Developmental effect criteria can assess associations in terms of whether they expand the horizons of members to recognize basic commonalities or empower individuals to see themselves as participants in global endeavors. In the case of the Olympics, the developmental effects remain only partial expressions of cosmopolitan mutual respect.

Shared Identity Effects

Cosmopolitan theorists have written not only about establishing just institutional relations or the moral development of individuals but also about cosmopolitanism as a way of life rooted to one's identity. Kwame Anthony Appiah considers cosmopolitan identity an identity beyond one's local community but compatible with more partial allegiances. He calls this "rooted" or "patriotic" cosmopolitanism. It can be cultivated through "conversations across boundaries of identity" that involve not only "literal talk but also . . . engagement with the experience and the idea of others."[47] Cosmopolitanism in this view involves an obligation to engage in cross-cultural exchanges to consider oneself part of the human community as well as more partial communities.

If cosmopolitanism is not to lose its moral force and simply accept all forms of diversity one needs to ask what makes the solidarity formed by associations cosmopolitan. One can assess whether the partial identities formed by membership in an association can foster cosmopolitanism. Focusing on a sense of a community, even one not based on common humanity, requires evaluating the different kinds of relations and duties each person has as an active member of a community. One can also ask whether associations do indeed cultivate a sense of membership in a common *human* community. In a particularly grandiose statement, former president of the IOC Baillet-Latour claimed that "the Olympic Games are not held in Berlin, Los Angeles or in Amsterdam. When the 5-circled Olympic flag is raised over the Stadium it becomes sacred Olympic territory and theoretically, and for all practical purposes, the Games are held in ancient Olympia. There, I am master."[48] Is this desirable? Cosmopolitanism is more than simply transnational ties. It is relevant for cosmopolitan purposes to ask whether that shared identity is based on relations of equal respect and recognition of obligations to fellow members.

Before considering if there is any sense of a human community, one can start with the question of whether partial shared identities formed through the Olympics support cosmopolitan norms. One such shared identity is the transnational community among elite athletes that exists independent of the countries these athletes represent. Athletes often compete against each other not merely for national victory but also for the purpose of breaking world records of human achievement.[49] They see each other at world championships and keep track of each other's achievements. At times, athletes have even taken a role in shaping the Games. John Ian Wang, a British-Chinese athlete, suggested at the Melbourne Olympics in 1956 that all athletes appear together in the closing ceremonies to show unity rather than appearing in national teams.[50] This is now a common practice in the closing ceremonies.

During the Olympic Games, the community of athletes is also located in the actual space of the Olympic Village. It was first established in 1932 to be "the symbolic home of the global citizens of this sporting fraternity, a place where the world's youth gathered in peaceful competition."[51] During the Cold War the Soviet Union sought to isolate its athletes, demanding that they be housed in a separate part of the Olympic Village from non-communist countries. Everyday interactions among athletes in the Village, however, undermined this attempt to maintain separation along ideological lines.[52] As athletes move out of the Olympic Village to stay in hotels (for security reasons or for comfort) there is not the same interaction among athletes of different nations.

Once they have participated in the Games, there are also associations that continue to engage athletes as part of a community of fellow Olympians. The World Olympians Association (WOA), formed in 1994, "unites Olympians from around the world regardless of their age, sport, nationality . . . in the promotion of the values and virtues that make the Olympic Movement."[53] The WOA consists of a global network of around eighty thousand Olympians holding reunions to discuss how better to serve their community through mentoring or education as well as how to spread Olympic ideals. "Olympian" is a shared identity that carries with it not only a sense of belonging among those with a similar experience but also a sense of obligations.

Some athletes argue that Olympians have special obligations or responsibilities. Before the Beijing Olympics, gold medalist speed skater Joey Cheek, one of the founders of Team Darfur, declared that he would donate all bonuses from his gold medal to youth sports programs in Darfur and encouraged all athletes to do the same.[54] French athletes started a petition protesting human rights abuses in China, an action that "prioritized professional status over political loyalty."[55] In these ways Olympians, for whom the crowds cheer, gain responsibilities beyond their direct participation in the athletic competitions.

This transnational shared identity created through participation in the Olympics vies with attempts to solidify another form of partial identity—a national one. The Olympics is not a perfectly cosmopolitan association. One must recognize that nations seek to show how they comply with Olympic ideas by developing sanitized stories that wash over real social inequalities.[56] Even the viewing experience of audiences tends to focus on athletes from one's own nation ensuring there is no global or universal viewing experience. Cosmopolitans should not overlook these aspects of the Olympics any more than critics should ignore transnational aspects. In the later case, there are ways the Olympics can affect how membership in the state is perceived. For example, even countries with more ethnic understandings of citizenship have adapted in order to attract superstar athletes that do not fit the traditional understanding of national membership.[57]

Beyond the more exclusive transnational community of elite athletes and national identities, athletes, participants, and audiences are supposed to feel membership in an Olympic community. Sport is not only the prevue or language of elites. It has a potential to forge broader ties. This is particularly true of certain sports. Large numbers of people can watch and understand many of the sports in the Olympics. Speaking of soccer, one scholar writes that, "the use of English and vocabularies of science and mathematics must run football close for universality, but they remain the lingua francas of the world's elites, not of its masses."[58] Spectators can participate in the drama of sports. "Sport's popularity is a function of the inherent unpredictability of every contest, which produces genuine drama, and of its capacity to create a uniquely powerful emotional bond between spectators and participants."[59] There are conscious efforts to draw an ever-increasing audience to the Games. Olympic committees have even sought to stage events during the opening ceremonies that include audience participation.[60] Broadcasting rights to reach audiences at home must go to those who can guarantee free-to-all coverage and maximum reach.[61] These goals need not arise solely from cosmopolitan motivations but can derive from the desire to promote forms of mass consumption.[62] "As the twentieth century unfolded, commercial corporations increasingly recognized that few if any cultural forms have as much potential to be cosmopolitan as modern sports."[63] These commercial goals are a good example of why one ought to evaluate indirect rather than only intended effects of the Olympics.

Symbols and rituals are more direct attempts to represent the global Olympic community. "Much of the mass attention given to the Olympics is laid at the door of these alluring, consistent, and powerful rites, the closest we have been able to come to true world rituals."[64] Like the nation is an imagined community the world of sports becomes an "imagined world."[65] Although international governmental or non-governmental organizations rarely seem to develop rituals or ceremonies of this nature, the Olympics has its own flag, anthem, and even organizes the world under a single calendar. In fact, the flag, which Coubertin introduced in 1914, with its logo of five interlocking rings has become one of the most recognized flags in the world.[66] When the Olympic flag is raised, it flies above the flags of other nations. In the victory ceremonies each winner receives first symbols of the Olympic community, namely the medals and the olive branch, and only then is the nation of the victor honored.

True, this human community is not culturally neutral. European heritage remains predominant in understanding the Olympics, in part because the tradition of the Olympics arises from ancient Greece. During the Beijing Olympics one scholar observed, "the chorus that sang the Olympic anthem was young and dressed in white, symbolically de-orientalising a country that held fast to its magnificent antiquity but sought to conform to Western civilizational standards to march in the future."[67] While sports such as soccer or track and field events may be nearly universally understood this is not the case for all sports. Certain sports are tied to particular cultural backgrounds. Judo and Taekwondo have been introduced into the Games in order to include sports from other parts of the world.[68] Being slightly more open to the cultural diversity of sports allows for sharing traditions and learning from others in the athletic realm not simply through cultural shows. Even so it is difficult "to construct categorically different forms of body culture to those institutionalized by Western organizations like the IOC."[69] Evaluating the cosmopolitan shared identity effects of the Olympics over time requires considering how contributions of members from different parts of the world are incorporated.

To summarize, a transnational identity with an informal set of ethics exists among elite athletes—Olympians—that has some cosmopolitan implications even if this is a limited exclusive identity. A more general transnational Olympic community is represented through the use of symbols and rituals. Here the need to consider indirect effects becomes particularly interesting since the reasons for cultivating more global rituals or identities are not always necessarily cosmopolitan. Shared identity effects can emerge from partial identities or through cultivation of a common human community.

Public Sphere Effects

Finally, there is an approach to cosmopolitanism that focuses on how certain forms of public deliberation can generate cosmopolitan norms. Seyla Benhabib argues that, "discourse theory articulates a universalist moral standpoint, it cannot limit the scope of the *moral conversation* only to those who reside within nationally recognized boundaries; it must view the moral conversation as potentially extending to all of *humanity*."[70] Deliberative democratic cosmopolitans usually focus on political communities; however, transnational non-governmental associations can also be evaluated in terms of cosmopolitan public sphere effects even if they are not held to the same strict standards of deliberative ethics required in democratic political communities. Advocacy associations, for example, often seek to shock people or trigger certain emotional reactions rather than employ deliberative methods.[71] In staging protests or awareness-raising campaigns associations can start global discussion on issues that are being ignored in more formal forums of deliberation. One can therefore ask whether an association creates a space for public discussion (for example, international conferences or meetings), but also whether associations start global dialogue. The Olympics indirectly establishes a public sphere through the audience it attracts.

The IOC does create some spaces for discussion, although not public deliberation. Discussion occurs during the process of bidding to host the Olympic Games when cities must defend their claim to best embody Olympic ideals. In this process, debates can emerge over the best way to realize certain goals (for example, protecting the environment or human rights) both nationally and internationally. However, the IOC primarily emphasizes presenting a united front, and the goal of internal discussions is to arrive at one position. There are no minority reports and some issues are not made public at all. The Chinese bid for the 2008 Olympics, for example, was not made public. The IOC press office places tight control on what is released about IOC meetings. Critics of the IOC argue that "unregulated by democratic political processes or journalistic scrutiny, these transnational affinity groups have long served as refuges for the politically unsavory."[72] How deliberative this association is remains questionable.

The Olympics has indirectly been an arena which debates about the definitions of internationalism and sports have advanced in more inclusive cosmopolitan directions. One instance in which internal debates over membership led to cosmopolitan advances occurred when women demanded greater inclusion in the Olympic Games. Early stages of the internationalization of sports had led to the exclusion of women athletes as male athletes were considered symbols of national bravery and power.[73] The Olympics allowed a small women's program of sports deemed appropriate for women, such as figure skating. During the 1920s and 1930s, however, the International Women's Sports Federation put pressure on the Olympics to significantly expand its women's program. In 1922, it even hosted its own separate Women's Olympics. By 1928, it was able to negotiate the inclusion of more women's events in the Olympic program. The actions of this women's organization challenged the Olympics on its own terms—sports are not essentially gendered. In this instance, the Olympics indirectly provided a forum and a language within which debates over membership criteria led away from a more nationalist exclusive view and toward more inclusive Olympic Games. In instances like this even sports organizations can be places where understandings of internationalism and nationalism can be evaluated and debated.

The Olympics also indirectly results in public spheres beyond the institutions of the association as it became "a crucible of symbolic force into which the world poured its energies, and a stage upon which it plays out its hopes and its terrors every four years."[74] The audience the Olympics draws does not generate a formal public sphere for organized debate but it is a space for individuals to raise issues not directly initiated by the IOC. Bread not Circus, a coalition of community-based Olympic watchdog groups concerned with issues such as housing, homelessness, environmental damage, redevelopment, and other harmful social impacts of the Olympics, grew up in response to the Olympic Games.[75] Other associations like Amnesty International or Human Rights Watch also focus on exposing human rights violations that occur in conjunction with the Games. The IOC does not see these groups as partners in the Olympic public sphere.

An emphasis on unity has actually led the Olympics to attempt and remove political protest from touching the Games. The Olympics is a "sports group, organized and pledged to promote clean competition and sportsmanship. When we let politics, racial questions, religious or social disputes creep into our actions, we're in for trouble and plenty of it."[76] Yet, the IOC also appears to consider its political impact important in determining where to host the Games. When describing the reason for granting the 2008 Olympics to Beijing, the then IOC president Juan Antonio Samaranch argued that "many people say that we cannot give Olympic Games to Beijing because of the human rights, because they're not respecting human rights, but many other people, even the Dalai Lama, they say the Olympic Games will open the country and even the human rights can be much better than today."[77] Reform has occurred in the past. Only months before Seoul, South Korea was awarded the 1988 Games the highly repressive military regime had massacred hundreds of civilian protestors. In the lead up to the Games, domestic mobilization and protests garnered increased media attention. Faced with international questions over whether South Korea could hold successful Olympic Games, the regime gave in to the demands of protestors in June 1987 leading to the greatest democratic reforms in the country's history.[78] Such changes, however, should not be considered inevitable.

The spotlight will often result in critiques but how a country responds may differ. Due to outside pressure, China did make some changes to its foreign policy. Steven Spielberg, artistic advisor to the Olympic ceremonies, wrote to Chinese president Hu Jintao asking China to put pressure on the Sudanese government to allow in UN peacekeepers. China did change its position on peacekeepers. However, most internal human rights issues were not given the same attention despite international protest. "It is a mystery why the Chinese leaders and the IOC ever thought they could get away with throwing a party to celebrate China's accomplishments at which no one would mention China's shortcoming. . . . Evidently both parties were blinded by the claim of their own blarney, the line that sports is only sports."[79] Public criticism does not necessarily result in governments changing their policies, but the fact that criticism is considered warranted is relevant from a cosmopolitan perspective since it can generate public spheres.

An evaluation of the Olympics need not conclude that the Olympics must become an advocacy organization. The IOC could make associations that point out human rights violations partners with the job of ensuring human rights are not violated rather than considering them opponents or threats. Attempts to project a sense of complete unity at the expense of any debate undermine the cosmopolitan ideals of mutual understanding and cooperation that the Olympics seeks to foster. The Olympics, for example, requires countries not only to provide protection for athletes but also to guarantee that no protests are allowed near or in any Olympic venue. Requirements often remain in place around a venue well after the Olympics have left. Before the 2000 Olympics Sydney passed laws prohibiting speaking and the creation or distribution of political leaflets around Olympic venues in the name of Olympic security. The laws remained in place after the Olympic Games.[80] This has long-term negative effects on freedom of expression and freedom of association, both of which are liberties that cosmopolitans value as important to respecting the moral equality of individuals.

Internal discussions are cloaked in secrecy rather than being public. However, indirectly, the Olympics has generated public spheres; whether it be through athletes petitioning political leaders or Amnesty International reporting on human rights violations. The public sphere effects of the Olympics remain indirect and partial. Public sphere effects require evaluating both internal forms of deliberation and how an association responds to or cultivates public spheres beyond the association itself.

CONCLUSION: IMPLICATIONS OF THIS CASE

The Olympics is an interesting case of partial cosmopolitanism because, unlike other sports associations, the Olympic Games are steeped in ceremony and ritual with the goals of creating a transnational community and cultivating mutual understanding. Are these goals a sports association can hope to realize? Are the goals hampered by the presence of non-cosmopolitan components within the association? This chapter has aimed to defend the claim that a sports organization can advance cosmopolitanism in some ways.

Assessing the cosmopolitan potential of the Olympics means recognizing certain tensions between the cosmopolitan ideal of respecting moral equality of all humans and the non-cosmopolitan nationalistic aspects of the association. Developing a concept of indirect and partial cosmopolitanism enables recognition of an association's cosmopolitan effects despite such tensions. In fact, tensions may even result in advances to cosmopolitanism as was the case with the inclusion of a more extensive women's program in the Olympic Games. The commercial effects of the Olympics are also not motivated by moral respect but may have some indirect cosmopolitan effects. Maintaining certain values like fair play is important for the market value of the Olympics. Associations are dynamic entities that can be transformed. As has been suggested, the criteria may indicate possible ways an association could shift in cosmopolitan or non-cosmopolitan directions. What partial and indirect effects show, however, is that one ought not expect that associations will eliminate all tensions. An association need not be transformed into an advocacy organization in order to have cosmopolitan effects.

The Olympics demonstrates that cosmopolitans should think broadly about which transnational associations advance cosmopolitanism including associations not directly focused on advancing cosmopolitan principles. Shared rules, for example, need not arise only through formal political or economic institutions. In fact, the universal potential of sports rules may be lodged in their arbitrary nature. The rules of sports are also inclusive, applying to professional athletes but also potentially to anyone else playing the sport. They form a kind of common transnational language. Acknowledging others as participants in shared practices and the expectation of adherence to certain codes of conduct provide a framework within which individuals interact on grounds of greater equality and mutual respect. Cosmopolitans also have not often focused on the importance of rituals and symbols in developing a sense of inclusive transnational community. States have many rituals and symbols to reinforce a sense of community. What the Olympics demonstrates is that secular non-governmental associations can also achieve transnational solidarity based on a community with shared rituals.

Because the Olympic Games spread cosmopolitan norms and attitudes among those who play or watch the Games it can spread norms among individuals not already committed to cosmopolitan principles. Incorporating into cosmopolitan theory criteria based on developmental, institutional, shared identity, and public sphere effects can show how associations might indirectly advance cosmopolitanism. The public sphere effects of the Olympics are a key example of why an indirect conception of cosmopolitan effects is necessary to recognize how an association might advance moral equality. The potential of associations like the Olympics to promote cosmopolitanism does not rest in transforming sporting competitions into events that directly and intentionally seek to promote certain principled causes. Other associations may advance aspects of cosmopolitanism the Olympics does not. The Olympics should not be expected to usher in cosmopolitanism on its own. Recognizing that does not mean overlooking the contributions the Olympics has made and can make to advancing cosmopolitanism in the world.

NOTES

This chapter was originally published in *Global Society* 26, no. 4 (2012) available at www.tandfonline.com.

1. George Orwell, "The Sporting Spirit," in *Shooting an Elephant, and Other Essays* (New York: Harcourt, Brace & World, 1950), 152.

2. Andrew Jacobs, "Olympic Official Calls Protests a 'Crisis,'" *New York Times,* April 11, 2008.

3. Pierre de Coubertin, "The Olympic Games of 1896," *Century* 53, no. 1 (November 1896): 53.

4. John Keane, *Global Civil Society?* (Cambridge, UK: Cambridge University Press, 2003), 66.

5. Barry Smart, "Not Playing Around: Global Capitalism, Modern Sport and Consumer Culture," in *Globalization and Sport,* ed. Richard Giulianotti and Roland Robertson (Malden, MA: Blackwell Publishing, 2007), 14.

6. Mark E. Warren, *Democracy and Association* (Princeton, NJ: Princeton University Press, 2001).

7. Stuart Hall describes strong cosmopolitanism in the first quote from "Political Belonging in a World of Multiple Identities," in *Conceiving Cosmopolitanism: Theory, Context, and Practice,* ed. Steven Vertovec and Robin Cohen (New York: Oxford University Press, 2002), 26. David Miller defines weak cosmopolitanism in the second quote from *National Responsibility and Global Justice* (New York: Oxford University Press, 2007), 27.

8. See Craig Calhoun's discussion of soft cosmopolitanism in "The Class Consciousness of Frequent Travellers: Towards a Critique of Actually Existing Cosmopolitanism," in Vertovec and Cohen, *Conceiving Cosmopolitanism,* 109.

9. A few examples include: Simon Caney, *Justice Beyond Borders: A Global Political Theory* (New York: Oxford University Press, 2005); Simon Caney, "Cosmopolitan Justice and Cultural Diversity," *Global Society* 14, no. 4 (2000): 525–551; Kwame Anthony Appiah, *Cosmopolitanism: Ethics in a World of Strangers* (Princeton, NJ: W.W. Norton & Company, 2006); Thomas Pogge, "Cosmopolitanism and Sovereignty," *Ethics* 103, no. 1 (1992): 48–75.

10. John Hoberman, "Toward a Theory of Olympic Internationalism," *Journal of Sport History* 22, no. 1 (1995): 8.

11. Swantje Scharenberg, "Religion and Sport," in *The International Politics of Sport in the Twentieth Century,* ed. James Riordan and Arnd Krüger (New York: E & FN Spon, 1999), 91–93.

12. Ibid., 92.

13. Ibid.

14. Hoberman, "Toward a Theory of Olympic Internationalism," 71–72.

15. Richard Mandell, *The First Modern Olympics* (Berkeley: University of California Press, 1976), 123.

16. Paul Close, David Askew, and Xu Xin, *The Beijing Olympiad: The Political Economy of a Sporting Mega-Event* (New York: Routledge, 2007), 19.

17. John Rennie Short, *Global Metropolitan: Globalizing Cities in a Capitalist World* (New York: Routledge, 2004), 95.

18. Darrel Moellendorf, *Cosmopolitan Justice* (Cambridge, MA: Westview Press, 2002), 32.

19. Thomas Pogge, *World Poverty and Human Rights: Cosmopolitan Responsibilities and Reforms* (Malden, MA: Polity, 2002).

20. Charles Beitz, *Political Theory and International Relations* (Princeton, NJ: Princeton University Press, 1979), 166.

21. Quoted in John Hoberman, *The Olympic Crisis: Sport, Politics and the Moral Order* (New Rochelle, NY: Astride D. Caratzas, 1986), 57.

22. Quoted in Andrew Strenk, "What Price Victory? The World of International Sports and Politics," *Annals of the American Academy of Political and Social Science* 445 (1979): 135.

23. William J. Morgan, "Cosmopolitanism, Olympism, and Nationalism: A Critical Interpretation of Coubertin's Ideal of International Sporting Life," in *Rethinking the Olympics: Cultural Histories of the Modern Olympic Games*, ed. Robert K. Barney (Morgantown, WV: West Virginia University, 2010), 107.

24. Maurice Roche, "Mega-events and Modernity Revisited: Globalization and the Case of the Olympics," in *Sports Mega-Events: Social Scientific Analyses of a Global Phenomenon*, ed. John Horne and Wolfram Manzenreiter (Malden, MA: Blackwell Publishing, 2006), 32. Andrei S. Markovits and Lars Rensmann also discuss this in terms of the second wave of sports globalization in *Gaming the World: How Sports are Reshaping Global Politics and Culture* (Princeton, NJ: Princeton University Press, 2010), 26.

25. How sports can lead to a community of competitors is a theme in Barbara Keyes's book *Globalizing Sport: National Rivarly and International Community in the 1930s* (Cambridge, MA: Harvard University Press, 2006).

26. Ibid., 8.

27. Roger Levermore, "Sport's Role in Constructing the 'Inter-State' Worldview," in *Sport and International Relations: An Emerging Relationship*, ed. Roger Levermore and Adrian Budd (New York: Routledge, 2004), 27.

28. David Goldblatt, "The Odd Couple: Football and Global Civil Society," in *Global Civil Society 2006/2007*, ed. Mary Kaldor, Martin Albrow, Helmut Anheier, and Marlies Glasius (London: Sage Publications, 2007), 167.

29. Markovits and Rensmann, *Gaming the World*, 45.

30. Scharenberg, "Religion and Sport," 90.

31. David L. Andrews, "Coming to Terms with Cultural Studies," *Journal of Sport & Social Issues*, 26, no. 1 (2002): 116.

32. Martha Nussbaum, *Frontiers of Justice: Disability, Nationality, Species Membership* (Cambridge, MA: Belknap Press of Harvard University Press, 2006): 258, 410–412. Catherine Lu makes a similar point in "The One and Many Faces of Cosmopolitanism," *The Journal of Political Philosophy* 8, no. 2 (2000): 244–267.

33. Goldblatt makes this point with regard to football. "The Odd Couple," 167. It can be extended to sports more generally.

34. Pierre de Coubertin, "Sports as Peacemaker," in *Olympism: Selected Writings*, ed. Norbert Müller (Lausanne: International Olympic Committee, [1935] 2000), 241.

35. Ibid., 240.

36. Richard Giulianotti, "Human Rights, Globalization and Sentimental Education: The Case of Sport," *Sport in Society* 7, no. 3 (2004): 366.

37. Markovits and Rensmann, *Gaming the World*, 36.

38. Keyes, *Globalizing Sport*, 39.

39. Markovits and Rensmann, *Gaming the World*, 35.

40. Michael Payne, *Olympic Turnaround: How the Olympic Games Stepped Back from the Brink of Extinction to Become the World's Best Known Brand* (Westport, CT: Praeger, 2006), 278.

41. The IOC quoted in Kristine Toohey and A.J. Veal, *The Olympic Games: A Social Science Perspective* (New York: CABI Publishing, 2000), 60.

42. John J. MacAloon, "Double Visions: Olympic Games and American Culture," in *The Olympic Games in Transition*, ed. Jeffrey O. Segrave and Donald Chu (Champaign, IL: Human Kinetics Books, 1988), 290.

43. David R. Black and Janis Van Der Westhuizen, "The Allure of Global Games for 'Semi-Peripheral' Politics and Spaces: A Research Agenda," *Third World Quarterly* 25, no. 7 (2004): 1200.

44. Ibid., 1210.

45. John Hoberman, "Sportive Nationalism and Globalization," in *Post-Olympism? Questioning Sport in the Twenty-first Century,* ed. John Bale and Mette Krogh Christensen (New York: Berg, 2004), 183.

46. Sabine Selchow, "The 2008 Beijing Olympics: A 'Once-in-a-Lifetime Opportunity' for Global Civil Society," in *Global Civil Society 2007/2008*, ed. Mary Kaldor et al. (London: Sage, 2008), 88.

47. Appiah, *Cosmopolitanism*, 85.

48. Quoted in Jean M. Leiper, "Politics and Nationalism in the Olympic Games," in *The Olympic Games in Transition*, ed. Jeffrey O. Segrave and Donald Chu (Champaign, IL: Human Kinetics Books, 1988), 337.

49. Keyes, *Globalizing Sport,* 11.

50. Pere Miro, "Athletes in Olympic Ceremonies," in *Olympic Ceremonies: Historical Continuity and Cultural Exchange*, International Symposium on Olympic Ceremonies Barcelona—Lausanne, 1995, eds. Miquel de Moragas, John MacAloon, and Montserrat Llinés, (Lausanne: International Olympic Committee, 1996), 48.

51. Keyes, *Globalizing Sport,*14.

52. Toohey and Veal, *The Olympic Games*, 84.

53. World Olympians Association, "About the World Olympians Association," accessed May 3, 2008, http://www.woaolympians.com/index.php?action=kiir&id=woa.tpl. The WOA is not a formal part of the institutional structure of the IOC; however, the IOC does fund it.

54. "Team Darfur is an international coalition of athletes. . . . Team Darfur aims to educate the global public through the unique voice of elite athletes." Team Darfur, "About Us," accessed September 2008, http://www.teamdarfur.org/aboutus.

55. Rodanthi Tzanelli, "Mediating Cosmopolitanism: Crafting an Allegorical Imperative through Beijing 2008," *International Review of Sociology* 20, no. 2 (2010): 230.

56. Ibid., 217.

57. Markovits and Rensmann, *Gaming the World*, 34.

58. Goldblatt, "The Odd Couple," 163.

59. Keyes, *Globalizing Sport*, 8.

60. Amy Bass, "Objectivity Be Damned, or Why I go to the Olympic Games: A Hands-On Lesson in Performative Nationalism," *The South Atlantic Quarterly* 105, no. 2, (2006): 349–371.

61. "The IOC takes all necessary steps in order to ensure the fullest coverage by the different media and the widest possible audience in the world for the Olympic Games." *Olympic Charter*, July 7, 2007 (Lausanne: International Olympic Committee).

62. Smart,"Not Playing Around," 11.

63. Ibid., 24.

64. MacAloon, "Double Vision," 287.

65. Keyes, *Globalizing Sport*, 2.

66. Close, Askew, and Xin, *The Beijing Olympiad*, 19.

67. Tzanelli, "Mediating Cosmopolitanism," 233.

68. Susan Brownell, *Beijing's Games: What the Olympics Mean to China* (New York: Rowman & Littlefield, 2008), 51.

69. Giulianotti, "Human Rights, Globalization and Sentimental Education," 363.

70. Seyla Benhabib, *The Rights of Others: Aliens, Residents, and Citizens* (New York: Cambridge University Press, 2004), 4. Italics in the original.

71. A point that Mark E. Warren makes in discussing domestic associations in *Democracy and Association.*

72. Hoberman is referring specifically to the ties some IOC members had to the Nazis and other fascist regimes. Hoberman, "Toward a Theory of Olympic Internationalism," 35.

73. Leena Laine, "Women's Movements in Sports: National and International Issues," in *Crossing Borders: Remapping Women's Movements at the Turn of the 21st Century,* ed. H.R. Christensen, B. Halsaa, and A. Saarinen (Odense: University Press of Southern Denmark, 2004), 127.

74. John J. MacAloon, *This Great Symbol: Pierre de Coubertin and the Origins of the Modern Olympic Games* (Chicago: University of Chicago Press, 1981), 4.

75. For a discussion of critics see Helen Jefferson Lenskyj, "The Olympic Industry and Civil Liberties: The Threat to Free Speech and Freedom of Assembly," in *Sport, Civil Liberties, and Human Rights,* ed. Richard Giulianotti and David McArdle (New York: Routledge, 2006), 78–92.

76. Avery Brundage, IOC president from 1952 to 1972, quoted in Toohey and Veal, *The Olympic Games,* 81.

77. Bill Nichols, Vicki Michaelis, Paul Wiseman, "Why China is Likely to Land the Olympics, IOC Expected to Give 2008 Games to Beijing as an Incentive to Lift Repressive Rule," *USA Today,* July 9, 2001, 1A.

78. See Black and Westhuizen, "The Allure," 1211.

79. Andrew J. Nathan, " Medals and Rights: What the Olympics reveal, and conceal, about China," *The New Republic,* July 9, 2008, 46.

80. Lenskyj, "The Olympic Industry," 88.

SEVEN

Transnational Solidarity through Exclusion in the Anglican Communion Crisis

Recent dissent in the Anglican Communion poses a challenging test case for whether a cosmopolitan transnational community, in which all humans are respected as moral equals, can be advanced through indirect and partial expressions of cosmopolitanism. Conservative Anglicans from England as well as from the Episcopal Church of the United States of America (ECUSA), the official church of the Anglican Communion in the United States, have united globally with Anglicans from South America, Africa, and Asia in support of an interpretation of the Bible that excludes gay men and women from ordained ministry and same-sex marriage within the church.[1] This goal does not promote moral equality between those of different sexual orientations; however, for cosmopolitan theorists entirely to dismiss the effects of dissident Anglicans would be a mistake. Even cosmopolitans who hold the equality of sexual orientation as critical can learn lessons from studying the actions of these conservatives, particularly when it comes to the expansion of individual imagination and the strengthening of global ties across borders as well as divisions of wealth and race.

The Anglican Communion also represents a third type of transnational association relevant for cosmopolitanism, namely a religious association. This is not a type of association that is usually considered to be advancing cosmopolitan understandings of individual liberty. Commonly religious associations require members follow more robust conceptions of morality based on a specific way of life. Missionary activity, which I will discuss later, can be perceived to entail a presumption of the truth rather than a sense of fallibility. All of this may well be tolerable within cosmopolitanism's protection of individual liberty but it is not usually studied as a source for advancing cosmopolitanism in the world. Rather than evaluating the association's declared purpose in terms of whether it is compatible with cosmopolitan theory's core principles, I explore the association's effects. Specifically, does the association have effects that cultivate cosmopolitan norms and dispositions? Using the criteria I develop in chapter 4 I analyze the Anglican Communion in terms of (1) shifts in institutional structure, (2) impact on moral development, (3) creation of shared identities, and (4) formation of new spaces for discussion. In each case one can ask if the effects are cosmopolitan. It is important to determine not only whether shared identities, for example, are established but also whether the identities formed foster respectful reciprocal relations among members. Not all forms of solidarity are compatible with a cosmopolitanism that respects individual moral equality.

Applying cosmopolitan criteria to exclusive associations tests the possibility for associations to partially or indirectly advance expressions of cosmopolitanism. Exclusive associations may have limiting membership criteria (you must be a medical professional, an athlete, or believe in certain religious truths, in order to be a member), and they may not speak to all humanity. There are different kinds of exclusion exhibited in the Anglican example. On the one hand, there is an attempt to define roles such as bishop or priest to exclude women and non-celibate gay men. On the other hand, there is an attempt to advocate for laws penalizing gay or lesbian individuals. Both are forms of exclusion, but the first case does not violate human rights. So long as statements, such as "faithfulness to Christ means abstinence or celibacy,"[2] refer to religious rather than civil dictates, then human rights are not violated. Laws that call for the punishment of gay and lesbian individuals who are not celibate violate individual liberty that is vital to equal moral respect because individuals can no longer freely choose to reject the message by simply exiting the association. Anglican dissidents come very close to, and at times cross, the threshold of what cosmopolitanism will tolerate. But so long as groups do not cross the threshold, respect for freedom of association means allowing certain forms of exclusion or else one could not freely associate.[3] One "need not think these discriminations are morally benign" in order to conclude that they ought to be tolerated.[4] A question not usually asked is whether associations close to the threshold of toleration advance cosmopolitanism. This association will help to test the claim that associations can partially realize cosmopolitanism by satisfying only some of the criteria.

The Anglican Communion is a useful case precisely because it draws out tensions that can arise from partial forms of cosmopolitanism. There are clear cosmopolitan and non-cosmopolitan components to this association. Two tensions in particular bear on the indirect and partial nature of this association's cosmopolitan effects. One tension arises through trans-national ties being formed for the purpose of excluding gay men in rela-tionships from certain roles and rites in the association. It is true that a sense of transnational community is reinforced along with obligations to fellow Anglicans that cross national borders, but the cosmopolitan princi-ple of moral equality of all individuals is not advanced by discrimination based on sexual orientation. A second tension between cosmopolitan and non-cosmopolitan components of the association emerges out of liberal Anglican demands that the independence of the ECUSA be respected. Respect for individual liberty seems to come at the expense of cultivating a transnational community. Exploring liberal Anglican objections to the reverse missionary activity carried out by overseas bishops setting up missionary outposts in US parishes exposes some of their concerns with forming transnational allegiances.

Exploring recent changes within the Anglican Communion due to the controversy over what constitutes scripturally acceptable forms of hu-man sexuality show the complexity of evaluating associations' effects. They also show how associations that do not embrace cosmopolitan prin-ciples can nevertheless have partial expressions of cosmopolitanism, even if this is not the association's actual intention. Cosmopolitans, even liberal cosmopolitans who oppose conservative views on sexuality, ought to consider the implications of this case in order to understand why con-servatives in the Anglican Communion were so successful at uniting glo-bally. Even more so than in the case of the Olympics, the potential for spreading cosmopolitan norms among those not already committed to cosmopolitan principles lies in associations where support for cosmopoli-tanism cannot be presumed.

THE CASE OF THE ANGLICAN COMMUNION IN BRIEF

One reason the Anglican Communion serves as an interesting religious association to study is that it is undergoing shifts toward a more global organization and toward more global perspectives among its members. Unlike the Roman Catholic Church, with its long tradition of a global authority structure, provinces within the Anglican Communion have been largely autonomous and independent. Conservative members of the ECUSA, however, are invoking the global Communion in support of their cause. This differs from previous conservative Anglican dissidents who retreated into local communities.

The conservative or traditionalist dissatisfaction in the ECUSA did not begin from a global motivation or with the intent to form global relation-ships. It arose in response to a shift in the Episcopal leadership beginning in the mid-1960s toward greater emphasis on matters of social justice. Whether it was defenses of the ordination of women or use of gender-neutral language in prayer or the granting of same-sex marriages and the ordination of gay men, conservatives found these changes threatening. In the case of evangelical Episcopalians (a form of more conservative or traditionalist Episcopalianism) the threat was to the authenticity of Scripture, which forbid many of the changes. Evangelical Episcopalians read the Bible more literally. Although they were interested in social and political causes, those the ECUSA leadership was advocating were not in accordance with Scripture. For Anglo-Catholic Episcopalians (another conservative element within the ECUSA) the threat was to traditional practices and decreased the likelihood of forming connections to the Roman Catholic Church. Dissatisfaction and unhappiness grew greater in the 1970s and 1980s.[5] These two previously distinct groups (evangelical and Anglo-Catholic) found common ground in their rejection of what they considered the liberal or progressive agenda of the church leadership. Attempts to halt the new agenda failed. A critical example of this is the failure of the 1995 heresy trial a group of conservative bishops brought against Bishop Walter Righter. Bishop Righter was accused of teaching false doctrine because he approved the ordination of gay men, including those in a relationship. He had ordained Reverend Barry Stopfel, a non-celibate gay man, as deacon in the Diocese of Newark in 1990. The committee of bishops that heard the case dismissed the charges against Righter because ordaining a gay man did not violate any specific core doctrine of the church. Previous resolutions opposing such ordinations, it was argued, were not to be enforced as law but rather viewed as advisory.[6] The ECUSA's General Convention would have to revise canon law to forbid such ordinations.[7] Stymied in their attempts to reform the Episcopal Church from within, conservative dissidents turned to conservative Anglicans in Africa, South America, and Asia for support in their attempts to halt the practices of ordaining gay bishops and the blessing of same-sex marriages.

At the 1998 Lambeth Conference (an international conference of Anglicans hosted every ten years at the University of Kent by invitation of the Archbishop of Canterbury) efforts were made to shift Communion policy in the direction of banning ordinations of non-celibate gay men. Conservatives and their allies were able to pass a resolution that includes the following language:

- "the teaching of Scripture, upholds faithfulness in marriage between a man and a woman"
- "while rejecting homosexual practice as incompatible with Scripture, [Scripture] calls on all our people to minister pastorally and sensitively to all irrespective of sexual orientation"
- "We must confess that we are not of one mind about homosexuality."

- "The challenge to our Church is to maintain its unity while we seek, under the guidance of the Holy Spirit, to discern the way of Christ for the world today with respect to human sexuality."[8]

However, Lambeth resolutions, including this one on human sexuality, are only advisory. As a result, despite the resolution, Gene Robinson, a gay man living with a partner, was elected to be bishop in New Hampshire. In protest conservative dissidents began to break with the Episcopal Church. At one point sixty-five of the approximately 7,600 parishes in the ECUSA had left to become missionary outposts appointed by sympathetic archbishops from abroad.[9] These churches became members of the Anglican Mission in America (AMiA).

The conservative movement began to form global ties in order to pressure the ECUSA by claiming support from the wider Communion rather than out of any cosmopolitan motivations. However, the implications of their actions extend well beyond the domestic agenda of reforming the ECUSA. In order to determine the association's cosmopolitan impact I will apply my criteria to the case of this moment in the Anglican Communion. Associations are dynamic entities, as I have already mentioned, so one can only really evaluate an association at a particular point and time. This dissident movement in the Anglican Communion serves as a good case for illustrating what partial and indirect cosmopolitanism might look like in each category of effects.

DETERMINING COSMOPOLITAN EFFECTS

Institutional Effects

As I did with the other two cases, I will begin assessing the potential cosmopolitanism of this association by looking at its institutional effects. These effects could be cosmopolitan in two ways. First, changes in an association's institutions or organization could make its structure more cosmopolitan in the sense of less oriented toward national distinctions. Transnational institutions may generate cosmopolitan obligations due to the cross-border relations among members. The second way an institutional effect could meet cosmopolitan criteria would be if an association institutionalizes rules or standards that help to advance cosmopolitan norms.

The Anglican Communion has had an international organizational structure for centuries. The worldwide association of Anglican churches was spread globally as part of the British Empire with centers of power emerging in the United Kingdom and later in the United States. The international structure that unites the different parts of the Anglican Communion has been understood as a loose connection of independent local provinces. The international ties are that of a global communion of

churches not a global church. Regular international conferences, such as
the Lambeth Conference, are opportunities for bishops from different
parts of the Communion to discuss theology and other common concerns
in order to provide consultation and guidance to the Communion as a
whole. Liberal Anglicans defend a view of the Communion as based on
independent provinces without a strong hierarchical structure. The loose
institutional structure is seen as protecting the value of "inclusion as the
broad intention" of an Anglican concept of justice.[10] This allows for the
inclusion of an array of practices across different provinces. Some provinces permit while others forbid, for example, the ordination of women
clergy. Liberal Anglicans are also increasingly wary of missionary activity because it is seen as interfering in another province's internal affairs.
When the controversy over the scriptural status of homosexuality arose
during the 1998 Lambeth Conference, liberals sought to protect the
autonomy of provinces to determine such matters on their own.[11]

Acting on their understanding of independence, the Episcopal leadership felt free to endorse the election of Gene Robinson, a gay man, as
Bishop of New Hampshire in 2003. They did so despite the Lambeth
resolution, which rejected "homosexual practice" as incompatible with
Scripture.[12] In the view of one member from a Church of England parish
with a "reputation for engaging in social justice issues":[13] why should
anyone "refuse to allow the American church to elect a gay bishop if they
so wish." Stopping them, the parishoner continued, is actually "forcing
them culturally," which is "what you're saying that the American church
is doing."[14] The view of a bishop from the Province of Southeast Asia
was quite different. The election of Gene Robinson was arrogant and
disrespectful. He argued that "knowing the gravity of the matter, [ECU-
SA] did not deem it necessary to seriously seek and consult the wider
body of the Communion" continuing that such a "callous process of non-
consultation . . . cannot but be seen as arrogant, with total disregard and
contempt for the sacramental unity of the Communion."[15] Even the then
Archbishop of Canterbury Rowan Williams, who was sympathetic to the
liberal position, felt the "reason for the ECUSA's deviance, as he and
many others saw it, was that the American church does not care about
the rest of the world. ECUSA was behaving like President Bush!"[16]
Claims that liberals do not care about the world are exaggerated. After
all, their actions could be seen as privileging toleration of certain forms of
diversity rather than rejection of diversity. The crux of the matter is that
according to critics, progressives were seen to "act locally without thinking globally."[17]

Just as parishes with a liberal orientation began taking a more local
focus, conservative evangelical Episcopalians were increasing their missions abroad. This provided a basis for global ties among conservative
dissidents in North America and bishops from the global South.[18] These
ties among conservatives are novel in significant ways. Rather than

breaking off from the local church, as was the pattern for dissident movements in the past, or seeking aid externally from other denominations, conservatives have chosen to keep their focus within the Anglican Communion but have looked beyond their local communities to form institutional relations with members of the global Communion.[19] They saw possibilities in calling on the vast numbers of Anglicans in countries of the global South, because many Anglicans there were more culturally conservative on issues of sexuality. There were more Anglicans in Kenya, roughly 3 million, than in the ECUSA, roughly 2.2 million. In Uganda there are about 9 million Anglicans and in Nigeria there are between 17 and 20 million Anglicans.[20] In fact, there is speculation that some of these former colonial churches now wield more power within the Communion than the British or North American churches.[21] This goes a bit far. Anglicans from England and the United States are still powerful figures within the Communion. However, profound changes are occurring as conservative Anglicans alter how they perceive the institutional structures of the Communion.

One of these profound changes relevant to a discussion of cosmopolitanism is the new tendency to invoke claims to global obligations. In the words of Archbishop Akinola: "those dioceses most tempted to indulge themselves with unilateral actions, taken without consulting the wider Communion, seem so often to be among those materially most advantaged, and to be in the global north. Should this not occasion reflection? Do we not see here . . . a new imperialism?"[22] The shift from a view of independence and non-interference to a view of Anglicans as a global family with obligations to intervene irrespective of geography represents a shift toward a more cosmopolitan way of viewing transnational relations. This shift arose for strategic reasons rather than cosmopolitan reasons but generated a more cosmopolitan view of institutional relations in the association. The language conservatives employ includes the "vehement insistence that their problems are of global relevance and require global responses," evidenced by "invocations of the 'global,' the 'Two-Thirds World,' the 'worldwide,' and the heightened level of talk about the Anglican Communion."[23] A global accountability view challenges Anglicans not to ignore the situation of others beyond their borders and to make the needs of others a concern for all.[24]

These changes were institutional as well as rhetorical. Also passed at Lambeth 1998 was Resolution 3.6, which "imbues the archbishops of the Anglican Communion with heretofore unheard of pan-Anglican authority and power."[25] Conservative Episcopalians, who were not receiving support at home where they were in the minority, claimed that those outside the United States had an obligation to hear and respond to their cries for assistance in reforming the wayward Episcopal Church. The actions of churches in one province should be answerable to the whole Communion. Henry Orombi, a Ugandan bishop, put it in these terms:

"bishops in America are one part of the Anglican Communion. Whatever they do should be found acceptable within the wider church. . . . We are not local priests, we are global priests."[26] In doing so Orombi differs considerably from the position expressed by the local Church of England parishioner quoted earlier arguing that provinces should be allowed to make their own choices without interference.[27]

Although conservatives argued that global obligations entailed chastising the ECUSA for certain liberal beliefs and practices, this need not be the specific transnational obligation that arises from invoking the global Communion. Liberal Anglicans could adopt a view of transnational obligations and direct it toward defending a different set of obligations such as respect for the equality of those with different sexual orientations. This would enable liberals to embrace a cosmopolitan shift in institutional relations without adopting an opposition toward homosexuality. In fact, liberal Anglicans support issues that benefit from being conceived in terms of transnational obligations such as debt relief and other global poverty issues. This requires moving away from a stance emphasizing local independence and isolation. It also requires liberals defend their views on the global level. It may even entail reshaping the role of missionary work in creating transnational institutional relations. In 2003 the Standing Commission on World Mission challenged churches like the ECUSA by "calling for dramatically enhanced forms of worldwide companionship."[28]

The case of the Anglican Communion dissidents represents a particularly challenging example of how tensions can arise between cosmopolitan effects (here institutional ones) and non-cosmopolitan effects. This becomes particularly evident when turning to the second cosmopolitan criterion, namely institutionalizing cosmopolitan rules or standards. Here a significant tension emerges in the actions of conservative Anglicans. They formed transnational communities across borders, race, and wealth in order to support discrimination against gay men and women. The resolution the conservative dissidents institutionalized at the 1998 Lambeth conference, Resolution 1.10, declares homosexual practices incompatible with Scripture. This establishes discrimination based on sexual orientation within the association, which does not extend liberal cosmopolitan theory's principle of individual liberty to those with different sexual orientations. Although cosmopolitan principles are not violated, they are not promoted.

In exploring this tension—forming transnational ties to institutionalize forms of discrimination within the association—it is important to remember that the Anglican Communion is a voluntary association. Those not happy with the rules of the organization are free to leave. As I argued in chapter 1, the understanding of cosmopolitanism I employ requires protecting individual freedom to join non-liberal associations as long as the association does not prevent individuals from acting on their individual liberties. No one has a human right to be an Anglican priest or bishop, and no one has a human right to be married in an Anglican wedding ceremony. It is certainly the perspective of some conservative dissidents that the disagreement is over the rules and rights of membership within the association (not civil legislation). The disagreement is over biblical interpretation, more specifically "two mutually exclusive accounts of Christian theology and the Church."[29] In fact, "the church's view on the matter [of homosexuality] affects neither most of the non-church attending population, nor a majority of secular gays."[30] Even the statements made by church leaders that oppose homosexual practices make the specifically religious element clear: "I think homosexuality is the presenting issue of a much deeper problem, which is how faithful to the teaching of the Bible will the church be?"[31]

Some members of the conservative movement do go too far, becoming a threat to cosmopolitanism by advocating for the institutionalization of laws that violate respect for moral equality. The former Archbishop of Nigeria, Akinola, a powerful conservative leader, supported legislation in Nigeria that makes same-sex relationships (including public displays of affection) punishable through civil law.[32] This was also the case in Uganda. In fact, "American missionaries wrote and promoted Uganda's nefarious 'Kill the Gays' bill."[33] While such laws violate a principle that individual basic liberties ought to be protected no matter an individuals' sexual orientation, Akinola's actions or those of some missionaries do not necessarily mean the whole conservative movement should be dismissed as anti-cosmopolitan. These examples do serve as an important caution that if actions begin to violate human rights or advocate for their violation, then transnational ties can cease to have even indirect and partial cosmopolitan effects.

Despite failing to institutionalize rules that advance a norm of respecting individuals with different sexual orientations, even analyzing just this one type of effect—institutional effect—shows how an association could partially advance cosmopolitan norms and also do so indirectly. An organization professing non-cosmopolitan values (as opposed to the anti-cosmopolitan actions of those legalizing bans on homosexuality) can nevertheless generate institutional cosmopolitan effects by invoking a new understanding of obligations as transnational. This need not be motivated by a desire to unite globally for its own sake. A great deal is missed by simply determining whether the association's purpose is tolerable or not. What this association illustrates is the complexity of assessing transnational associations' effects.

Developmental Effects

Evaluating the developmental effects of an association shifts the focus from the implications of institutional arrangements to the impact associa-

tions have on individual moral development. One can assess the cosmopolitan potential of an association's effects on individuals in two ways.
First, does the association expand the imagination of its members to recognize commonalities among fellow humans that assist in the recognition
of moral equality? Second, does an association cultivate in individuals a
sense that they are or can be transnational actors by shifting their perspective to see opportunities in transnational terms or even recast local
concerns within a transnational framework? In evaluating the impact of
associations on the disposition of individuals it is also worth considering
whether the effects are only felt by elites or by the broader membership
of an association. It is precisely the broad effect that the dissident Anglican movement has on ordinary Anglicans that makes it a significant case
to explore.

Conservatives generated the first kind of cosmopolitan developmental
effect by creating opportunities for members to expand their imaginations beyond their national or local churches. This is particularly the case
in churches that left the ECUSA to officially become missionary outposts
of African parishes. In US churches that joined African parishes, church
meetings started to include readings of political news related to the
African country of their new bishop. This cultivated a greater awareness
of fellow Anglicans beyond their local church. Some parishioners even
traveled to Africa. While these were not necessarily parish-sponsored
trips, anthropologist Miranda Hassett describes how "the whole congregation experienced intensified learning about Rwanda by participating in
preparations for the trip and especially by hearing about the journey
afterward through the number of sermons, special presentations, and
discussions."[34] Even though only three Americans from a parish went on
a trip to the new home parish of Kigali, Rwanda, the congregation back at
home was impacted.

The impact of these travels developed more cosmopolitan attitudes
toward African Anglicans. Talking with Rwandan Anglicans was a learning experience that strengthened relationships across global cleavages of
wealth, culture, and race helping to overcome certain stereotypes. In
many cases the conservative American parishes were wealthy, largely
white communities. Now they were reaching out and finding commonalities with poorer African communities. Hassett recorded the following
remarks make by parishioners in a US church under the Archbishop of
Rwanda. One parishioner commented that "'most folks here only know
Africa as Africa, and the people there are dark skinned, and they'd heard
about the genocide' but, he explained, once the Rwandan church helped
them in their difficulties, they began to see the Rwandans as human
beings and to care about what had happened to them."[35] Another said,
"she thinks a lot of people 'have a wrong conception about Africa as a lot
of black people running around' and that meeting people like John [a
visiting priest from Nigeria] and Archbishop Kolini helps Americans re-

alize that Africans are 'just like us, or even a little better.'" In language that certainly still has patronizing tones, these parishioners argue that they began to see Africans as human beings. The development of cosmopolitan attitudes is limited because the effects on individuals remain indirect and partial. Travelers to Africa were not interested in learning about others as such and they traveled to communities that shared their theological views. Yet, this did have some impact on expanding imaginations and reshaping the Americans' view of fellow Anglican Africans.

The second key developmental impact of the association affected the clergy in particular, especially bishops from the global South. They have developed an increased sense of empowerment within the international association of the Anglican Communion. Associations can function as places for global empowerment even if these associations are not formal political or economic institutions. It is only recently that many African bishops have felt that they were able to navigate and have influence on the international level of the Communion.[36] In the past, bishops from the global South often felt powerless and alienated from the rest of the Communion. The difficulty in navigating international conference procedures with specific rules for debate and participation led one Ugandan Anglican to comment: "this is not our way of doing things, so we just leave you to it."[37] It is certainly the case that historically the leadership and power have been concentrated in the ECUSA and the Church of England. During the 1978 Lambeth Conference, Archbishop of Nigeria Joseph Adetiloye had to stand at the microphone for twenty minutes refusing to be seated before the chair recognized him, but he predicted that "in ten years, when African bishops come to the microphone at this conference, we will be so numerous and influential that you will have to recognize us."[38]

The feeling of powerlessness has shown signs of dissipating. In February 1997 bishops and archbishops from the global South gathered in Kuala Lumpur to create their own agenda that spoke to their views on issues such as: witnessing to injustice, mission, relation to other faiths, the role of youth, the place and role of diversity, the family, and human sexuality.[39] Conservative dissidents in the United States picked up on similarities to their own views and held an international conference in September 1997 in Dallas, Texas, to coordinate with bishops from the global South. The goal was to teach the Lambeth procedures and how to maneuver within the Anglican Communion's bureaucratic institutions. Conservative groups such as the American Anglican Council (AAC), which helped to organize the Dallas conference, hoped to "bring Anglican bishops from around the world for teaching missions in the USA" and to "provide opportunities for AAC parishes to broaden their experience of our global Anglican Fellowship."[40] The immediate goal was to strategize for the upcoming Lambeth. The result was that at the Lambeth Conference a year later, in 1998, conservatives from the global North and South were able to pass a resolution that declared homosexual practices incompatible with Scripture—Resolution 1.10. The resolution even refers to the Kuala Lumpur Conference.

The development of a sense of efficacy as global actors extends beyond Lambeth 1998. Conferences and ties formed among bishops of the global South help in developing their own agenda and finding solutions to similar problems that confront them. A sense of greater empowerment can also help overcome the colonial heritage of relations within the Communion. Travel throughout the Communion, for example, ought to aim "to cross-pollinate. . . . The West come to the South, the South go to the West, West go to the East, let's move around, let's influence each other!"[41] Of course existing balances of power continue to be far from equal. Some bishops still feel as though members from the United States and England are forcing particular agendas on them. After all, African bishops were not primarily interested in pursuing the issue of homosexuality before international alliances were formed. Nevertheless, there are significant indications that Anglicans in the global South are beginning to feel that they can influence decisions made in the Communion.

In summary then, there are some limited elements of both types of developmental effects. Increased awareness of certain commonalities with Africans has developed in some congregations. Leaders from the global South are also learning skills and expanding their international agency within institutional structures. Issues are being crafted in regional and transnational terms.

Shared Identity Effects

Cultivating a shared identity among members of an association involves drawing on commonalities, but it also aims to generate a sense of shared community among members. Therefore, while a developmental impact could potentially be realized through learning about others without direct interaction, shared identity effects imply a sense of community or solidarity, which often involves shared practices, symbols, traditions, and ties of identity. Cosmopolitan criteria for evaluating shared identities entail exploring not only the scope of the identity formed by also whether ties of community are based on terms of mutual respect and reciprocity rather than paternalism and charity.

Anglicanism is a transnational identity that has existed for centuries, but the sense of what that entails—the ties and community it describes— is changing. There has been a much greater emphasis on transnational rather than local or national church identity, and there is also a change in how relations between members across the Communion are perceived. The conservative American parishes that joined African parishes took this the farthest, rejecting geographic designations in favor of ties of affinity. Developmentally this has the effect of educating individuals to recognize that there are others beyond their borders with certain commonalities. It has also resulted in an interest in and feeling of connection with African Anglicans that is better understood in terms of a shared identity effect. Parishioners buy African art from the East African Market to decorate their homes. "We are all Africans," declared a guest preacher at a parish in the United States that was now under the province of the Archbishop of Rwanda.[42] As mentioned under developmental effects, some parishioners even travel to Africa. There they meet fellow Anglicans and share in spiritual communion.

The comments of a few parishioners indicate a sense of renegotiating their identity as Anglicans now that they are a part of African provinces, although this should not be understood to mean that local identities become irrelevant. In a passage meant to demonstrate the force of local ties the idea that this could be overcome by travel appears as a side note. "I think that most [parishioners] would have only an awareness that we're part of a wider whole but it doesn't really feature in people's lives . . . unless people have travelled . . . widely and gone specifically also to Anglican Churches in other countries."[43] While perhaps only a minor step in the direction of greater moral equality and transnational community, travel due to new institutional relationships can be a partial step in the direction of more cosmopolitan identities. Moreover, it is a step that liberals who place less emphasis on travel and missionary activity may fail to fully recognize. Confronting challenging disagreements within the association can be helped by "committed (and preferably delighted) experience in some African community."[44] This experience is hampered if avoiding "colonialist intrusions" results in a "refusal of relationship" leaving people unconnected rather than members of a shared liturgical family.[45]

Moreover, what ought to be noted about the relationships and identities being formed among the conservatives is that these often involve the construction of new identities. As already mentioned some of the alliances are bridging internal divides between evangelical and Anglo-Catholic Episcopalians as well as across borders. The intent is to overcome differences through the construction of a new identity of Anglican Orthodoxy, which "becomes a means of bringing together groups which would have previously had little common cause."[46] This new identity also involves the construction of the opposition identity. The danger is that such opposition can become so entrenched that it hampers discourse. Amartya Sen's work on identity and violence warns of the dangers of identities that bifurcate instead of unite. He argues that identity must be seen as flexible and changing or else it can become a source of division.[47] Bishop Timothy explains that issues like homosexuality may not be the primary source of conflict (he sees underlying views of the Scripture as more central); nevertheless, they can "have a visceral connection with identity . . . with who people are. So they are nonnegotiable."[48] Once identities become non-negotiable they can lose the potential to have cosmopolitan effects. Identity, cultural cosmopolitans tell us, should not be presented as non-negotiable.

Because identities can change, cosmopolitan potential is still possible. It is important to build reciprocal relations across global divisions of vast wealth disparities and historical relations of colonialism. This requires that members recognize different contributions to the Communion as valuable. This is a challenge when dealing with communities of vastly different wealth and resource distribution. Much of the funding poorer parishes receive comes from North America or Britain. Such one-directional giving can result in one-sided power structures in which some feel beholden to others rather than equal to or full members in the association. After Lambeth 1998, accusations were made that African bishops had their votes bought by rich conservatives in the North. This certainly indicates how unequal relations can generate divisions or tensions within the association no matter if the perspectives of vote buying are right or wrong.[49] In some cases, liberal Anglicans have undermined the possibility of relationships based on respect through their paternalistic attempts to absolve African bishops of their arguments against homosexuality as being motivated by an eagerness to "assert themselves in the presence of their former 'masters.'"[50]

Some forms of reciprocity do emerge. Rwandan Anglicans are seen as helping Americans. North Americans traveling to Africa often had the goal of establishing channels of charitable giving, in which Africans were to play the passive role of recipient. However, traveling to African communities changed views. Through conversation with African Anglicans, one parishioner describes how "I felt like they taught me so much more than I could give them."[51] The visits led to discussions on theology as well as broader church needs, far beyond the material needs of the African hosts. As a result, American and African Anglicans came to recognize similarities and commonalities across cleavages where there had not been much interaction let alone interaction on terms of equality. This speaks to the importance of travel and conversation rather than simply learning about others from books or media outlets. Through travel and face-to-face interaction there was a shift in the perception of the Province of Rwanda "that used to be an abstraction. It no longer is. Being part of the Province of Rwanda is a very special gift."[52]

While the institutional effects of transnational ties focus on who owes what based on one's respective place in the institutional relations of the association, building community focuses on the contributions members make to other members in the community. Shared identities can bridge differences by building relations of greater respect. In the words of one American Anglican talking about African Anglicans: "They're black, yeah, but they're faithful!"[53] The idea that Africans have something to contribute to the conservative cause is significant in building a sense of empowerment but also in fostering a sense of community. African bishops provide conservatives with spiritual support by consecrating bishops, preaching, administering sacraments, as well as generally providing moral support. This establishes a more reciprocal relation between American and African co-religionists. It is not merely a relationship of benefactor to recipient.

There are limits to the cosmopolitan nature of the shared identity formed. It should be noted that in certain cases the members of US churches under African bishops still see their primary ties to the Anglican Mission in America, or other local associations, not to the Rwandan church. There are also still substantial prejudices to be overcome before the identity of "fellow Anglican" becomes a shared identity based on complete mutual respect. New prejudices also pose a problem. In the rhetoric conservative dissidents employ, Africans are sometimes presented as better than the Americans: poverty and hardship are seen as making for a more pure practice of Christian values.[54] This highlights the stereotypical way in which Africa is still viewed, even though the stereotype might have shifted. African Anglicans must also be careful that they do not make the basis of their new identity a claim about purity in contrast to the decadent West. Such vague and sweeping distinctions could hamper their relations with Western Anglicans. Despite these obstacles there can be some cosmopolitan potential through perceiving one another as part of a transnational community of co-religionists with different meaningful ways of contributing to the community.

Public Sphere Effects

The last category of effects deals with whether associations contribute to public spheres of discussion. Cosmopolitanism does not require or entail that members of the group agree on all issues or represent complete unity. Deliberation not consensus is the focus of this category of effects. Therefore, even considering an association like the Anglican Communion, which is undergoing tense debates, is relevant. There are two ways in which one can evaluate associations' contributions to deliberation and debate on the global level. One can ask: Does an association introduce issues into global debate that spread cosmopolitan norms, thereby shaping transnational public opinion? Introducing new issues is not a significant impact of the conservative Anglican movement. The association is attempting to engage in a discussion of human sexuality, but not necessarily in ways that advance cosmopolitan norms. More importantly in this case is the possibility that an association could establish a separate sphere of deliberation by creating a space for discussion—the second criterion. In this case, one can ask whether an association creates a space for deliberation within the association itself and/or cultivate skills of public deliberation. As the conservative movement seeks to advance its own goals, deliberation and debate spring up within the shared organizational structures of the Anglican Communion.

The Anglican Communion has institutions and organizations within which to hold deliberation and within which groups form to represent their views. Conferences can serve as gathering places where individuals talk to one another even without the expectation of reaching consensus. Archbishop of Wales Barry Morgan describes Lambeth Conferences as places of interaction in a setting that encourages conversation. Morgan stresses the importance of informal conversations. This also harkens back to Kwame Anthony Appiah's idea that cosmopolitanism is about engagement with others. Here is what Morgan says about Lambeth conversations.

> You realize when you come here why the Anglican Communion matters, as old friendships are renewed and new ones are forged from people who on the face of it have very little in common but who are fellow members of the Body of Christ. . . . People underestimate the value of talking leisurely and at length to all sorts of people. No doubt that has helped to lessen the tensions.[55]

New spheres for discussion have emerged in addition to the existing conferences. Pre-Lambeth Conferences have helped to build a greater sense of global agency and have also established new traditions of international meetings, which conservatives built on with their own conferences. There has also been increased global activity among gay and lesbian Anglican activists in response to conservative actions. These activist organizations hold their own meetings, issue reports, and contribute to blogs (for example, the liberal blog "Thinking Anglicans"). The Alliance of Lesbian and Gay Anglicans works "for the unconditional inclusion and full participation of lesbian and gay people in every facet of the Church's life throughout the Anglican Communion," and the International Gay and Lesbian Christian Network "promotes broadening the discussion regarding lesbian and gay Christians within the WCC [World Council of Churches] and within the Council's member churches."[56] A flurry of debates and discussion within the Communion has emerged from conservative dissidents' actions on human sexuality. The indirect result is a flourishing of norms of activism and, in some cases, new forums for deliberation all of which contribute to a practice of transnational dialogue.

However, there are limits to the cosmopolitan potential of the spaces for discussion formed around the debates on homosexuality. First of all, discussions outside of key Communion meetings, like Lambeth, often occur among those with similar beliefs rather than among those with different views. A more global vision is not necessarily more cosmopolitan in all respects. It would be worrisome, from a cosmopolitan perspective, if the dissidents' attempts to define Anglicanism did not allow for any internal disagreement on issues of theology or the ethics of social practices. Not that this would prevent all cosmopolitan effects but it would certainly hamper public sphere effects. The National Evangelical Anglican Congress gathering in September 2003 wanted "to demonstrate Evangelicalism's vibrancy and unity, and indeed the organizers went out of the way to discourage a diversity of opinion. . . . The message was clear: Evangelicals had to be all of one mind to face the threats confronting them and their beliefs."[57] In June 2008, a group of conservatives boycotted the Lambeth meeting in favor of holding their own conference, the Global Anglican Future Conference, GAFCON. It was held in Jerusalem, one month before Lambeth. GAFCON reaffirmed participants' "Christian faith as it relates to some prime topics: Anglican identity and orthodoxy, the Lordship of Jesus Christ and its implications for personal morality and missions, and the whole issue of authority, Christ's authority in the church and the authority of the Bible."[58] Attending conferences like this in lieu of Lambeth hampers deliberation with those who are not of like mind. Conferences among only like-minded individuals can undermine cosmopolitan goals of cultivating mutual understanding instead creating battle lines that become harder and harder to cross. The fact that the conservative movement is being challenged shows that different sides on the controversy over the relationship between homosexuality and Scripture are still participating in the debate. Some norms of deliberation and active participation are still present.

Liberals have not ceded the global arena and did attend Lambeth 2008, but there is a possibility that liberal Anglicans might retreat when they see their view losing ground. Shifts in the Communion seem to threaten their positions most. Talking about the shift from colonial relations with the global South to a post-colonial Communion, one American Anglican writes, "transitions in the Anglican world are terrifying, especially for those of us who historically have been the most privileged, most in control, most secure in the colonial Enlightenment world."[59]

If liberals retreat from global discussion, then public sphere effects would be undermined just as if conservatives stifle discussion in the name of unity.

One very interesting project that has emerged from the crisis in the Anglican Communion is the Continuing Indaba project, which facilitates conversation based in an idea of mission. As described on the project's website, it aims "to enable Anglicans worldwide to live reconciliation by facing our own conflicts, celebrate our diversity and difference and so become agents of God's reconciling Mission in the world."[60] This project is particularly interesting from a cosmopolitan perspective because it aims to foster conversations across cultures based not on Western foundations of deliberative democracy but on Indaba, a Zulu word "describing a community process for discernment on matters of significance."[61] The aim of Indaba "is to further community life, not to solve issues.

Continuing Indaba uses journeys to establish relationships and build community so that genuine conversation on matters of significance can energize mission."[62] The project was developed through the work of theologians from Africa, Asia, North America, the West Indies, and the United Kingdom. It works by connecting three dioceses from different Provinces. Then local clergy and lay members at each site are brought together in facilitated conservations through which they "will encourage and challenge one another in order to further mission in each place."[63] Resources will be exchanged to provide context for the different cultural backgrounds of contributing members. In the words of Archbishop Paul Kwong, Primate, Hong Kong Sheng Kung Hui, "The Indaba process also encourages genuine conversation across differences. It seeks to build trust and . . . emphasizes mutual and intense listening to deeply held opinions and a willingness to dig deeper in order to find the shared values that lie at the root of our common faith."[64] Although this may not serve as an example of building large public spheres that shape public opinion on the global level, this models a kind of conversation that fits well with cosmopolitan goals of developing ways to encourage conversation with strangers in a respectful manner.

Without the ability to engage in conversation, it will be impossible to solve common concerns and build communities rooted in mutual understanding. Indaba conversation aims to build community outside the traditional forms of authority as well as across the global North and global South cleavage, fostering "deep relationships between Anglicans in different parts of the Communion, based on an experiential knowledge of the contexts in which other participants live."[65] Projects such as this contribute interesting ways of understanding what creating a cosmopolitan public sphere for ethical dialogue could look like. They also serve as potential counterbalances to actions that seek to create deliberation among those who think alike.

CONCLUSION: IMPLICATIONS OF THE CASE

Applying the cosmopolitan criteria to different associational effects shows that associations like the Anglican Communion with non-cosmopolitan components can nevertheless have lessons for cosmopolitans. Conservative Anglican dissidents have worked to build transnational ties of solidarity. In doing so they have indirectly helped members to recognize certain commonalities across borders and taken partial steps toward increasing some forms of mutual respect through reciprocal relations. Anglicans from the global South have gained a greater sense of themselves as active participants within the international structure of the Communion rather than mainly being perceived as recipients of Northern largesse. However, because these effects are only partially cosmopolitan, significant tensions remain. Conservative Anglicans build new institutional relations in order to exclude gay men as well as women from aspects of membership. This hampers institutionalization of cosmopolitan norms of equal respect. If conservatives seek to dampen discussion in the name of unity or liberals retreat from transnational discussion, then the ability for the discussion to generate cosmopolitan public spheres is undermined. These tensions test the potential of indirect and partial cosmopolitanism in associations that do not aim to advance cosmopolitan principles.

One challenge that emerges from a discussion of tensions is whether the broader context surrounding the association matters. With the exception of those working to criminalize homosexuality, the conservative position does not necessarily threaten cosmopolitanism. Yet, one might still ask whether, in the absence of a world state that could enforce the human rights of gay and lesbian individuals, the actions of the Anglican Communion conservatives do not threaten the cultivation of cosmopolitan norms and attitudes of mutual respect. One could argue that because "homosexuals are a minority" this "makes it more (not less) imperative that the church bear witness to the justice issue."[66] Cosmopolitans should certainly work toward justice for those with different sexual orientations but if cosmopolitans want to accommodate freedom of association this requires tolerating the choices individuals make in ordering their lives. Expecting all associations on the global level to conform to liberal cosmopolitan principles in their internal organization would undermine the liberty of individuals to freely choose associations to shape their lives. In fact, Appiah argues, "a tenable cosmopolitanism . . . must take seriously the value of human life, and the value of particular human lives."[67] This does not mean that cosmopolitans need to see illiberal positions as advancing cosmopolitanism fully. To expect cosmopolitanism to be advanced as a whole would hamper the freedom of individuals to form associations based on their religious views. In fact, as this case has illustrated, liberal groups may be only partially cosmopolitan themselves.

There is a second significant tension emerging in the actions of some liberal Anglicans in ECUSA who advocate for norms of equality to be extended to sexual orientation but who are also wary of forming transnational ties and shared identities. Liberal Anglican responses to missionary activity as culturally imperialistic reveal critical differences between liberal and conservative attitudes toward building transnational relations. The transnational ties conservatives have formed have led to reverse missionary activity. Unlike traditional patterns of missionary activity from the United States or Europe to the global South, Africans and Latin Americans minister to individuals in North American and Europe. For conservative Americans "orthodoxy travels from the South to the North" in a way that "offers a perfect symbol for the termination of the paternalistic relationship between the churches of the Old and New

Christian Worlds."[68] However, North American liberal Anglicans vehemently oppose the interference of bishops from outside provinces: "Bishops are not intercontinental ballistic missiles, manufactured on one continent and fired into another as an act of aggression."[69] To argue against reverse missionary activity, liberal Anglicans employ language that was in the past used against missionaries to Africa, namely claims of cultural imperialism.[70] The response of liberals to reverse missionary activity is rooted in their preference for independence and its emphasis on tolerating diversity as well as avoiding hubris.

Although the reduction in missionary activity may stem from a sense of guilt over past colonial and imperialistic relationships with Anglicans in other parts of the world, the redirection of funds from programs abroad to domestic concerns may result not in tolerance of diversity but in indifference toward those abroad. One scholar cautions that, "for all their vast wealth, many churches in North America and Europe have far less interest or commitment in the global South than they once had" and this "at just the point it is most desperately needed, at the peak of the current surge of Christian numbers."[71] Another scholar, Maria Rovisco, finds that missionary projects can provide opportunities and motivation for young people to travel or volunteer abroad rather than at home.[72] As liberal Anglicans are "retreating from the multiculturalist dreams of diversity globalism, they pull back into a defensive posture, anxious to protect their churches from Southern influences."[73] This tension between liberal Anglicans' cosmopolitan ideals of respecting individual liberty and their wariness of forming transnational ties highlights that even where cosmopolitan norms are more consciously part of a group's activities cosmopolitan effects may still only be partial. Cutting back on missionary activity may have implications of undermining the development of cosmopolitan dispositions if not offset with other efforts to forge relationships across borders.

Perhaps there are ways to cultivate ties outside of traditional missionary activities.[74] Missionary activity creates certain common practices and shared experiences, but it is also still a practice with potentially paternalistic elements. Despite significant changes in missionary practices, which now consider evangelism to include learning local dialogues and socializing with local communities as opposed to simply saving heathens,[75] the "symbolic boundaries between 'us' and 'them'" are not necessarily being challenged.[76] The Indaba project hints at the possibility of ways to re-envision practices of mission. Cultural sensitivity requires a willingness to ask for forgiveness, which in turn requires recognition of one's own fallibility.[77]

Liberal Anglicans and liberal cosmopolitans can learn from conservatives. There are important benefits in forming transnational relations in order to cultivate relationships of respect and defend certain ideals. Belief in the importance of diversity and toleration does not necessarily build international communities that bridge global divides. It can take on the attitude of leave well enough alone. In order to generate strong institutional relations and to form shared identities that can support these institutional ties, liberals need to see Africans as potential partners. Some Anglicans are issuing calls for liberals to unite and defend their positions. "Our inclusiveness needs to be protected if it is to survive. . . . We therefore need to do the opposite of what we normally do. . . . To retain our inclusiveness we now need, formally, to reject as incompatible with Anglicanism, the view that Churches should be exclusive."[78] There are issues for liberal Anglicans to unite around. After all, the agenda of Anglicans from the global South shows that homosexuality is not the limit of their concerns. However, liberal Anglicans have not been as successful in building shared identities despite supporting issues such as debt relief, which resonates with bishops in the global South. This case highlights the importance of cultivating shared identities that incorporate reciprocal relations. Anglicans from Africa contributed spiritual support to their relationship with conservative Americans.

A very brief look at the issue of international debt relief shows the problems with a failure to build a sense of global community based on reciprocal relations. Anglicans were a part of the large international social movement Jubilee, launched in 1995 as an independent charity with the Anglican's Most Reverent Desmond Tutu from South Africa as its president.[79] The goal of this movement was to raise awareness of the problems international debt caused for some of the poorest countries in the world and to call for creditor nations to forgive the debt of those countries. The movement was largely driven by Northern NGOs: Southern NGOs played a role in supporting the Northern initiatives and lending credibility.[80] Anglicans might have used this issue of debt relief to form ties within the Anglican Communion that could be invoked for cooperation on other issues beyond debt relief.[81] Not providing opportunities for many in the global South to play a role as active members hampered developing ties among co-religionists. Therefore, while the goal of debt relief was compatible with recognition of our shared humanity (namely, attacking the inhuman conditions caused by international debt), those they sought to aid were not necessarily empowered. Attempts to strengthen a sense of transnational community among fellow Anglicans could have cultivated a more sustained sense of global outlook.

The example of conservative dissidents in this association shows that religious groups can have some expressions of cosmopolitanism worth studying. Religion plays an important role in many people's lives. Religious associations also seem particularly important for exploring the potential cosmopolitanism of associations from the global South since "the more we look at the Southern Hemisphere in particular, the more we see that while universal and supranational ideas are flourishing, they are not secular in the least."[82] The case of Anglican dissidents once again raises the point that a discussion of associational criteria ought not aim to develop a comprehensive conception of cosmopolitanism. As David Held describes cosmopolitanism, it "must always be an ensemble of organizations, associations and agencies pursuing their own projects, whether these be economic, social or cultural; but these projects must always also be subject to the constraints of democratic processes and a common structure of political action."[83] We are not at this cosmopolitan world yet. My criteria reveal places where associations fail to realize cosmopolitanism as well as where cosmopolitanism emerges from unlikely sources. The presence of tensions does not make a case less valuable because cosmopolitans can learn lessons from it. Even if missionary work may intensify exclusive religious identity[84] that does not necessarily make expressions of cosmopolitanism within the religious association irrelevant. The Anglican Communion helps flesh out the encouraging idea that cosmopolitan norms can be spread piecemeal.

This piecemeal advancement may occur indirectly and unintentionally. Associations can have cosmopolitanism effects if they generate ties between individuals, shape identities, cultivate certain moral dispositions, and encourage global dialogue. It is necessary to explore a range of associations to see if together they spread different cosmopolitan norms, perhaps other associations advance elements that the Anglican Communion is not good at advancing. Together with the other two cases of associations explored in detail, Médecins Sans Frontières and the Olympics, these examples show how associations might affect individuals in different ways. These cases demonstrate the key idea that realizing cosmopolitanism need not always depend on committed cosmopolitans advocating for their principles. The Anglican case in particular reveals the force of transnational ties of identity and community. The conclusion ought not necessarily be that such ties are a threat to cosmopolitanism but rather that cosmopolitans ought to consider how to better cultivate such ties.

NOTES

1. The focus of this chapter will be on the exclusion of non-celibate gay men from the clergy and the banning of same-sex marriage because that is largely the focus of the dissidents I am discussing. They also oppose women as clergy. Lesbian, gay, bisexual, transgendered, and queer (LGBTQ) activists within the Anglican Communion often have much broader agendas.

2. Wallace Been, Suffragan Bishop of Lewes, quoted in Stephen Bates, *A Church at War: Anglicans and Homosexuality* (New York: I.B. Tauris, 2004), 16–17.

3. Amy Gutmann, "Freedom of Association: An Introductory Essay" in *Freedom of Association,* ed. Amy Gutmann (Princeton, NJ: Princeton University Press, 1998), 22–23.

4. Ibid., 17.

5. Miranda Hassett, *Anglican Communion in Crisis: How Episcopal Dissidents and Their African Allies are Reshaping Anglicanism* (Princeton, NJ: Princeton University

Press, 2007), 32–33. This is also discussed by Jason Bruner in "Divided We Stand: North American Evangelicals and the Crisis in the Anglican Communion," *Journal of Anglican Studies* 8 (2009): 102–109. William L. Sachs discusses the liberal or progressive nature of the leadership in *Homosexuality and the Crisis of Anglicanism* (New York: Cambridge University Press, 2009), 34–35.

6. Gustav Niebuhr, "Hearing Begins for Bishop who Ordained Gay Deacon," *The New York Times*, February 28, 1996, accessed January 18, 2014, http://www.nytimes .com/1996/02/28/us/hearing-begins-for-bishop-who-ordained-gay-deacon.html.   See also Gustav Niebuhr, "Episcopal Bishop Absolved in Gay Ordination," *The New York Times*, May 16, 1996, accessed January 18, 2014, http://www.nytimes .com/1996/05/16/us/episcopal-bishop-absolved-in-gay-ordination.html. In addition see Hassett, *Anglican Communion in Crisis,* 33 and Bruner, "Divided We Stand,"108.

7. Niebuhr, "Episcopal Bishop Absolved in Gay Ordination."

8. *Resolution I.10 Human Sexuality*, Lambeth Conference 1998, accessed January 18, 2014 on the Lambeth Conference Official Website, http://www.lambethconference.org/ resolutions/1998/1998-1-10.cfm.

9. Rachel Zoll, "Anglicans say US Episcopalians trying to heal split over gays, but want more done," *Associated Press Worldstream* (New York), October 4, 2007.

10. Sachs, *Homosexuality,* 232.

11. Hassett, *Anglican Communion in Crisis,* 121.

12. *Resolution 1.10 Human Sexuality*, Lambeth Conference 1998.

13. Gill Valentine et al., "Transnational Religious Networks: Sexuality and the Changing Power Geometries of the Anglican Communion," *Transactions of the Institute of British Geographers* 38 (2013): Table 1 p. 54.

14. Interviewee from Church of England-1 focus group quoted in Valentine et al., "Transnational Religious Networks," 56.

15. Willis Jenkins, "Episcopalians, Homosexuality, and World Mission," *Anglican Theological Review* 86, no. 2 (2004): 296.

16. Described in Ian Markham, "Episcopalians, Homosexuality and the General Convention," *Reviews in Religion and Theology* 14, no. 1 (2007): 2.

17. Sachs, *Homosexuality,* 234.

18. The term global South is used in the literature on the Anglican controversy to mean South America, Africa, and Asia, although much of scholarship on which I draw relates to Africa. Any negative connotations associated with this term are not intended by the author.

19. Hassett discusses how previous dissidents in the Episcopal Church broke off from the church to form their own communities not recognized by the Anglican Communion. *Anglican Communion in Crisis,* 25. Christopher Craig Brittain and Andrew MacKinnon mention that in the past conservative dissidents often looked for support in other denominations. "Homosexuality and the Construction of 'Anglican Orthodoxy': The Symbolic Politics of the Anglican Communion," *Sociology of Religion* 72, no. 3 (2011): 370.

20. Peter Boyer, "A Church Asunder," *The New Yorker,* April 17, 2006.

21. The view that the global South is now the power base of Anglicanism arises, in part, out of Philip Jenkins's research. He argues the number of Anglicans in the global South compared to the North has caused a power shift toward the South. Philip Jenkins, *The Next Christendom: The Coming of Global Christianity* (New York: Oxford University Press, 2002). My view takes into account Hassett's caution that one must consider the role powerful figures in the North play in affecting the positions that bishops from the global South adopt.

22. "Statement from Archbishop Peter Akinola, Primate of the Church of Nigeria" quoted in Willis Jenkins, "Episcopalians," 306–307.

23. Hassett, *Anglican Communion in Crisis,* 65.

24. Hassett uses the terms global diversity *vs.* global accountability to describe the two different global visions within the Anglican Communion.

25. Ian Douglas, "Authority after Colonialism," *The Witness* (March 2000), accessed September 28, 2009, http://www.thewitness.org.

26. Quoted in Hassett, *Anglican Communion in Crisis*, 126–127.

27. See endnote 14 for the earlier reference to this quote from Valentine et al., "Transnational Religious Networks," 56.

28. Willis Jenkins, "Episcopalians," 299.

29. Jonathan Clatworthy, "Inclusiveness and Unity," in *The Windsor Report: A Liberal Response*, ed. Jonathan Clatworthy and David Taylor (New York: O Books, 2005), 85.

30. Bates, *A Church at War*, 5.

31. Wallace Benn, Suffragan Bishop of Lewes, quoted in Bates, *A Church at War*, 16–17.

32. Sarah Simpson, "An African archbishop finds common ground in Virginia," *The Christian Science Monitor*, January 8, 2007.

33. Jay Michaelson, "Could an African LGBT Activist Win the Nobel Peace Prize?" *The Daily Beast*, May 5, 2012, accessed May 20, 2014, http://www.thedailybeast.com/articles/2012/05/05/could-an-african-lgbt-activist-win-the-nobel-peace-prize.html. Dr. Michaelson, author of works on religion and LGBT issues, is not talking specifically about Anglicans or Episcopalians; however, his arguments relate to how the actions of missionary associations can have anti-cosmopolitan effects that should not be tolerated. Drafting anti-gay laws is anti-cosmopolitan. For a discussion of those advocating for harming gay and lesbian individuals and their allies see also Jeffrey Gettleman's article "Ugandan Who Spoke Up for Gays Is Beaten to Death" *The New York Times* January 27, 2011, accessed June 5, 2014, http://www.nytimes.com/2011/01/28/world/africa/28uganda.html.

34. Hassett, *Anglican Communion in Crisis*, 161.

35. This quote and the one below are from Hassett, *Anglican Communion in Crisis*, 159–160.

36. Desmond Tutu, former Archbishop of Cape Town and bishop of the Anglican Church of South Africa, is a famous exception. He is a very influential activist.

37. Hassett, *Anglican Communion in Crisis*, 54.

38. Joseph Adetiloye, former Archbishop of Nigeria, quoted in Boyer, "A Church Asunder."

39. *Second Trumpet* from 2nd Anglican Encounter in the South, Kuala Lumpur 10–15 February 1997. Print version November 1, 2005, accessed January 19, 2014 from Global South Anglican Online, http://www.globalsouthanglican.org/index.php/blog/comments/second_trumpet_from_2nd_anglican_encounter_in_the_south_kuala_lumpur_10_15.

40. American Anglican Council, "Who We Are," American Anglican Council website (1996); no longer available online, quoted in Hassett, *Anglican Communion in Crisis*, 51. Today the brochure "Defending the Faith and Guarding the Faithful" reads: "Founded in 1996, the American Anglican Council is building and strengthening a society of great communion churches in the Anglican tradition in the United States and worldwide. The AAC began as a response to unbiblical teachings that crept into The Episcopal Church (TEC) and the larger Anglican Communion. As a not-for-profit 501(c)3 network of individuals, clergy, organizations and churches, the AAC works to help rebuild a unified, orthodox, missional Anglicanism in North America. The AAC is a non-profit advocacy and equipping ministry, not a church. We link thousands of individuals, hundreds of churches and many ministries within TEC and the Anglican Church in North America (AC-NA), all working to spread the Gospel and reform the church." American Anglican Council, accessed January 19, 2012, https://americananglican.org/wp-content/uploads/2013/08/AAC-BrochureDefending-the-Faith.pdf.

41. Bishop Thomas, a Ugandan, quoted in Hassett, *Anglican Communion in Crisis*, 145.

42. Hassett, *Anglican Communion in Crisis*, 140.

43. A vicar from an Anglican Church of South Africa parish quoted in Valentine et al., "Transnational Religious Networks," 59.

44. Willis Jenkins, "Episcopalians," 309–310.

45. Ibid., 310.

46. Brittain and MacKinnon, "Homosexuality," 355.

47. Amartya Sen, *Identity and Violence: The Illusion of Destiny* (New York: W.W. Norton & Company, 2006), 3.

48. Quoted in Brittain and MacKinnon, "Homosexuality," 364.

49. This is discussed in Hassett, *Anglican Communion in Crisis,* 110–111 and in Valentine et al., "Transnational Religious Networks," 54.

50. Bishop Hays Rockwell quoted in Hassett, *Anglican Communion in Crisis,* 110–111.

51. A parishioner from an unidentified church in the southeastern United States quoted in Hassett, *Anglican Communion in Crisis,* 162.

52. A parishioner from the United States quoted in Hassett, *Anglican Communion in Crisis,* 164.

53. A United States parishioner quoted in Hassett, *Anglican Communion in Crisis,* 173.

54. Hassett, *Anglican Communion in Crisis,* 111, 174–175. See also Maria Rovisco, "Religion and the Challenges of Cosmopolitanism: Young Portuguese Volunteers in Africa" in *Cosmopolitanism in Practice,* ed. Magdalena Nowicka and Maria Rovisco (Burlington, VT: Ashgate, 2009), 193.

55. Bess Twiston Davies, "Lambeth Voices: A panel of Anglican bishops share their views with Faith Online," *Times Online* (July 30, 2008), accessed on August 14, 2009.

56. *Anglicans Online,* accessed on August 14, 2009, http://anglicansonline.org/resources/assn.html.

57. Bates, *A Church at War,* 15.

58. From a GAFCON press release quoting Most Rev. Nicholas D. Okoh, Archbishop of Bendel, Nigeria, chairman of the Theological Resource Team. GAFCON's website, news section, accessed on August 14, 2009, http://www.gafcon.org.

59. Douglas, "Authority after Colonialism."

60. "About," on the Continuing Indaba project website, accessed on May 20, 2014, http://continuingindaba.com/about-2/.

61. Ibid.

62. Ibid. Italics in the original.

63. "What is conversing," from the Frequently Ask Questions section of the Continuing Indaba website's History of the Development of the Project Page, accessed May 20, 2014, http://aco.org/ministry/continuingindaba/whatis/faq.cfm.

64. "About," on the Continuing Indaba project website.

65. Valentine et al., "Transnational Religious Networks," 62. In the context of this discussion, they also raise the point that because of the frequent tensions between belief and conduct (which they recorded between beliefs that homosexuality is immoral and respectful attitudes toward particular gay and lesbian individuals), placing conversation in local context rather than in large Communion-level discussions, like at Lambeth, might facilitate greater mutual respect and understanding.

66. Markham, "Episcopalians, Homosexuality," 4.

67. Kwame Anthony Appiah, *The Ethics of Identity* (Princeton, NJ: Princeton University Press, 2005), 222–223.

68. Philip Jenkins, *Next Christendom,* 204.

69. Former Presiding Bishop of the US Episcopal Church, Frank Griswold, originally quoted in Douglas LeBlanc, "Intercontinental Ballistic Bishops?" *CT,* posted April 25, 2000, quoted in Philip Jenkins, *Next Christendom,* 203–204.

70. For example, Bishop Spong concludes that "no church anywhere can survive an attempted imposition of cultural uniformity." John Shelby Spong, foreword to *The Windsor Report: A Liberal Response,* ed. Jonathan Clatworthy and David Taylor (New York: O Books, 2005), xi. Spong is the retired Episcopal Bishop of Newark, New Jersey. He is a leading spokesperson for progressive Christianity.

71. Philip Jenkins, *Next Christendom,* 212, 213.

72. Rovisco, "Religion and the Challenges of Cosmopolitanism,"188.

73. Hassett, *Anglican Communion in Crisis,* 256.

74. Willis Jenkins, "Episcopalians," 300.

75. Rovisco, "Religion and the Challenges," 192. She goes on to quote someone volunteering in Cape Verde as saying: "People have a bit this idea that 'we go there and we change that.' I think we have to go there with our own experiences, to share our experiences, but also to understand why they are like they are. This is what I attempted to do with the children from the orphanage. The orphanage had children between four and twenty-two years old. With the little ones we played and organized fun activities. With the eldest we offered informal training courses."

76. Ibid., 193, 197–198.

77. These are two criteria that Michael S. Merry and Doret J. de Ruyter see as critical to a cosmopolitan moral perspective. They go on to argue that those who have a literal belief in the truth of the Bible cannot be true cosmopolitans but that those with less literal views have the potential to act as cosmopolitans. They discuss this in "Cosmopolitanism and the Deeply Religious," *Journal of Beliefs & Values* 30, no. 1 (2009): 58–59. My own argument comes to a different conclusion because of the understanding of cosmopolitanism I employ.

78. Clatworthy, "Inclusiveness and Unity," 105.

79. Elizabeth A. Donnelly, "Making the Case of Jubilee: The Catholic Church and the Poor Country Debt Movement," *Ethics & International Affairs* 21, no. 1 (2007): 121–123. Paola Grenier, "Jubilee 2000: Laying the Foundations for a Social Movement," in *Global Civic Engagement,* ed. John Clark (Sterling, VA: Earthscan, 2003), 90.

80. Elizabeth A. Donnelly, "Proclaiming Jubilee: The Debt and Structural Adjustment Network," in *Restructuring World Politics: Transnational Social Movements, Networks, and Norms,* ed. Sanjeev Khagram, James V. Riker, and Kathryn Sikkink (Minneapolis: University of Minnesota Press, 2002), 167.

81. Greiner argues that a movement oriented toward advocacy and lobbying states is not as good at forming shared identities or permanent ties. The goal is not to form a lasting association. "Jubilee 2000."

82. Philip Jenkins, *Next Christendom,* 11.

83. David Held, *Democracy and the Global Order: From the Modern State to Cosmopolitan Governance* (Stanford, CA: Stanford University Press, 1995), 278.

84. Rovisco, "Religion and the Challenges," 194. She discusses how missionary work can institutionally reinforce religious identity through training and other mission related activities that seek to keep religious identity strong.

Conclusion

I began this project by pointing to a tension between universal principles, which apply to all individuals equally, and partial exclusive associations, which do not encompass all humans. The tension seems to disappear in many contemporary cosmopolitan theories because respect for individual liberty is at least partly manifest in the right to freedom of association. Cosmopolitan theory can therefore tolerate individuals freely joining associations with a variety of purposes as long as they do not violate basic human rights. A religious association that forbids non-celibate gay men from being priests may not embrace norms that cosmopolitans want to endorse, but the association also does not violate any basic human rights. Merely categorizing associations as tolerable or intolerable fails to adequately appreciate the potential of associations to advance or even generate cosmopolitan norms and obligations. In order to determine whether associations advance cosmopolitanism one needs to ask: What ought cosmopolitans expect of associations? There is no obvious answer to this question. Cosmopolitans defend or prioritize different values, even if one focuses only on moral theories of cosmopolitanism. In order to recognize the potential of a diverse range of associations one must draw on elements from different cosmopolitan theories, rather than select one to apply in all cases.

A middle-level theory of cosmopolitan criteria categorizes cosmopolitan theories in terms of standards for just transnational institutions, duties to fellow humans, respectful solidarity, and inclusive deliberation in order to apply these expressions of cosmopolitanism to research on the institutional, developmental, shared identity, and public sphere effects of associations. Focusing on elements of cosmopolitanism, rather than any one theory as a whole, turns out to be a particularly good approach for assessing associations. Ideal comprehensive theories of cosmopolitanism are ill suited for providing a normative framework broad enough to understand the impact of a plurality of associations. Even though existing theories are individually inadequate for assessing a diverse range of associations, understanding cosmopolitan moral theories is still central to assessing associations. A middle-level theory that combines different cosmopolitan theories aims to avoid the danger of "general moral guidelines fray[ing] under the strain of concrete application."[1] On the one hand, the criteria are rooted in normative theory with moral guidelines for assessing associations. On the other hand, drawing on not one but different

expressions of moral cosmopolitanism ensures flexibility and accommo-
dates some plurality.

Few, if any, associations will advance all possible expressions of cosmopolitanism. Even associations with a purpose very much in line with
cosmopolitan principles, such as an anti-slavery association or a humanitarian relief organization, do not necessarily have all possible cosmopolitan effects. Moreover, members of associations like Amnesty International or Human Rights Watch, which have missions congruent with respecting the moral equality of all individuals, may already hold cosmopolitan
views. In that case the association does not spread cosmopolitan norms
among members. Associations that individuals join for a variety of reasons not related to advancing cosmopolitanism may actually help to develop cosmopolitan dispositions in members. In that case, membership in
the association plays a role in advancing cosmopolitanism. Studying specific cases of associations reveals more precisely how partial and indirect
effects of exclusive associations help cosmopolitanism come about in the
world. Applying the criteria to associations without a cosmopolitan purpose presents the greatest potential for spreading cosmopolitan. At the
same time, recognizing that not all associations advance all cosmopolitan
expressions means that tensions may arise. It is worth spending a few
final words summarizing first the criteria of partial cosmopolitanism and
second the tensions that a middle-level theory of cosmopolitanism must
navigate in order to embrace indirect and partial cosmopolitanism.

PARTIAL EXPRESSIONS OF INDIRECT OR DIRECT
COSMOPOLITANISM

It is challenging to apply cosmopolitan theories to the effects of associations because those effects are complex and varied. The very plurality
emerging from freedom of association may lead one to conclude that it is
impossible to generalize about the effects associations have. Perhaps it
would be better to just focus on norms that are being developed rather
than on associations. Newly institutionalized norms such as responsibility to protect self-consciously aim to foster a greater sense of transnational moral responsibility. In the 1990s, an international commission worked
to institutionalize a responsibility to protect in international law. If a state
fails to fulfill its responsibility to protect the rights of its citizens, then it
becomes the responsibility of the rest of the international community to
step in and protect those individuals' rights.[2] While this is certainly an
important development, focusing on norms does not always address
transnational voluntary associations. They are not the only actors spreading norms. Moreover, it could miss cosmopolitanism arising in unlikely
places because it focuses on norms that more obviously connect to cosmopolitanism, such as those framed in ways that challenge state sove-

reignty or that advance human rights. This would overlook the cosmopolitan potential of MSF's attempts to transform the norms within medical research practices in order to draw greater attention to neglected diseases and those that suffer from them. Medical research comes more in line with cosmopolitan norms of moral equality but the focus is limited to medical research not challenging state borders. Matters become even more complex when considering indirect effects that do not self-consciously aim to be cosmopolitan. The Olympics may result in debates over how to prioritize public projects without actually aiming to do so.

In studying associations it is critical to evaluate the effects not only the association's declared purpose. Categories of effects also ought to allow for flexibility within each type of effect. Institutional effects, for example, could be exhibited through a variety of different actions. By applying cosmopolitan theories to the categories of effects it is possible to get a sense of the kind of things cosmopolitans could expect of associations. Some specific lessons emerge from applying my criteria to the three cases of exclusive associations in part II.

The first category of effects explores institutional effects. The challenge of applying theories of institutional cosmopolitanism to associations is determining what they have to say about voluntary associations as opposed to the formal coercive political and economic institutions that these theories usually address in order to determine our transnational obligations. When determining what makes for good cosmopolitan institutional arrangements, there are also no obvious global or cosmopolitan institutions for associations to mirror. Nevertheless, membership in the transnational institutional relations of an association can generate new obligations and/or help to enforce other cosmopolitan obligations.

Exploring Médecins Sans Frontières (MSF), the Olympics, and Anglican Communion dissidents shows how institutional effects can overcome state boundaries without an association's institutions being fully global or membership being all-encompassing. Institutional relations can be formed around ties of affinity, as with the Anglicans, or around particular expertise, as with doctors in MSF. These illustrate ways to organize institutions around commonalities other than mere nationality or citizenship. In forging such institutional relations members of the association also come to have specific obligations. MSF expatriates have to consider what they owe to each other as well as what they owe to the national staff hired on field missions. In the case of the Anglican Communion, conservatives draw on shared membership in a worldwide Communion as the basis for holding members accountable to each other. They not only argued that Anglicans anywhere in the world had obligations to fellow Anglicans; they also established new institutional relations joining US and African parishes.

An association can also spread cosmopolitan norms through institutionalizing transnational rules or codes of conduct (sometimes in institutions outside the association). MSF aims to change existing institutions of patent law and policies of the World Health Organization that hamper medical aid going to those most in need. The International Olympic Committee, in conjunction with international sports federations, institutes rules of sports that make competitions among individuals from different parts of the world possible. Indirectly, however, these rules of sports establish a shared framework in which participants interact on terms of fair play that respect their opponents or challengers.

None of these associations are perfectly cosmopolitan or without flaw, but they entail certain lessons. First of all, studying associations can help illustrate some of the creative options for organizing transnationally. This can help in imagining what cosmopolitan institutional structures might look like. The potential of associations to serve as spaces for innovation is something cosmopolitans should explore in greater depth. Second of all, it is important to recognize that obligations can emerge even when membership in institutional relations is voluntary. The Olympics shows that there are ways of creating conditions that demand respect for others without requiring cosmopolitan motivations. Individuals may just want to win a game but to do so they ought to abide by the rules. Once MSF takes action to aid in an emergency, MSF workers find themselves with new obligations. The fact that these obligations are the result of a voluntary decision to join MSF does not make them insignificant.

The second category of effects where cosmopolitanism can be applied is that of its developmental effects. Associations need not have extensive institutions in order to advance cosmopolitan norms and dispositions. They can do so by educating people about their obligations to aid others as well as connecting local issues to global problems and solutions. Individuals join associations for a variety of reasons; yet, the cases I explore highlight how membership in partial associations can indirectly play a powerful role in spreading cosmopolitanism among those not already committed to its principles. Imagination can be expanded if individuals begin to study and travel to Africa in order to meet co-religionists. Those looking for adventure and excitement end up grappling with what impartial relief aid means in conflict zones. Individuals can be empowered by learning to navigate international religious conferences or by orchestrating worldwide sporting events.

One must nevertheless be cautious to recognize the limits of some of these educative effects. Developing more cosmopolitan norms in one area does not necessarily nor automatically transfer to other realms. Conservative Anglican dissidents in the United States have drawn commonalities across certain race, class, and nationality divides to forms ties with African Anglicans; however, one cannot assume that the international shift in race relations carries over toward a shift in race relations with African Americans at home in the United States.[3] Crossing boundaries in one arena may not result in complete moral equality across all differences. As the case of the Anglican dissidents also makes clear developing more transnational attitudes in one way may solidify divides in other areas (sexual orientation). This is one reason why membership in a variety of different associations can be important. It may be challenging to always think in terms of common humanity but it is less difficult to image one person having different points of commonality with many different people. The experience of plurality can be critical to sustaining respect and toleration among individuals in a diverse community.[4]

Associations not only provide opportunities to expand individuals' horizons but also serve as places to develop skills that can positively affect an individual's life. Women and former slaves, for example, gained a public voice in discussions and activism on the topic of abolition. Ignoring these effects because they are partial (women did not suddenly gain access to all public spheres of politics) would be missing something significant. Acknowledging the effects as more than partial expressions of cosmopolitanism would undercut cosmopolitanism's moral force by locating it everywhere.

The third category of effects consists of shared identity effects. Shared identity construction is one effect that many moral cosmopolitan theories do not adequately address. Defining cosmopolitan shared identity may at first seem to require establishing one type of ideal identity, thereby threatening diversity. This need not be the case if partial identities can be cosmopolitan. Cultural cosmopolitans tell us some partial identities are more acceptable than others. Interaction across borders raises awareness of similarities but also differences among individuals. It is one thing to recognize commonalities with others and another to actually engage with them. Moreover, shared norms or shared interests are not necessarily sufficient to generate common identities or forge transnational communities as the case of the Society for Effecting the Abolition of the Slave Trade demonstrates. Most slaves and former slaves were absent from the Society's activities.

How then can associations create cosmopolitan identities or generate solidarity? The power of symbols and shared traditions or practices seems important in the cases I explored. Religious associations like the Anglican Communion have extensive rituals and shared beliefs that create ways for members to interact with each other. Americans traveling to Africa found a form of equality and mutual support through theological discussions. Rituals need not be religious. Combining the rules of a worldwide sporting event with shared symbols and practices at the Olympic Games is meant to evoke a sense of global Olympic community. While not necessarily a strong human identity, Olympians do form friendships and in some cases a sense of obligation connected to being an Olympian.

It is critical not to disconnect concepts of identity from cosmopolitanism understood as a theory of obligations of justice. Associations that create partial transnational communities can be evaluated in terms of whether those relations respect cosmopolitan responsibilities. MSF expatriates describe the challenge of connecting with local communities given the temporary nature of their stay, the conditions of emergency aid, as well as the stark differences between life experiences between expatriates and their patients. Patronizing attitudes that see individuals as charity cases can undercut a cosmopolitan sense of community. Maintaining the importance of cosmopolitan identity through drawing on cultural cosmopolitan theories can help remind individuals that moral obligations should not be acted upon in a paternalistic fashion. Reciprocal relationships and shaping common ways of life are an important part of assessing cosmopolitan effects.

The fourth and final category of effects is the category of public sphere effects. Associations can influence public opinion by raising issues in global debates or shaping a legitimate language for public discourse on particular issues as well as by fostering skills of deliberation. The International Olympic Committee was a space in which discussions about women's equality in the world of sports took place in the context of determining who should be allowed to compete in the Olympic Games. MSF witnesses human rights violations the world ignores. It also works diligently to protect the language of humanitarianism from states misusing it to justify military projects.

As with the other categories of effects, analyzing public sphere effects highlights the difference between direct and indirect expressions of cosmopolitanism. The Olympics indirectly creates public sphere effects because it attracts a worldwide audience. It does not intend to create a forum for discussion. The IOC actually tries to craft a single public image and united message for its audience. Both the IOC and certain Anglican dissidents want to realize unity at the expense of dialogue. The result, however, is not always what the group intends. A cacophony of voices surrounds the Olympic Games, and the IOC cannot fully silence them. The IOC should not consider all those speaking out as a threat but instead use the public sphere that is formed around it in order to work with those associations that aid its goals. It gains obligations from its own insistence at addressing and even representing a world community of sports based on fair competition.

One cannot fully determine the potential cosmopolitan effects of associations by evaluating self-conscious actions that aim to promote human equality or human rights. There may be effects on individuals who are not explicitly or self-consciously advocates of cosmopolitan philosophy. The benefit of using all four categories of effects (institutional, developmental, shared identity, and public sphere) for locating expressions of cosmopolitanism is not only a clearer understanding of associations' impact but also an important recognition of the potential of partial and indirect expressions of cosmopolitanism.

IMPLICATIONS OF COSMOPOLITANISM
EMBRACING PARTIALITY

The three associations in part II also reveal cautionary notes about partial cosmopolitanism in an imperfectly cosmopolitan world. After all, embracing pluralism should not come at the expense of cosmopolitan principles. I have repeatedly defined associations as partial because they do not include all of humanity in their membership. Applying the criteria to actual associations also reveals ways in which an association could be partially cosmopolitan because it does not advance all possible elements of cosmopolitanism, a different form of partiality. A middle-level cosmopolitan theory can accommodate associations partial in both senses—exclusive membership and limited effects. The three cases reveal not only the potential but also the limits of partial cosmopolitanism. The previous section emphasized the potential of partiality. Let me now address some of the tensions that arise. Two tensions in particular merit attention. The first is a tension that emerges between core values of cosmopolitanism. The second tension has to do with patterns of membership in associations that may reify inequalities rather than overcome them to advance moral equality. Exploring what it would mean for cosmopolitanism to embrace partiality requires navigating these tensions.

Partiality: Tensions Within
Cosmopolitanism and Among Effects

In each case of partial cosmopolitanism I addressed tensions between cosmopolitan and non-cosmopolitan components that persist in the association. This is the case even in MSF, the more cosmopolitan-oriented association of the three. Since my theory does not require that associations realize all expressions of cosmopolitanism, these kinds of tensions will remain and need not undermine the cosmopolitan expression of an association.

Another kind of tension emerges as part of the middle-level theory itself, namely tensions between elements of cosmopolitanism. Might an association emphasize one cosmopolitan effect particularly well precisely because it does not emphasize another?[5] When this is the case—that some aspects of cosmopolitanism are best spread separately—the partiality of associations actually becomes crucial to realizing cosmopolitan ideals. What may seem like a drawback or weakness within the theory—the presence of tensions—may not be. The limits are in existing comprehensive theories of cosmopolitanism. They are inadequate on their own for understanding associations. It also means that a middle-level theory of cosmopolitanism will necessarily involve tensions among its ideals.

Let me show how tensions among effects emerge between developmental and shared identity effects. MSF teaches that at the core individuals are all the same: everyone bleeds red. In striving to ensure the broader public does not forget such commonalities MSF seeks to cultivate a sense of empathy for fellow members, who are living under inhumane conditions. At the same time, the professional nature of MSF's medical aid creates distance between doctors and patients. Dr. James Maskalyk's experience reveals that an expatriate doctor could live in a community for weeks and not know anything about the culture of the community.[6] The professional ties that serve as a source of cosmopolitan obligation make the impartiality of medical care difficult to realize without maintaining some distance. This makes it very difficult to forge a sense of community beyond biological commonality. In the past, it also made it challenging to recognize obligations to national staff, whose experiences may be different from that of expatriates. The existence of this tension should not mean that MSF needs to reform its organization in order to also construct a global shared identity. There are lessons MSF can learn from considering shared identity criteria, such as the importance of reciprocity and humility in building relations of respect that do not require a radical shift in the goals of the association. To give up their crisis relief work because of tensions between cosmopolitan ideals would belie the importance of medical relief aid in restoring basic human dignity to inhumane conditions.

What this potential tension between developmental and shared identity effects points to is the need for an array of types of associations. Not every association ought to aim at realizing all cosmopolitan effects. In the domestic context, Warren talks of the need for a democratic ecology of associations consisting of an optional balance of associations realizing different elements of democracy.[7] There is no world state on the transnational level to regulate or foster the right associational diversity but individuals could evaluate whether the associations they support, form, or join are advancing elements of cosmopolitanism. An individual may have the full range of cosmopolitan obligations of responsibility and identity but could realize those through different types of associations. An individual could begin by considering whether his or her membership in an association creates an identity that is based on respect for moral equality, in particular whether moral respect is advanced in a way that avoids paternalistic hubris.

Recognition of tensions should not only result in discussions about how to achieve the right kind of balance of associations, but also in theoretical discussions about the meaning of cosmopolitanism. The tensions can help to inform the debate within cosmopolitan theory between understanding cosmopolitanism as a thesis about responsibility and cosmopolitanism understood as a thesis about identity. Instead of choosing between them, both are critical elements of cosmopolitanism. They may, however, not be advanced in the same ways through the work of one association. Focusing only on shared identity misses the need for moral criteria to evaluate identities. Not any identity with a global scope is cosmopolitan (as evidenced by transnational criminal and terrorist organizations) so moral criteria are necessarily to evaluate shared identity. Are the identities ones that foster respect for moral equality and build a sense of reciprocity through shared experiences and actual interactions? At the same time, moral obligations without some focus on cosmopolitanism as a way of life may slide into paternalism. There are lessons for associations from both approaches to cosmopolitanism. The two ideals are very much connected and relevant no matter the association, but one need not conclude that associations must have robust effects in both categories. Development effects could be less paternalistic if informed by cultural cosmopolitanism without rejecting associations that do not foster a strong form of global identity. In other words, a middle-level theory of criteria requires identity and responsibility understandings of cosmopolitanism but one association need not have both developmental and shared identity effects. As a result, tensions remain within associations but also within a cosmopolitan theory that aims to navigate between universal moral responsibility and particular relations.

*Partiality: Tensions within Membership
and the North/South Cleavage*

Besides elements of cosmopolitanism coming into tension with each other the partiality of membership—not being inclusive of all humanity—also has implications that arise as a common theme in the three cases. Exclusivity itself, I have argued, is not a problem for cosmopolitanism. Elite associations may not aim to create large membership bases (although they may target global audiences). MSF's membership consists of medical professionals and those that support them. The Olympics consists of a membership base of elite athletes. The IOC is largely made up of wealthy global elites. The Anglican Communion is interesting precisely because it has effects on lay people not just the clergy.

Exclusive partial membership need not be a concern for cosmopolitans; however, one form of exclusivity emerged in each case, namely the divide between the global North and the global South. This cleavage is important to acknowledge because it rests on a history of global inequality that often remains the context for contemporary transnational relations. The three associations I discuss all originated in Western Europe, and their power bases remain, to a large part, still in Europe and North America. This can create problems for generating cosmopolitan effects, as MSF and the Anglican Communion cases indicate. If members from the global South are perceived in a way that undermines respect for their moral equality, even as members they may not be equals. One way of further evaluating the cosmopolitanism of partial membership may require expanding cosmopolitanism's focus on bridging state borders to also address membership ties that connect individuals from wealthier nations in the global North to individuals from poorer countries in the global South. Engaging in this is beyond the scope of my project but it is a critical avenue for further exploration. The associations I have chosen are important to analyze because of their impact and influence but they do not (and should not) represent the full range of associations on the global level.

There are certainly cases of transnational associations forming in the global South that are helping to advance cosmopolitanism. Cosmopolitans ought to consider the effects of associations such as transnational indigenous associations.[8] Indigenous peoples' associations have worked to develop a shared sense of identity on a more global level, one which recognizes their common concerns despite vast geographic, linguistic, and economic development differences. Including a broader array of associations might have the effect of broadening or re-shaping our understanding of cosmopolitanism. Some of the indigenous groups seek to advance their own worldview and the very idea of protecting people may come into tension with a cosmopolitan focus on individuals. Perhaps a cosmopolitanism that allows for groups to play a larger role could address these kinds of views. This is well beyond the scope of my project. At this point all I can say is that a middle-level theory is meant to evaluate actual associations and as a result needs to be open to considering how research on associations may provide lessons for understanding what cosmopolitanism would look like in partial forms in an imperfectly cosmopolitan world.

Another example of an organization formed in the global South is the World Social Forum, which was established by southern associations who reject neo-liberal globalization. It is a worldwide public sphere for discussions on the global economy.[9] Its aim is to "empower global civil society through a long-term unguided, but ever growing (and not necessarily converging), pedagogic process of consciousness-building and mobilization that ultimately transforms national and global governance."[10] Those interested in global civil society and global justice have increasingly sought to understand the impact of the World Social Forum. Might studying it impact our understanding of cosmopolitan public sphere effects or institutional effects?

Acknowledging transnational associations formed in the global South by those who have, in recent history, not held international power could still lead to a world where associations fall along a North-South divide. The focus may simply have shifted from associations in the global North to associations in the global South. This is certainly an improvement in terms of recognizing power differences but one could still ask whether there are ways to build more global communities or transform existing associations to make them more cosmopolitan. MSF South Africa, for example, is trying to transform MSF from a European organization to a more international one. The Anglican Communion case indicated another way in which actors in the global South can play a role in shaping the association, although Hassett pointed out that the focus on homosexuality was partly influenced by conservatives in the United States and England. The lesson the Anglican Communion case teaches to cosmopolitans is the importance of liberal Anglicans learning to forge alliances with Anglicans in Africa.

There are some other examples of transformation through including membership across the North/South divide. Opposition to construction of the Narmada Dam in India shows how local grassroots groups that joined forces with international anti-dam associations shifted international norms. The main focus of the international movement was on environmental conservation until the actions of local Indian associations and their concern with unfair resettlement plans changed the language to one of human and indigenous rights.[11] Collaborations with international networks are particularly important where local groups do not have the resources to mount global campaigns, establish international commissions, or challenge international organizations like the World Bank. By participating in transnational networks individuals from different parts of the world can shift norms in a more cosmopolitan direction even if they are addressing a matter that impacts them locally. Cosmopolitans ought to pay greater attention to how the participation and interaction of local or national non-state actors from across the globe can shape cosmopolitan norms.

IMPLICATIONS OF THE THREE CASES: WHICH NORMS ARE ADVANCED? ARE THEY COSMOPOLITAN?

Focusing on associations and their effects rather than only on norms is important to understanding how cosmopolitanism comes about in the world. This does not mean that it is irrelevant to explore which norms are advanced through the effects of an association. Let me briefly highlight the creative cosmopolitanism of the three cases from part II by considering which norms the three associations advance. Were they cosmopolitan norms?

MSF is the most self-consciously cosmopolitan group of the three I explore. The association certainly challenges state boundaries in its goal to access patients but it also challenges states' actions on an international level. During the recent wars in Afghanistan and Iraq, MSF USA came out strongly in opposition to attempts by the US government to use the legitimacy of humanitarian organizations as part of their military strategy. The danger is that humanitarianism becomes co-opted into the language military conflict, which is usually far from impartial. MSF leaders such as Nicholas de Torrente have become outspoken critics of this, ar-

guing that humanitarian associations need to be considered neutral parties to complete their work. The neutrality norm of humanitarianism is
something MSF is attempting to defend even as governments such as the
United States seek to transform the norm in their own ways.[12] However,
even in this association cosmopolitan norms are not only about challenging state sovereignty. Beyond challenging states in the name of respecting humanitarian neutrality, MSF has been an active participant, along
with other NGOs, in re-shaping norms governing transnational medicine. MSF takes existing drugs and uses them in innovative ways. It also
draws connections between medicine and transnational trade regulations
in its Campaign for the Access to Essential Medicines.[13] MSF has used its
Noble Prize money to help fund research on neglected diseases. To fully
grasp MSF's impact one must consider its challenges to norms of sovereignty and the power of states but also its attempts to transform the
norms of medical research and patent laws in more cosmopolitan directions.

The Olympics are a different kind of association. While rhetorically
supporting goals of global unity, the association is not a humanitarian or
advocacy organization. It aims to unite the world through sports competitions. Norms of fair play are critical to realizing its goal and recently the
IOC has sought to advance this more thoroughly by confronting issues of
doping or cheating in sports. As I discussed in chapter 6, the IOC itself
needs to be careful that its lack of transparency and demands for unity do
not undermine its ability to foster such norms. If people come to associate
the Olympics and IOC with corruption then the ability to foster norms of
fair play can be undermined. Certain forms of hypocrisy that circumvent
ethical standards can be seen not as "a temporary way state in difficult
circumstances" but rather "in favor of more venal objectives."[14] One area
where problems seem to emerge in particular is in how the Olympics
handles the process by which cities bid to host the Games.

Despite changes in the bidding requirements to make it feasible for
more cities to be able to host the Olympic Games (usually by addressing
issues of cost), there has been a trend against hosting the Olympic Games
as costs rise and frustration with the IOC mounts. Some cities have even
withdrawn applications due to public votes of dissatisfaction. Most recently, in 2014 Oslo, Norway, withdrew its bid for hosting the Winter
Olympics in 2022 leaving only two remaining cities: Beijing, China, and
Almaty, Kazakhstan. Norway withdrew after Parliament refused to pass
the necessary legislation to guarantee funding for the games (something
the IOC requires) and rejected demands of IOC members that there be
special lanes for them to avoid traffic, that traffic lights prioritize them,
that bars stay open later, and that VIP lounges serve special food.[15] As I
write, my home state of Massachusetts is embroiled in discussions over
Boston's bid for the 2024 Olympics. One *Boston Globe* columnist describes
the IOC and those crafting the Boston bid as a "cabal of corporate titans

and political heavyweights."[16] The IOC advances ideals of fair play in rhetoric and then seems to ignore them in its own actions. In order to foster a desire for cities to welcome the world in hosting international events, the inconveniences and costs to residents need to be offset by persuasive and consistent arguments for the importance of international hospitality and the value of cross-cultural learning experiences and global empowerment.

The case of the Anglican Communion involves some pretty unique norm shifts given past dissident movements within the organization. However, it serves as a cautionary tale (not of the danger of hypocrisy) but of how norm shifts in one direction may give rise to new problems rather than inevitably usher in cosmopolitanism.[17] Norms of global accountability are forming as common views of religious authority unite conservatives in the United States with African parishes. This shift is accompanied by (or even driven by) a more conservative view of social practices (including opposition to homosexuality and to women's ordination). Moral progress toward greater respect for equality in one area (among Americans and Africans) can lead to new moral dilemmas rather than a complete solution to all problems. Cosmopolitanism is not an inevitable trajectory. Philip Jenkins's study of Christianity led him to conclude that, while Christianity in the global South tends to be conservative on issues of human sexuality, this need not be the case. He points out that "the most powerful theme that recurs in the text [of the Bible] concerns outsiders, those rejected by the world, for whom is reserved a special place at the divine banquet."[18] As I argued in chapter 7, liberals in the United States and England could unite with Christians in other parts of the world along such themes as defending the inclusion and respect for individuals who face oppression (which would include those of different sexual orientations).

It may seem as though focusing on the specific case of Anglican dissidents or the IOC or MSF and the norm shifts in their particular areas pulls against the goal of establishing criteria that can be applied in different contexts to determine whether cosmopolitanism is being advanced in the world. Constructivists like Richard Price argue that the emergence of new moral challenges requires paying attention to the context in which morality or ethical principles play out.[19] A middle-level theory attempts to navigate between specificity and generality in order to provide some ways for universal cosmopolitan ideals to be explored in the contexts of a variety of associations. As I have said many times now, this will result in tensions as elements from different theories are combined to account for a range of different effects. Given the plurality of associations, differences in cosmopolitan theory can become a benefit rather than a drawback as they provide ways of thinking about cosmopolitanism in different situations. For example, Catherine Lu defends a non-utopian cosmopolitanism that focuses on common vulnerabilities in a non-cosmopolitan world. [20] This approach may see a cosmopolitan potential in our shared human biology that MSF can draw on in contexts of emergency and crisis. Kwame Anthony Appiah, however, is skeptical that shared biology is enough to generate the cultural engagement around shared practices he sees as critical in a cosmopolitan life. [21] Such disagreements among cosmopolitan theories raise tensions but need not require cosmopolitans pick either/or—common vulnerability or shared experiences. Tensions need not signal a flaw in middle-level cosmopolitan theory. It is rather the extreme versions of universalism and partiality that are problematic. Cosmopolitans want to distance themselves from universal civilizing missions and, at the same time, reject cultural relativism. Wading into the murky in-between will likely make it more difficult to determine what counts as cosmopolitan effects but it need not mean we navigate blindly. There are certain ways individuals in association with others can foster cosmopolitan norms and ideals even if only in partial ways.

Membership can transform individuals and it is important for cosmopolitan theorists to not only focus on international law or distributive justice but also on how membership in associations can generate cosmopolitan norms and dispositions. Individuals belong to many different kinds of associations. The same individual can belong to a wide range of orgainizations with different effects. Just as an individual's belief system is not necessarily always logically consistent, an individual's membership in associations can be quite varied. Even those who already embrace cosmopolitanism can learn lessons from a middle-level theory. The criteria can provide a guide for self-reflection on the effects of an association irrespective of its goals. Addressing each association one belongs to using the types of effects and their corresponding cosmopolitan ideals could help to assess whether one's memberships are helping to advance cosmopolitan norms.

Rather than primarily defending a theory of individual responsibility, a middle-level theory of cosmopolitan criteria for associations remains focused on the effects of associations. It seeks to answer the question: What ought cosmopolitans expect of the many different associations that emerge from respecting freedom of association? There is also the important follow up question: How can one answer this question in a way that respects diversity as well as cosmopolitanism's core principles of moral equality? These are not the only relevant questions about cosmopolitanism and associations. There are many avenues for further research on the place of associations in cosmopolitan theory. A systemic study of associations might consider the relation of associations to a range of political institutions and other actors on the global level. Relating associations to other actors is important because my middle-level theory does not embrace a teleological view of the advancement of cosmopolitan norms or dispositions. There is no inevitable chain of progress that leads to a cosmopolitan world community. The lessons of constructivist theories and the scholarship on actual associations show that norms are not advanced in a unidirectional mode. Individuals' attitudes can be shaped in a variety of ways and actually transforming standards of acceptable behavior is not easy. Even moral progress such as abolishing slavery was far from without its setbacks. In fact, slavery exists in many parts of the world today (although not legal, human trafficking continues to occur even in Europe and North America). Shifting norms against the legitimacy of slavery does not mean slavery is completely eliminated. All three associations that I discussed in part II have had an impact on transforming norms that cosmopolitans ought to consider relevant. None of the paths are completely unidirectional. Each association continues to face challenges in remaining an association that advances cosmopolitan norms (some greater than others).

Despite my emphasis on tensions and partiality, I see recognizing partial and indirect forms of cosmopolitanism as a sign of hope for those who believe in cosmopolitan ideals. Even partial or exclusive associations can advance cosmopolitan values. In fact, membership in associations with only partial expressions of cosmopolitanism offers great potential for spreading norms and attitudes that advance morality equality. Recognizing the effects of a broad plurality of associations leads one to a better understanding of how cosmopolitanism can arise in our imperfectly cosmopolitan world, often in unexpected ways, through the actions of exclusive associations not committed to cosmopolitan principles.

NOTES

1. Richard Price, "Progress with a Price," in *Moral Limit and Possibility in World Politics*, ed. Richard Price (New York: Cambridge University Press, 2008), 283.

2. For an in-depth analysis of responsibility to protect see Gareth Evans, *The Responsibility to Protect: Ending Mass Atrocity Crimes Once and For All* (Washington, D.C.: Brookings Institute Press, 2008).

3. Miranda Hassett, *Anglican Communion in Crisis: How Episcopal Dissidents and Their African Allies are Reshaping Anglicanism* (Princeton, NJ: Princeton University Press, 2007), 173.

4. Nancy L. Rosenblum, *Membership and Morals: The Personal Uses of Pluralism in America* (Princeton, NJ: Princeton University Press, 1998), 46, 70.

5. Mark E. Warren makes this point about associations on the domestic level: advancing one element of democracy may make it harder for the association to realize other democratic norms. *Democracy and Association* (Princeton, NJ: Princeton University Press, 2001), 27, 36.

6. I related this example in chapter 5. It is from Dr. James Maskalyk's book on his experience in Abyei, Sudan. He had lived there for five or six weeks and found that he "couldn't tell you one particular thing about the place, one custom, one habit of its people" and while some of this was due to his self-described tendency "to retreat when I need respite," it was also due to the very large difference between life in Canada and in Abyei, where "I see the poorest, the ones with no mosquito nets, or no access to clean water. Not only does our language seem irreconcilable, so do our worlds." James Maskalyk, *Six Months in Sudan: A Young Doctor in a War-torn Village* (New York: Spiegel & Grau, 2009), 112.

7. Warren, *Democracy and Association,* 12–13.

8. Transnational associations have been formed to take up the cause of indigenous people's rights. In addition, indigenous people have formed their own organizations. The World Council of Indigenous Peoples in 1975 was the first indigenous NGO to receive consultative status with the UN. The Indigenous Peoples' Network has as one of its goals to advance a worldview unique to indigenous people. Franke Wilmer, *The Indigenous Voice in World Politics: Since Time Immemorial* (Newbury Park, CA: Sage, 1993), 140–141.

9. Günter Schönleitner, "World Social Forum: Making Another World Possible," in *Globalizing Civic Engagement: Civil Society and Transnational Action,* ed. John Clark (Sterling, VA: Earthscan, 2003), 128.

10. Ibid., 142.

11. "IRN (International Rivers Network) had evolved into a structured organization and our vision had expanded and changed. While our analysis of the problem remained the same, we now understood that the destruction of rivers was as much a social and human rights issue as environmental." Philip Williams, a member of the IRN, quoted in Sanjeev Khagram, *Dams and Development: Transnational Struggles for Water and Power* (Ithaca, NY: Cornell University Press, 2004), 188.

12. Nicholas de Torrente discusses this in "Challenges to Humanitarian Action," *Ethics & International Affairs* 16, no. 2 (2002): 2–8. James Orbinski critiques "military-humanitarian operations" and defends "independent civilian humanitarianism," quoted in Renée Fox, *Doctors Without Borders: Humanitarian Quests, Impossible Dreams of Médecines Sans Frontières* (Baltimore: Johns Hopkins University Press, 2014), 69–70. David Rieff mentions this theme in an article about MSF's Nobel Peace Prize. David Rieff, "Good Doctors: Humanitarianism at Century's End," *The New Republic* 221, no. 19 (November 8, 1999): 23.

13. Jean-Hervé Bardol, "Caring for Health," in *Humanitarian Negotiations Revealed: The MSF Experience,* ed. Claire Magone, Michael Neuman, and Fabrice Weissman (New York: Columbia University Press, 2011), 210, 218.

14. Price, "Progress with a Price," 297.

15. For a full list of demands seem David Crouch and Roger Blitz, "IOC hits out as Norway withdraws Winter Olympic bid," *Financial Times,* October 2, 2014, accessed January 17, 2014, http://www.ft.com/cms/s/0/d8938ffc-4a04-11e4-8de3-00144feab7de. html#axzz3P6cyC9LE.

16. Christopher L. Gasper, "All that glitters about Boston's Olympic bid isn't gold," *The Boston Globe,* January 10, 2015, accessed January 14, 2015, http://www.bostonglobe.com/sports/2015/01/10/boston-doesn-need-olympics/u9Uvy2Ltc JSmLyJOCVKEKN/story.html.

17. Price argues that it is important for scholars to adopt a level of humility even as they defend certain norm shifts as progress. "Progress with a Price," 296.

18. Philip Jenkins, *The New Faces of Christianity: Believing the Bible in the Global South* (New York: Oxford University Press, 2006), 175.

19. Price, "Progress with a Price," 281–282.

20. Catherine Lu, "The One and Many Faces of Cosmopolitanism," *The Journal of Political Philosophy* 8, no. 2 (2000): 244–267.

21. Kwame Anthony Appiah, *The Ethics of Identity* (Princeton, NJ: Princeton University Press, 2005), 267.

Bibliography

Aeberhard, Patrick. "A Historical Survey of Humanitarian Action." *Health and Human Rights* 2, no. 1 (1996): 30–44.

Ahmed, Shamima, and David Potter. *NGOs in International Politics*. Bloomfield, CT: Kumarian Press, 2006.

Allié, Marie-Pierre. "Introduction: Acting at Any Price?" In *Humanitarian Negotiations Revealed: The MSF Experience*, edited by Claire Magone, Michael Neuman, and Fabrice Weissman, 1–11. New York: Columbia University Press, 2011.

Anderson, Kenneth, and David Rieff. "'Global Civil Society': A Skeptical View." In *Global Civil Society 2004–2005*, ed. Helmut Anheier, Marlies Glasius, and Mary Kaldor, 26–40. London: Sage, 2004.

Andrews, David L. "Coming to Terms with Cultural Studies." *Journal of Sport & Social Issues* 26, no. 1 (2002): 110–117.

Anheier, Helmut, Marlies Glasius, and Mary Kaldor, ed. *Global Civil Society 2001*. New York: Oxford University Press, 2002.

Appiah, Kwame Anthony. *Cosmopolitanism: Ethics in a World of Strangers*. Princeton, NJ: W.W. Norton & Company, 2006.

———. *The Ethics of Identity*. Princeton, NJ: Princeton University Press, 2005.

———. "Cosmopolitan Patriots." In *For Love of Country*, ed. Joshua Cohen, 21–29. Boston: Beacon Press, 2002.

Archibugi, Daniele, "Cosmopolitan Democracy and Its Critics: A Review." *European Journal of International Relations* 10, no. 3 (2004): 437–473.

Baker, Gideon. "Cosmopolitanism as Hospitality: Revisiting Identity and Difference in Cosmopolitanism." *Alternatives* 34 (2009): 107–128.

———. "Problems in the Theorisation of Global Civil Society." *Political Studies* 50 (2002): 928–943.

Bardol, Jean-Hervé. "Caring for Health." In *Humanitarian Negotiations Revealed: The MSF Experience*, edited by Claire Magone, Michael Neuman, and Fabrice Weissman, 199–218. New York: Columbia University Press, 2011.

Bass, Amy. "Objectivity Be Damned, or Why I Go to the Olympic Games: A Hands-On Lesson in Performative Nationalism." *The South Atlantic Quarterly* 105, no. 2 (2006): 349–371.

Bates, Stephen. *A Church at War: Anglicans and Homosexuality*. New York: I.B. Tauris, 2004.

Beck, Ulrich. "Cosmopolitical Realism: On the Distinction between Cosmopolitanism in Philosophy and the Social Sciences." *Global Networks* 4, no. 2 (2004): 131–156.

Beitz, Charles. "Human Rights as a Common Concern." *The American Political Science Review* 95, no. 2 (2001): 269–282.

———. "Social and Cosmopolitan Liberalism." *International Affairs* 75, no. 3 (1999): 515–529.

———. *Political Theory and International Relations*. Princeton, NJ: Princeton University Press, 1979.

Bell, David A., and Jean-Marc Coicaud, ed. *Ethics in Action: The Ethical Challenges of International Human Rights Nongovernmental Organizations*. New York: Cambridge University Press and United Nations University, 2007.

Benhabib, Seyla. "Democratic Iterations: The Local, the National, and the Global." In *Another Cosmopolitanism*, edited by Robert Post, 45–80. New York: Oxford University Press, 2006.

———. *The Rights of Others: Aliens, Residents, and Citizens.* New York: Cambridge University Press, 2004.

Berger, Peter. "Religion and Global Civil Society." In *Religion and Global Civil Society*, edited by Mark Juergensmeyer, 11–22. New York: Oxford University Press, 2005.

Bhaba, Homi K. "Unsatisfied: Notes on Vernacular Cosmopolitanism." In *Text and Nation: Cross-Disciplinary Essays on Cultural and National Identities*, edited by Laura García-Moreno and Peter C. Pfeiffer, 191–207. Columbia, SC: Camden House, 1996.

Black, David R., and Janis Van Der Westhuizen. "The Allure of Global Games for 'Semi Peripheral' Politics and Spaces: A Research Agenda." *Third World Quarterly* 25, no. 7 (2004): 1195–1214.

Bohman, James. "From *Demos* to *Demoi*: Democracy across Borders." *Ratio Juris* 18, no. 3 (2005): 293–314.

———. "Republican Cosmopolitanism." *Journal of Political Philosophy* 12, no. 3 (2004): 336–352.

———. "The Public Spheres of the World Citizen." In *Perpetual Peace: Essays on Kant's Cosmopolitan Ideal*, edited by James Bohman and Matthias Lutz-Bachmann, 179–200. Cambridge, MA: MIT Press, 1997.

Bortolotti, Dan. *Hope in Hell: Inside the World of Doctors Without Borders.* Buffalo, NY: Firefly Books, 2004.

Brauman, Rony. Forword to *The World in Crisis: The Politics of Survival at the End of the Twentieth Century*, edited by Médecins Sans Frontières, MSF project coordinator Julia Groenwold, and Associate Editor Eve Porter, xix–xxvi. New York: Routledge, 1997.

———. "The Médecines Sans Frontières Experience." In *A Framework for Survival: Health, Human Rights, and Humanitarian Assistance in Conflicts and Disasters*, edited by Kevin M. Cahill, M.D., 202–220. New York: BasicBooks and Council on Foreign Relations, 1993.

———. "When Suffering Makes a Good Story." In *Life and Death and Aid: The Medécins Sans Frontières Report on World Crisis Intervention*, edited by Francois Jean, 149–158. New York: Routledge, 1993.

Brittain, Christopher Craig and Andrew MacKinnon. "Homosexuality and the Construction of 'Anglican Orthodoxy': The Symbolic Politics of the Anglican Communion." *Sociology of Religion* 72, no. 3 (2011): 351–373.

Brock, Gillian, and Harry Brighouse. Introduction to *The Political Philosophy of Cosmopolitanism*, edited by Gillian Brock and Harry Brighouse, 1–9. New York: Cambridge University Press, 2005.

Brooks, Ethel. "Transnational Campaigns against Child Labor: The Garment Industry in Bangladesh." In *Coalitions Across Borders: Transnational Protest and the Neoliberal Order*, edited by Joe Bandy and Jackie Smith, 121–139. Lanham, MD: Rowman & Littlefield, 2005.

Brown, Chris. "Cosmopolitanism, World Citizenship and Global Civil Society." *Critical Review of International Social and Political Philosophy* 3, no. 1 (2000): 7–26.

Brownell, Susan. *Beijing's Games: What the Olympics Mean to China.* New York: Rowman & Littlefield, 2008.

Bruner, Jason. "Divided We Stand: North American Evangelicals and the Crisis in the Anglican Communion." *Journal of Anglican Studies* 8 (2009): 101–125.

Calhoun, Craig. "The Class Consciousness of Frequent Travellers: Towards a Critique of Actually Existing Cosmopolitanism." In *Conceiving Cosmopolitanism: Theory, Context, and Practice*, edited by Steven Vertovec and Robin Cohen, 86–109. New York: Oxford University Press, 2002.

Caney, Simon. *Justice Beyond Borders: A Global Political Theory.* New York: Oxford University Press, 2005.

———. "Cosmopolitan Justice and Cultural Diversity." *Global Society* 14, no. 4 (2000): 525–551.

Casanova, José. "Global Catholicism and the Politics of Civil Society." *Sociological Inquiry* 66, no. 3 (1996): 356–373.

Chapman, John W. "Voluntary Associations and the Political Theory of Pluralism." In *Voluntary Associations Nomos XI*, edited by J. Roland Pennock and John W. Chapman, 87–118. New York: Atherton Press, 1969.

Clark, Ian. *International Legitimacy and World Society*. Oxford: Oxford University Press, 2007.

Clatworthy, Jonathan. "Inclusiveness and Unity." In *The Windsor Report: A Liberal Response*, ed. Jonathan Clatworthy and David Taylor, 83–106. New York: O Books, 2005.

Close, Paul, David Askew, and Xu Xin. *The Beijing Olympiad: The Political Economy of a Sporting Mega-Event*. New York: Routledge, 2007.

Cohen, Joshua, ed. *For Love of Country?* Boston: Beacon Press, 2002.

Cohen, Joshua and Charles Sabel. "Extra Rempublicam Nulla Justitia?" *Philosophy & Public Affairs* 34, no. 2 (2006): 147–175.

Commissiong, Anand Bertrand. *Cosmopolitanism in Modernity: Human Dignity in a Global Age*. New York: Lexington Books, 2012.

Coubertin, Pierre de. "Sports as Peacemaker." In *Olympism: Selected Writings*, edited by Norbert Müller. Lausanne: International Olympic Committee, [1935] 2000.

———. "The Olympic Games of 1896." *Century* 53, no. 1 (November 1896).

Darieva, Tsypylma. "Rethinking Homecoming: Diasporic Cosmopolitanism in Post-Soviet Armenia," *Ethnic and Racial Studies* 34 (2011): 490–508.

Davis, David Brion. "The Universal Attractions of Slavery." Review of *Abolition: A History of Slavery and Anti-Slavery*, by Seymour Drescher. *The New York Review of Books*, 56, no. 20 (2009): 72–74.

———. *Slavery and Human Progress*. New York: Oxford University Press, 1984.

Dawes, James. *That the World May Know: Bearing Witness to Atrocity*. Cambridge, MA: Harvard University Press, 2007.

Debrix, Francois. "Deterritorialised Territories, Borderless Borders: The New Geography of International Medical Assistance," *Third World Quarterly* 19, no. 5 (1998): 827–846.

Donnelly, Elizabeth A. "Making the Case of Jubilee: The Catholic Church and the Poor Country Debt Movement." *Ethics & International Affairs* 21, no. 1 (2007): 107–133.

———. "Proclaiming Jubilee: The Debt and Structural Adjustment Network." In *Restructuring World Politics: Transnational Social Movements, Networks, and Norms*, edited by Sanjeev Khagram, James V. Riker, and Kathryn Sikkink, 155–180. Minneapolis: University of Minnesota Press, 2002.

Douglas, Ian. "Authority after Colonialism." *The Witness*, March 2000. Accessed September 28, 2009. http://www.thewitness.org.

Drescher, Seymour. *Abolition: A History of Slavery and Antislavery*. New York: Cambridge University Press, 2009.

———. "History's Engines: British Mobilization in the Age of Revolution." *The William and Mary Quarterly* 66, no. 4 (2009): 737–756.

———. *The Mighty Experiment: Free Labor versus Slavery in British Emancipation*. New York: Oxford University Press, 2004.

———. "Whose Abolition? Popular Pressure and the Ending of the British Slave Trade." *Past and Present* 143 (1994): 136–166.

Dryzek, John. *Deliberative Global Politics: Discourse and Democracy in a Divided World*. Malden, MA: Polity, 2006.

Dryzek, John, and Patrick Dunleavy. *Theories of the Democratic State*. New York: Palgrave Macmillan, 2009.

Eade, John, and Darren O'Byrne, eds. *Global Ethics and Civil Society*. Burlington, VT: Ashgate, 2005.

Ellis, Elizabeth. *Provisional Politics: Kantian Arguments in Policy Context*. New Haven, CT: Yale University Press, 2008

Ericksson, Cynthia B., Jeff P. Bjorck, Linnea C. Larson, Sherry M. Walling, Gary A. Trice, John Fawcett, Alexis D. Abernethy, and David W. Foy. "Social Support, Organizational Support, and Religious Support in Relation to Burnout in Expatriate

Humanitarian Aid Workers." *Mental Health, Religion & Culture* 12, no. 7 (2009): 671–686.

Erskine, Toni. *Embedded Cosmopolitanism: Duties to Strangers and Enemies in a World of "Disloacated Communities."* New York: Oxford University Press, 2008.

Evans, Gareth. *The Responsibility to Protect: Ending Mass Atrocity Crimes Once and For All.* Washington, D.C.: Brookings Institute Press, 2008.

Falk, Richard. "Global Civil Society and the Democratic Prospect." In *Global Democracy: Key Debates*, edited by Barry Holden, 162–178. New York: Routledge, 2000.

———. "Global Civil Society: Perspectives, Initiatives, Movements." *Oxford Development Studies* 26, no. 1 (1998): 99–104.

———. "Resisting 'Globalisation-from-above' through 'Globalisation-from-below.'" *New Political Economy* 2, no. 1 (1997): 17–24.

———. *On Humane Governance: Toward a New Global Politics.* University Park, PA: Pennsylvania State University, 1995.

Finnemore, Martha, and Katheryn Sikknik. "International Norm Dynamics and Political Change." *International Organization* 52, no. 4 (1998): 887–917.

Forsythe, David P. "The Red Cross as Transnational Movement: Conserving and Changing the Nation-State System." *International Organization* 30, no. 4 (1976): 607–630.

Fox, Renée C. *Doctors Without Borders: Humanitarian Quests, Impossible Dreams of Médecines Sans Frontières.* Baltimore: Johns Hopkins University Press, 2014.

———. "Medical Humanitarianism and Human Rights: Reflections on Doctors without Borders and Doctors of the World." *Social Sciences & Medicine* 41, no. 12 (1995): 1607–1616.

Gatehouse, Mike, and Miguel Angel Reyes. *Soft Drink/Hard Labor: Guatemalan Workers Take on Coca-Cola.* Edited by James Painter. London: Latin American Bureau, 1987.

Giulianotti, Richard. "Human Rights, Globalization and Sentimental Education: The Case of Sport." *Sport in Society* 7, no. 3 (2004): 355–369.

Goldblatt, David. "The Odd Couple: Football and Global Civil Society." In *Global Civil Society 2006/2007*, edited by Mary Kaldor, Martin Albrow, Helmut Anheier, and Marlies Glasius, 160–184. London: Sage Publications, 2007.

Gould, Carol C. "Transnational Solidarities." *Journal of Social Philosophy* 38, no. 1 (2007): 148–164.

Grenier, Paola. "Jubilee 2000: Laying the Foundations for a Social Movement." In *Globalizing Civic Engagement: Civil Society and Transnational Action*, edited by John Clark, 86–108. Sterling, VA: Earthscan, 2003.

Gutmann, Amy. "Freedom of Associations: An Introductory Essay." In *Freedom of Association*, edited by Amy Gutmann, 3–34. Princeton, NJ: Princeton University Press, 1998.

Gutmann, Amy, and Dennis Thompson. *Why Deliberative Democracy?* Princeton, NJ: Princeton University Press, 2004.

Haas, Peter. "Introduction: Epistemic Communities and International Policy Coordination." *International Organization* 46, no. 1 (1992): 1–35.

Habermas, Jürgen. *The Postnational Constellation: Political Essays.* Translated and edited by Max Pensky. Cambridge, MA: MIT Press, 2001.

———. *Between Facts and Norms: Contributions to a Discourse Theory of Law and Democracy.* Translated by William Rehg. Cambridge, MA: MIT Press, 1996.

Hall, Stuart. "Political Belonging in a World of Multiple Identities." In *Conceiving Cosmopolitanism: Theory, Context, and Practice*, edited by Steven Vertovec and Robin Cohen, 25–31. New York: Oxford University Press, 2002.

Hassett, Miranda. *Anglican Communion in Crisis: How Episcopal Dissidents and Their African Allies are Reshaping Anglicanism.* Princeton, NJ: Princeton University Press, 2007.

Heater, Derek. *World Citizenship and Government: Cosmopolitan Ideas in the History of Western Political Thought.* New York: St. Martin, 1996.

Held, David. "The Transformation of Political Community: Rethinking Democracy in the Context of Globalization." In *Democracy's Edges*, edited by Ian Shapiro and Casiano Hacker-Cordón, 84–111. Cambridge: Cambridge University Press, 1999.

———. *Democracy and the Global Order: From the Modern State to Cosmopolitan Governance*. Stanford, CA: Stanford University Press, 1995.

Herzlich, Claudine. "Comments: Professionals, Intellectuals, Visible Practitioners? The Case of 'Medical Humanitarianism.'" *Social Sciences & Medicine* 41, no. 12 (1995): 1617–1619.

Hoberman, John. "Sportive Nationalism and Globalization." In *Post-Olympism? Questioning Sport in the Twenty-first Century*, edited by John Bale and Mette Krogh Christensen, 177–188. New York: Berg, 2004.

———. "Toward a Theory of Olympic Internationalism." *Journal of Sport History* 22, no. 1 (1995): 1–37.

———. *The Olympic Crisis: Sport, Politics and the Moral Order*. New Rochelle, NY: Astride D. Caratzas, 1986.

Hochschild, Adam. *Bury the Chains: Prophets and Rebels in the Fight to Free an Empire's Slaves*. Boston: Houghton Mifflin Company, 2005.

Hollinger, David A. "Not Universalists, Not Pluralists: The New Cosmopolitans Find Their Own Way." *Constellations* 8, no. 2 (2001): 236–248.

Jenkins, Philip. *The New Faces of Christianity: Believing the Bible in the Global South*. New York: Oxford University Press, 2006.

———. *The Next Christendom: The Coming of Global Christianity*. New York: Oxford University Press, 2002.

Jenkins, Willis. "Episcopalians, Homosexuality, and World Mission," *Anglican Theological Review* 86, no. 2 (2004): 293–316.

Jie, Chen. "Burgeoning Transnationalism of Taiwan's Social Movement NGOs." *Journal of Contemporary China* 10 (2001): 613–644.

Julius, A.J. "Nagel's Atlas." *Philosophy & Public Affairs* 34, no. 2 (2006): 176–192.

Kaldor, Mary. *Global Civil Society: An Answer to War*. Malden, MA: Polity, 2003.

Kant, Immanuel. "Perpetual Peace." In *Political Writings*, edited by Hans Reiss and translated by H.B. Nisbet, 93–130. 2nd ed. New York: Cambridge University Press, 1991.

Kateb, George. "The Value of Association." In *Freedom of Association*, edited by Amy Gutmann, 25–63. Princeton, NJ: Princeton University Press, 1998.

Kaufmann, Chaim D., and Robert A. Pape. "Explaining Costly International Moral Action: Britain's Sixty-Year Campaign against the Atlantic Slave Trade." *International Organization* 53, no. 4 (1999): 631–668.

Keane, John. *Global Civil Society?* Cambridge: Cambridge University Press, 2003.

Keck, Margaret E., and Kathryn Sikkink. *Activists Beyond Borders: Advocacy Networks in International Politics*. Ithaca, NY: Cornell University Press, 1998.

Keyes, Barbara. *Globalizing Sport: National Rivalry and International Community in the 1930s*. Cambridge, MA: Harvard University Press, 2006.

Khagram, Sanjeev. *Dams and Development: Transnational Struggles for Water and Power*. Ithaca, NY: Cornell University Press, 2004.

Kidder, Thalia G. "Networks in Transnational Labor Organizing." In *Restructuring World Politics: Transnational Social Movements, Networks, and Norms*, edited by Sanjeev Khagram, James V. Riker, and Kathryn Sikkink, 269–293. Minneapolis: University of Minnesota Press, 2002.

Kleingeld, Pauline. *Kant and Cosmopolitanism: The Philosophical Ideal of World Citizenship*. New York: Cambridge University Press, 2011.

Klotz, Audie. "Transnational Activism and Global Transformations: The Anti-Apartheid and Abolitionist Experiences." *European Journal of International Relations* 8, no. 1 (2002): 49–76.

Laine, Leena. "Women's Movements in Sports: National and International Issues." In *Crossing Borders: Remapping Women's Movements at the Turn of the 21st Century*, edited by H.R. Christensen, B. Halsaa, and A. Saarinen, 119–133. Odense: University Press of Southern Denmark, 2004.

Leiper, Jean M. "Politics and Nationalism in the Olympic Games." In *The Olympic Games in Transition,* edited by Jeffrey O. Segrave and Donald Chu, 329–344. Champaign, IL: Human Kinetics Books, 1988.

Lenskyj, Helen Jefferson. "The Olympic Industry and Civil Liberties: The Threat to Free Speech and Freedom of Assembly." In *Sport, Civil Liberties, and Human Rights,* edited by Richard Giulianotti and David McArdle, 78–92. New York: Routledge, 2006.

Levermore, Roger. "Sport's Role in Constructing the 'Inter-State' Worldview." In *Sport and International Relations: An Emerging Relationship,* edited by Roger Levermore and Adrian Budd, 16–30. New York: Routledge, 2004.

Levy, Jacob T. *The Multiculturalism of Fear.* New York: Oxford University Press, 2000.

Leyton, Elliott. *Touched by Fire: Doctors Without Borders in a Third World Crisis.* Photographer Greg Locke. Toronto: M&S, 1998.

Lipschutz, Ronnie D. "Reconstructing World Politics: The Emergence of Global Civil Society." *Millennium: Journal of International Studies* 21, no. 3 (1992): 389–420.

Lu, Catherine. "The One and Many Faces of Cosmopolitanism," *The Journal of Political Philosophy* 8, no. 2 (2000): 244–267.

MacAloon, John J. "Double Visions: Olympic Games and American Culture." In *The Olympic Games in Transition,* edited by Jeffrey O. Segrave and Donald Chu, 279–301. Champaign, IL: Human Kinetics Books, 1988.

———. *This Great Symbol: Pierre de Coubertin and the Origins of the Modern Olympic Games.* Chicago: University of Chicago Press, 1981.

Mandell, Richard. *The First Modern Olympics.* Berkeley: University of California Press, 1976.

Markham, Ian. "Episcopalians, Homosexuality and the General Convention." *Reviews in Religion and Theology* 14, no. 1 (2007): 1–5.

Markovits, Andrei S., and Lars Rensmann. *Gaming the World: How Sports are Reshaping Global Politics and Culture.* Princeton, NJ: Princeton University Press, 2010.

Maskalyk, James. *Six Months in Sudan: A Young Doctor in a War-torn Village.* New York: Speigel & Grau, 2009.

McConnell, Michael W. "Don't Neglect the Little Platoons." In *For Love of Country,* edited by Joshua Cohen, 78–84. Boston: Beacon Press, 2002.

McCorquodale, Robert. "An Inclusive International Legal System." *Leiden Journal of International Law* 17 (2004): 477–504.

Médecins Sans Frontières. *International Activity Report 2012.* Facts and Figures Section, HR Statistics. Accessed on July 12, 2013. www.msf.org.

Merry, Michael S., and Doret J. de Ruyter. "Cosmopolitanism and the Deeply Religious" *Journal of Beliefs & Values* 30, no. 1 (2009): 49–60.

Miller, David. *National Responsibility and Global Justice.* New York: Oxford University Press, 2007.

Miro, Pere. "Athletes in Olympic Ceremonies." In *Olympic Ceremonies: Historical Continuity and Cultural Exchange: International Symposium on Olympic Ceremonies Barcelona—Lausanne 1995,* edited by Miquel de Moragas, John MacAloon, and Montserrat Llinés, 45–52. Lausanne: International Olympic Committee, 1996.

Moellendorf, Darrel. *Cosmopolitan Justice.* Cambridge, MA: Westview Press, 2002.

Morgan, William J. "Cosmopolitanism, Olympism, and Nationalism: A Critical Interpretation of Coubertin's Ideal of Modern Sporting Life." In *Rethinking the Olympics: Cultural Histories of the Modern Olympic Games,* edited by Robert K. Barney. Morgantown, WV: West Virginia University, 2010.

Morton, Katherine. "The Emergence of NGOs in China and Their Transnational Linkages: Implications for Domestic Reform." *Australian Journal of International Affairs* 59, no. 4 (2005): 519–532.

Musa, Saif Ali, and Abdalla A.R.M. Hamid. "Psychological Problems among Aid Workers Operating in Darfur." *Social Behavior and Personality* 36, no. 3 (2008): 407–416.

Mutua, Makau. "Human Rights International NGOs: A Critical Evaluation." In *NGOs and Human Rights: Promise and Performance,* edited by Claude E. Welch Jr, 151–161. Philadelphia: University of Pennsylvania Press, 2001.

Nussbaum, Martha. *Frontiers of Justice: Disability, Nationality, Species Membership.* Cambridge, MA: Belknap Press of Harvard University Press, 2006.

———. "Patriotism and Cosmopolitanism." In *For Love of Country?* edited by Joshua Cohen, 2–17. Boston: Beacon Press, 2002.

Orbinski, James. *An Imperfect Offering: Humanitarian Action in the Twenty-First Century.* New York: Walker & Company, 2008.

———. "Médecins Sans Frontières—Nobel Lecture." The Nobel Foundation, 1999. Accessed on *Nobelprize.org.* Nobel Web AB 2014, http://www.nobelprize.org/nobel_prizes/ peace/laureates/1999/msf-lecture.html.

Orwell, George. "The Sporting Spirit." In *Shooting an Elephant, and Other Essays.* New York: Harcourt, Brace & World, Inc., 1950.

Payne, Michael. *Olympic Turnaround: How the Olympic Games Stepped Back from the Brink of Extinction to Become the World's Best Known Brand.* Westport, CT: Praeger, 2006.

Plewes, Betty, and Rieky Stuart. "The Pornography of Poverty: A Cautionary Fundraising Tale." In *Ethics in Action,* edited by Daniel A. Bell and Jean-Marc Coicaud, 23–37. New York: Cambridge University Press, 2007.

Pogge, Thomas. *World Poverty and Human Rights: Cosmopolitan Responsibilities and Reforms.* Malden, MA: Polity, 2002.

———. "Cosmopolitanism and Sovereignty." *Ethics* 103, no. 1 (1992): 48–75.

———. *Realizing Rawls.* Ithaca, NY: Cornell University Press, 1989.

Price, Richard. "The Ethics of Constructivism." In *The Oxford Handbook of International Relations,* edited by Christian Reus-Smit and Duncan Snidal, 317–326. New York: Oxford University Press, 2010.

———. "Moral Limit and Possibility in World Politics." In *Moral Limit and Possibility in World Politics,* edited by Richard Price, 1–52. New York: Cambridge University Press, 2008.

———. "Progress with a Price." In *Moral Limit and Possibility in World Politics,* edited by Richard Price, 281–303. New York: Cambridge University Press, 2008.

———. "Transnational Civil Society and Advocacy in World Politics." *World Politics* 55, no. 4 (2003): 579–606.

Putnam, Robert. *Bowling Alone: The Collapse and Revival of American Community.* New York: Touchstone Books by Simon & Schuster, 2001.

———. "Bowling Alone: America's Declining Social Capital." *Journal of Democracy* 6, no. 1 (1995): 65–78.

Rawls, John. *Justice as Fairness: A Restatement.* Edited by Erin Kelly. Cambridge, MA: The Belknap Press of Harvard University Press, 2001.

———. *The Law of Peoples with "The Idea of Public Reason Revisited."* Cambridge, MA: Harvard University Press, 1999.

———. *Political Liberalism.* New York: Columbia University Press, 1996.

———. "The Idea of the Overlapping Consensus." *Oxford Journal of Legal Studies* 7, no. 1 (Spring 1987).

Redfield, Peter. "Doctors, Borders, and Life in Crisis." *Cultural Anthropology* 20, no. 3 (2005): 328–361.

Reus-Smit, Christian, and Duncan Snidal. "Between Utopia and Reality: The Practical Discourses of International Relations." In *The Oxford Handbook of International Relations,* edited by Christian Reus-Smit and Duncan Snidal, 1–25. New York: Oxford University Press, 2010.

Rieff, David. "Good Doctors: Humanitarianism at Century's End." *The New Republic* 221, no. 19 (November 8, 1999).

Robbins, Bruce. "Actually Existing Cosmopolitanism." In *Cosmopolitics: Thinking and Feeling Beyond the Nation*, edited by Pheng Cheah and Bruce Robbins, 1–19. Minneapolis: University of Minnesota Press, 1998.

Roche, Maurice. "Mega-events and Modernity Revisited: Globalization and the Case of the Olympics." In *Sports Mega-Events: Social Scientific Analyses of a Global Phenomenon*, edited by John Horne and Wolfram Manzenreiter, 27–40. Malden, MA: Blackwell Publishing, 2006.

Rootes, Christopher. "Global Visions: Global Civil Society and the Lessons of European Environmentalism." *Voluntas: International Journal of Voluntary and Nonprofit Organizations* 13, no. 4 (2002): 411–429.

Rosenblum, Nancy L. *Membership and Morals: The Personal Uses of Pluralism in America.* Princeton, NJ: Princeton University Press, 1998.

Rovisco, Maria. "Religion and the Challenges of Cosmopolitanism: Young Portuguese Volunteers in Africa." In *Cosmopolitanism in Practice*, edited by Magdalena Nowicka and Maria Rovisco, 181–200. Burlington, VT: Ashgate, 2009.

Ruggie, John Gerard. "Reconstituting the Global Public Domain—Issues, Actors and Practices." *European Journal or International Relations* 10 (2004): 499–531.

———. "What Makes the World Hang Together? Neo-Utilitarianism and the Social Constructivist Challenge." *International Organization* 52, no. 4 (1998): 855–885.

Sachs, William L. *Homosexuality and the Crisis of Anglicanism.* New York: Cambridge University Press, 2009.

Salamon, Lester M. "The Rise of the Nonprofit Sector." *Foreign Affairs* 73, no. 4 (1994): 109–122.

Sandel, Michael. *Democracy's Discontents: America in Search of a Political Philosophy.* Cambridge, MA: The Belknap Press of Harvard University Press, 1996.

Scharenberg, Swantje. "Religion and Sport." In *The International Politics of Sport in the Twentieth Century*, edited by James Riordan and Arnd Krüger, 90–104. New York: E & FN Spon, 1999.

Scheffler, Samuel. "Conceptions of Cosmopolitanism." *Utilitas* 11, no. 3 (1999): 255–276.

Schönleitner, Günter. "World Social Forum: Making Another World Possible." In *Globalizing Civic Engagement: Civil Society and Transnational Action*, edited by John D. Clark, 127–149. Sterling, VA: Earthscan, 2003.

Scruton, Roger. "Cosmopolitanism." *The Palgrave Macmillan Dictionary of Political Thought*. 3rd ed. New York: Palgrave Macmillan, 2007.

Selchow, Sabine. "The 2008 Beijing Olympics: A 'Once-in-a-Lifetime Opportunity' for Global Civil Society." In *Global Civil Society 2007/2008*, edited by Mary Kaldor, Marlies Glasius, Helmut Anheier, Martin Albrow, and Monroe E. Price, 88–89. London: Sage, 2008.

Sen, Amartya. *Identity and Violence: The Illusion of Destiny.* New York: W.W. Norton & Co., 2006.

Shapcott, Richard. "Anti-cosmopolitanism, Pluralism and the Cosmopolitan Harm Principle." *Review of International Studies* 34 (2008): 185–205.

Short, John Rennie. *Global Metropolitan: Globalizing Cities in a Capitalist World.* New York: Routledge, 2004.

Sikkink, Kathryn. "The Role of Consequences, Comparison, and Counterfactuals in Constructivist Ethical Thought." In *Moral Limit and Possibility in World Politics*, edited by Richard Price, 83–111. New York: Cambridge University Press, 2008.

Smart, Barry. "Not Playing Around: Global Capitalism, Modern Sport and Consumer Culture." In *Globalization and Sport*, edited by Richard Giulianotti and Roland Robertson, 6–27. Malden, MA: Blackwell Publishing, 2007.

Smith, Jackie. "Global Civil Society? Transnational Social Movement Organizations and Social Capital." *American Behavior Scientist* 42, no. 1 (1998): 93–107.

Smith, Matt Baillie, and Katy Jenkins. "Disconnections and Exclusions: Professionalization, Cosmopolitanism and (Global?) Civil Society." *Global Networks* 11, no. 2 (2011): 160–179.

Snyder, Anna. "Fostering Transnational Dialogue: Lessons Learned from Women Peace Activists." *Globalizations* 3, no. 1 (2006): 31–47.
Sperling, Valerie, Myra Marx Ferree, and Barbara Risman. "Constructing Global Feminism: Transnational Advocacy Networks and Russian Women's Activism." *Signs* 26, no. 4 (2001): 1115–1186.
Spini, Debora. "The Double Face of Civil Society." In *The Search for a European Identity: Values, Policies and Legitimacy of the European Union,* edited by Furio Cerutti and Sonia Lucarelli, 142–156. New York: Routledge, 2008.
Spong, John Shelby. Foreword to *The Windsor Report: A Liberal Response,* edited by Jonathan Clatworthy and David Taylor, ix–xiv. New York: O Books, 2005.
Strenk, Andrew. "What Price Victory? The World of International Sports and Politics." *Annals of the American Academy of Political and Social Science* 445 (1979): 128–140.
Sypnowich, Christine. "Cosmopolitans, Cosmopolitanism, and Human Flourishing." In *The Political Philosophy of Cosmopolitanism,* edited by Gillian Brock and Harry Brighouse, 55–74. New York: Cambridge University Press, 2005.
Tan, Kok-Chor. "The Demands of Justice and National Allegiances." In *The Political Philosophy of Cosmopolitanism,* edited by Gillian Brock and Harry Brighouse, 164–179. New York: Cambridge University Press, 2005.
Tanguy, Joelle, and Fiona Terry. "Humanitarian Responsibility and Committed Action: Response to 'Principle, Politics, and Humanitarian Action.'" *Ethics & International Affairs* 13, no. 1 (1999): 29–34.
Tocqueville, Alexis de. *Democracy in America.* Translated and edited by Harvey C. Mansfield and Delba Winthrop. Chicago: University of Chicago Press, 2002.
Toohey, Kristine, and A.J. Veal. *The Olympic Games: A Social Science Perspective.* New York: CABI Publishing, 2000.
Toole, Mike. "Frontline Medicine: The Role of International Medical Groups in Emergency Relief." In *The World in Crisis: The Politics of Survival at the End of the Twentieth Century,* edited by Médecins Sans Frontières, MSF project coordinator Julia Groenwold, and Associate Editor Eve Porter, 16–36. New York: Routledge, 1997.
Torrente, Nicolas de. "Challenges to Humanitarian Action." *Ethics & International Affairs* 16, no. 2 (2002): 2–8.
Tzanelli, Rodanthi. "Mediating Cosmopolitanism: Crafting an Allegorical Imperative through Beijing 2008." *International Review of Sociology* 20, no. 2 (2010): 215–241.
Valentine, Gill, Robert M. Vanderbeck, Joanna Sadgrove, Johan Andersson, and Kevin Ward. "Transnational Religious Networks: Sexuality and the Changing Power Geometries of the Anglican Communion." *Transactions of the Institute of British Geographers* 38 (2013): 50–64.
Vertovec, Steven, and Robin Cohen. "Introduction: Conceiving Cosmopolitanism." In *Conceiving Cosmopolitanism: Theory, Context, and Practice,* edited by Steven Vertovec and Robin Cohen. New York: Oxford University Press, 2002.
Waal, Alexander de. *Famine Crimes: Politics & the Disaster of Relief Industry in Africa.* London: African Rights & the International African Institute, 1997.
Waldron, Jeremy. "What is Cosmopolitan?" *The Journal of Political Philosophy* 8, no. 2 (2000): 227–243.
Wapner, Paul. "Politics Beyond the State: Environmental Activism and World Civic Politics." *World Politics* 47, no. 3 (1995): 311–340.
Warren, Mark E. *Democracy and Association.* Princeton, NJ: Princeton University Press, 2001.
Welch, Cheryl B. *De Tocqueville.* New York: Oxford University Press, 2001.
Werbner, Pnina. "Vernacular Cosmopolitanism." *Theory Culture and Society* 23 (2006): 496–498.
Wilmer, Franke. *The Indigenous Voice in World Politics: Since Time Immemorial.* Newbury Park, CA: Sage, 1993.

Index

About the Author

Bettina Scholz is a political theorist specializing in cosmopolitanism and the normative impact of transnational associations. She received her PhD from Harvard University in 2010. Currently an assistant professor of political science at Stonehill College in Easton, Massachusetts, she teaches a range of courses in historical and contemporary political theory as well as global ethics.